Yukon Quest

The 1,000-mile dog sled race through the Yukon and Alaska

Includes 1998 race rules
and
1984 to 1998 musher lists and ~ *~*

D1360384

John Firth

Christine,

Happy Trails

Quest 2003

1998

Originally published in 1990 as *Yukon Challenge*

Published by Lost Moose, the Yukon Publishers
58 Kluane Crescent, Whitehorse, Yukon, Canada Y1A 3G7
phone: 867-668-5076, fax: 867-668-6223
e-mail: lmoose@yknet.yk.ca
web site: http://www.yukonweb.com/business/lost_moose

Canadian Cataloguing in Publication Data
Firth, John, 1953-
    Yukon Quest : the 1,000-mile dog sled race through the Yukon and Alaska

ISBN 1-896758-03-7

Includes an index.

1. Sled dog racing — Yukon Territory — History.
2. Sled dog racing — Alaska — History.
3. Sled dogs — Yukon Territory.
4. Sled dogs — Alaska.
5. Yukon Quest International Sled Dog Race.
I. Title.
II. Title: The 1,000-mile dog sled race through the Yukon and Alaska.

SF440.15F57 1997   798.8'3097191   C97-980480-9

Design by Patricia Halladay

Maps by Peter Long

Production by K-L Services, Whitehorse

Printed and bound in Canada   98 99 00 01 02 5 4 3 2 1

Cover photographs and photographs on pages 8, 59 (inset), 181 (inset) and 195 by Richard Hartmier. All other photographs courtesy of the *Whitehorse Star.*

Main cover photograph: The frozen Yukon River at Dawson City.
Front inset: Start of the Yukon Quest.
Back, top inset: Musher on King Solomon Dome.
Dog insets: Resting at Braeburn, 1997.

Note: Distances are given in miles, temperatures in degrees Fahrenheit, and weights in pounds.

The Yukon Quest is the result of years of dedication from the founders of the race. It is the reward for the volunteers who put in endless hours during the most bitter months of the year. It is the ultimate symbol of what it means to be a dog driver. It is the supreme achievement for the true athletes of this event, the dogs. This book is dedicated to all of them.

Preface

It's been almost 10 years since I first started to write this book, eight years since it was originally published, and four or so years since it was last on the bookshelves. But even after all that time, people still ask me where they can find a copy.

It did wonders for my ego, but really, the inquiries had little to do with the fact that this is a wonderful piece of literature. They had more to do with the emergence of the Yukon Quest onto the world stage as an international sporting event of note.

In 1990, when this book was first published, the Quest was little more than a local race that happened to cross an international boundary. Now, in 1998, it has major sponsors from around the globe who find its image can be easily marketed. It has an appeal that can lure the powerful down from their ivory towers to mingle with and idolize the lowly musher.

In 1997, the Chief Executive Officer of Fulda Reifen, Goodyear Tire's European manufacturer and distributor, posed with a German musher at the Yukon Quest start line while, down the way, the president of Japan's Mitsubishi Corporation grinned from ear to ear as the cameras captured him with one of his country's dog-driving citizens.

Sponsors dream of associating their products with this image. The race combines skill, strength, stamina, speed and, most important of all, integrity.

Television carries images of the event halfway around the world to living rooms across the continent of Europe where millions are now calling it "winter's Tour de France." Documentaries about competitors have won awards in Europe, the United States and Japan. Dog mushing can be found on the covers of *Paris Match*, *Der Spiegel* and *Outdoor Life*. It captures front page space in newspapers like the *Los Angeles Times* and the *Globe and Mail*.

How did the Quest mushroom from a small, back-country dog sled race to an international sporting event?

The first tangible action came with the president of the organization calling up a few people he knew — some of whom happened to be CEOs of fairly large corporations and one of whom happened to be Doug Phillips, the Yukon government's Minister of Tourism — to tell them the Quest needed support. Within those corporations and in the Yukon government was the marketing expertise, financing and connections that the Quest itself — an organization that operates, with few exceptions, entirely on volunteer labour — lacked.

With access to this expertise, succeeding boards were able to start getting the message out to the rest of the world — here is something worth being a part of.

The Yukon Quest is a race originally founded for the benefit of the small kennel, and its backbone consists of the residents and small communities in Alaska and the Yukon. It embodies all of the qualities of the land that northerners love and those that set northerners apart.

When times were tough and the Quest was on the ropes financially, it was the people of the north who rallied to save it — not once, but several times. The race has almost been torn apart by infighting. But every year, at the last minute, 1,000 people, spread out along a wilderness trail, come together to pull it off, again and again.

Things have not been, and will not be, easy for the world's toughest race, but success and quality are not achieved by taking the easy trail.

The Quest has become a northern emblem. It defines who we are, whether we are from Alaska, the Yukon or any other isolated northern region of the earth. In the end, the race, and everything it represents, is what is important to northerners and it is truly their dedication to this event that has brought it into the world spotlight.

For "outsiders" to be a part of the Quest is, for a moment, to capture a part of what it means to be a northerner.

When the decision was reached to re-title the book (from *Yukon Challenge* to *Yukon Quest*) and re-release it, it was obvious that the events and changes that had occurred in the following years should be included. I have tried in the additional material to continue in the same vein as in the original text.

There have been minor editorial changes to the original book and new pictures added. Some of the maps and descriptions no longer reflect the existing routes, but that is because of changes that have occurred in the following years. I have left the original descriptions in the book, then identified the changes in the new material. I have also ventured outside the event to discuss the political aspects of the organization and the role those struggles have played in the growth of this event.

In the section entitled "Rules and statistics," I have brought the race results up-to-date and included an alphabetical listing of all mushers who have been in the Yukon Quest, with their standings.

Last, I have attempted to look into the future to determine where the Quest should travel to maintain its distinctive role in this very unique sport.

Some of the proceeds from this book will go to the Yukon Quest. Despite its new worldwide image, it is still a community race and, like any local organization, it needs money to survive.

Come with me on the trail of the world's last great adventure. Enjoy!

John Firth
Whitehorse, Yukon, 1998

Acknowledgements

Like the Yukon Quest itself, the survival of this book is due to the unflagging dedication and contributions of those who believe in the event and in the book.

Those who contributed their invaluable assistance in both 1988 and 1997 have my deepest appreciation.

Laura Chapman. Roger Williams. Jocelyn Williams. Leroy Shank. Bob Eley. Tom Randall. Elsie Wain. Leo Oleson. Frenchy De Rushe. Jackie Pierce. Dave Monson. Bill Cotter. Kathy Swenson. Sonny Lindner. Joe Runyan. Harry and Sandy Sutherland. Jon Rudolph. Frank Turner. Lorrina Mitchell. Ralph and Shari Tingey. Gordie Mitchell. John Mitchell. Joe May. Senley Yuill. Stan Njootli. Hans Oettli. Jim Reiter. Lou and Carol Johnson. Dawn Dimond. Shane Horsnell. Jackie Parsons. Janice Drake. Barb Ballentyne. Joe May. David and Edna Knight. My apologies to all of those whom I inadvertently left out.

Thanks also to Lone Pine Publishing in Edmonton for originally publishing this book. Much appreciation to Wynne Krangle and Peter Long at Lost Moose Publishing for recognizing the potential in reprinting the book and dedicating many hours to ensuring the new and improved version of the book was of the highest quality.

All photographs in this book are printed with the permission of the Whitehorse Star (1977) Ltd., except, as indicated, those taken by Richard Hartmier. The 1984 mail cachet is from the collection of Jim McLeod.

Many thanks to Yukon Quest International for permission to print the 1998 rules and to use the title "Yukon Quest."

Contents

Maps

Introduction

This is not just a story about a race. It is a book about the kind of people who conceive of such an event, the individuals who take part in it and the dogs that make it a reality.

The driving of dogs is as much a philosophy of life as it is a necessary means of transportation or a recreational pastime. The romantic fantasies of pioneers in search of adventure, glory and wealth that were first publicized by Jack London, Robert Service and television's Sergeant Preston and his dog King — these are the idealistic images that lured many who now populate Alaska and the Yukon.

They portrayed an unforgiving world of deceptive beauty and ruthless winter, a land of environmental contradictions where the sun shone at midnight, the moon waxed at noon and the silent shroud of night was ripped by dancing lights and crackling music of unknown origin.

It was an eerie world that could only be conquered by dogs blessed with undying loyalty, unburdened affection, limitless endurance and quick intelligence. Behind them, riding sled runners and inspiring the dogs to even greater heights of accomplishment, were their drivers; the strong who somehow found a way to survive where the weak perished. They were men and women of stout heart and childlike innocence who triumphed through sheer intestinal fortitude and the gritty determination to succeed at any price. They endured the pain and loneliness of the trail to find comfort in the camaraderie of others who shared the same hardships.

It was a desire to find within themselves that romantic fantasy and pioneer spirit that drove a few modern northerners into the world of driving dogs. Some believe that dog drivers, or mushers, are the only genuine northerners left; that everyone else, with their creature comforts, has compromised with nature or hidden from it rather than confronting it head-on.

Some drivers hitched up dogs through necessity. Dogs and sleds are more reliable than gasoline-powered snowmachines for moving supplies, freight and mail to isolated communities and cabins in the dead of winter.

Others set foot on the runners for adventure. They simply enjoyed the satisfaction of merging with the wilderness, traversing virgin country and developing the skills that form the foundation of arctic survival.

Occasionally, the drivers would meet on a trail and it was always fun to race just to see who was the fastest. It was only a matter of time before their fun got serious and drivers started pitting themselves against each other, against a clock and against the environment.

The measured courses got longer and longer, from short 15-mile sprint tracks, to middle distance 400-mile events, until one day the drivers strove to surpass the magical figure of 1,000 miles in a single race.

In this era of space shuttles and jet planes carrying people around the world in a few hours, or satellite communications sending messages across continents in seconds, we tend to forget just how far 1,000 miles is or exactly what kind of an effort is required to travel it.

At one time, people and messages could only travel by horseback, stagecoach, on foot or by dog sled. What takes us a few hours or a few seconds to do today, used to take weeks, sometimes months or years, to complete. And this compression of time and effort hasn't taken hundreds of years to achieve. It has occurred entirely within the confines of the 20th century.

To gain some appreciation of this phenomenon, next time you commute from your home to work, leave the car behind or save your bus fare, and walk to your place of employment. Don't pick a nice sunny, warm day to do it. Try a blustery, cold day with some rain or sleet. If you haven't had the opportunity to wade knee-deep in snow, try walking along a beach with your shins immersed in the surf.

Then, think about what it would be like to do that 24 hours a day for two weeks — not because you have to do it, but because you want to.

That's what the Yukon Quest is like.

This book follows the running of the 1988 Yukon Quest for two reasons. First, the 1988 race runs in the direction that was followed when the race was first run in 1984 (Fairbanks to Whitehorse). And, second, it was a classic confrontation, possibly the last of its kind, between the best of the new scientific dog mushers and the great drivers of the traditional school of hard knocks.

John Firth, 1990

The Yukon Quest

The Yukon Quest is a measured test
Of man and dog versus trail
But more than that it's a statement
Of the strong will not to fail.

Where the musher stands, not against the land
But against unspoken fear...
The bitter cold and the loneliness
And silence that hurts to hear!

The Quest is more than finishing first,
It's more than how slow or how fast;
It's a thousand miles on the winter trail,
Where a winner may finish last.

The men and the women who live for the trail,
For the huskies' lonesome call,
And the bone weary camps at the end of the day;
They'd sell their souls for it all!

They love, and they live it and 12 months each year
They give it their very best,
And they dream of the long lonesome trail ahead,
Once again on the Yukon Quest.

W.M. Frenchy De Rushe, 1986

(over) Harry Sutherland approaching Eagle, 1984.

Mush! The race begins

Mush! The race begins

ebruary 20, 1988. In the night, the day begins to change. Just before warm weather turns to cold, there's a crispness in the air you can smell. Maybe it's the drop in humidity or the increased density of the environment. Whatever the source, once you've tasted it and know what it heralds, it's something you can never forget.

It doesn't tell you if it's going to snow, or whether there will be winds, or how cold it will get. It is simply one of nature's ways of letting you know there is a change on the way. This night you can smell it; tomorrow will be cold.

A mass of arctic air is rolling in. Sometime this afternoon the weather front is due to arrive over Fairbanks, Alaska. Fresh snow and high winds will precede it; then the Alaskan interior will be locked in a deep-freeze. The mercury, already starting to drop, will finally, reluctantly, stabilize around minus 50 degrees.

And the cold is going to stay around for a while. Well into next week, the city of 60,000 is going to be forced to deal with cars too frozen to start and roads barricaded by drifting snow.

Huddled in a small second-floor office, protected from the night air by groaning hot water heaters, Yukon Quest race manager Jack Niggemyer of Fairbanks is listening to the weather forecast with only half an ear.

He isn't too concerned about what the weather will be later today or tomorrow. He will still have to do what is necessary to ensure the success of the race, regardless of snow, cold and wind. On his shoulders rides the ultimate responsibility to make sure there's a trail to follow to the Canadian border and that the checkpoints en route are staffed.

Once the racers are across the boundary, his job is finished. At that point his Canadian counterpart, the tall, white-bearded Art Christensen, from Whitehorse, Yukon, takes over.

As the greys of dawn replace the dark of night outside his downtown office window, he heaves a sigh of aggravation through his untrimmed black goatee.

There is a multitude of last minute emergencies covering his desk with white paper and clogging his telephone lines. The outer offices and the Yukon Quest board room are filled with volunteers trying to resolve other hassles or to organize the starting line personnel.

A block north of him, on the Chena River, one problem can't be solved on paper or by phone. Unseasonably warm temperatures over the past two weeks have left the ice under the starting chute thinner than Niggemyer likes. It will probably support the teams and officials without buckling, but if the crowd of "mush-aholics" wanting to get close to the action becomes too big, there is the potential for disaster.

"The thing is," he says to the enquiring media crowded around the door to his office, "we're afraid the ice is in grave danger of collapsing if too many people stand on it."

He has been broadcasting that message, over the air and in print, for the past few days. The alternative, he has been saying, is to watch the start from the Chena River Bridge or the river bank. But Niggemyer knows that telling people is one thing; whether or not they listen is another.

Three Quest volunteers, Bob Goodwin, Randy Navin and Joe Calvin, are oblivious to the thin ice. In the early morning dusk, they are drilling holes in the ice into which they will set the 20-foot posts that will hold the yellow and red Yukon Quest start banner over the centre of the river. Around them stand 45-gallon gas drums filled with water that act as fence posts. Wired to the gas drums is the snow fencing used to hold back the crowd.

A hundred yards behind, up on the riverbank just past the bridge, the parking lot behind the Fairbanks North Star Borough administration

Fairbanks to Angel Creek

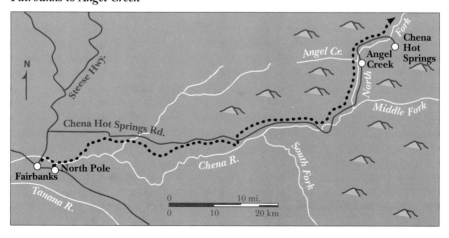

building (city hall) is starting to look surprisingly busy for a Saturday morning. But cars and trucks form the minority of the parking stall occupants on this day.

The dog lot and starting chute for a long distance race have to be seen to be believed. Kimberley Sessions, from Atlanta, Georgia, arrived in Fairbanks just yesterday to visit a friend. She has never seen a sled dog or a dog sled, much less a dog race of this nature.

Crammed in the crowd on the Chena River Bridge, kept warm by the closeness of the other bodies around her, she thinks about how different it is from back home. The winter. The people. And above all, the dogs. This reality vastly exceeds the fantasy.

"I'm amazed. My whole vision of the north was Jack London. White Fang. That kind of stuff. This is by far the most exciting thing I've ever seen."

Six hundred dogs are chained to the sides of vehicles or to cables stretched out across the ground. Or they are sticking their heads out of windows in the dog boxes on the backs of pick-ups and small trucks.

Inside their little cubbyholes, the dogs have enough room to stand, curl up and sleep, or stretch out on their straw beds. But the comforts of their boxes are the last thing on their minds now. The activity all around tells them this is the place and now is the time to RUN.

The parking lot is barely large enough to contain the mass of animals, people and machines. Inside that space, drivers are sending several confusing, unspoken signals to each other. The dogs, in close proximity

Dog heads poking out of the dog box, with sled stored on top.

with each other, are affected. There is a tremendous concentration of frustrated and anxious energy from both drivers and teams.

The dogs strain at their chains, crouch and yowl with excitement, or bound frantically into the air. Howling and barking, and the meaty-smelling clouds of their breath, thicken the air. All the time they are emptying their bladders and bowels. Some of them are digging up the frozen earth, turning the snow into a brownish slop.

In this canine-dominated world gone crazy, the dog mushers move confidently in the eyes of their hurricanes. They and their handlers wander unruffled through the bedlam, carrying bags of dog food, sleeping bags, campstoves, and boxes and bags of unknown content.

Among the mushers is a housewife, two lawyers, a sports promoter, an author, a dentist, a few fishers, an artist, some carpenters, a retired cattle rancher and his two sons, heavy equipment operators, the owner of a highway lodge, several trappers, a grandmother, and those who claim to have no profession at all or don't know what they do.

They come from Great Britain, Alaska, Illinois, Washington, France, the Yukon and British Columbia. Their homes are located in heavily populated metropolitan cores, in small towns, in villages that don't even get a dot on the map, or on the banks of lakes and rivers, miles from their nearest neighbour. There are five women and 42 men. The youngest is 21. The oldest is 58. Two have listed their ages as "unknown" and "forgotten."

They have only one thing in common — they all drive dogs.

Bill Cotter stands almost lost in the milling bystanders. The building contractor from Nenana, Alaska, isn't the kind of person who wants to stand out in a crowd. It was his ability to achieve that effect that won him the 1987 Yukon Quest championship.

His smile is shy. His eyes are deceptively soft. His voice barely climbs above a whisper. But there is a competitor's intensity about him. Even though he is not running this year, he still feels the starting line edge. Like the other drivers around him, he shows no reaction at the news of the encroaching arctic front.

"It's just one of the things we live with. Nothing else exists for you except the race. Your focus is narrowed down to one thing. The world economy, war, drought in the midwest — that has no meaning. The only thing that's important is your dog team, yourself, the environment around you, keeping your dogs and yourself healthy. Survival.

"I think the hardships we take for granted would kill most people. We almost look forward to the prospect of those hardships because we've adapted ourselves to deal with those circumstances."

A lot of the mushers don't even hear the weather report, but they know what's coming. They can smell it. Besides that, their dogs stopped shedding their excess fur a day or so ago, indicating they will still have need of their winter coats.

Drivers who stand in this parking lot today, who have stood in it in the past or will stand in it in the future, have their own reason for being there.

Kathy Swenson measures you with every glance. In this world of strategy and deception, this slightly-built mother of two has learned not to take anything at face value, at first sight. Her husband, Rick is a four-time winner of the Iditarod—the 1,000-mile sled dog race from Anchorage, on Alaska's south coast, through the interior to Nome, on the north coast of Norton Sound. Rick is a master of the head games that mushers play and some of his ability has rubbed off on her. But along with the acquired knowledge comes the pressure of being the wife of Rick Swenson.

"If I changed my name, it would be different," says the woman who had to adapt to the Alaska winter after being raised in the Florida sun, "but I'm Swenson. I'm expected to have a strong team and I'm expected to do well."

Learning to cope with pressure didn't come easily though. Swenson's first long distance race was the 1986 Quest. For the first three days, she was unable to eat. "I was in shock. But I finally relaxed and settled down."

Last minute consultation between Jeff King and his lead dog, 1988.

She finished that race in 17th place. In 1987, she became the first woman to finish in the top 10 — fourth overall, less than an hour behind Cotter. For anyone else, that might have been enough. But she is a Swenson; she feels she can do better. Kathy Swenson intends to win.

Bob Bright is better known as a sports promoter in Chicago, Illinois, but he's also a winter regular on the Alaskan sled dog racing circuit.

"It's a great adventure. Where else can you go and spend days on the back of a dog sled looking at some of the most beautiful country in the world?"

His technique for combating the cold and fatigue he faces on the trail is making sure he has the proper diet. Into his high-tech titanium sled he packs deep-dish pizzas and pork chops donated by a restaurant owned by another sporting personality, Chicago Bears coach Mike Ditka. On top sits chili and Chinese food.

"I'll tell you something. You get pretty damned hungry out there, especially in this kind of climate, if you don't have food you like to eat."

The trail philosopher is the diminutive Frank Turner, who lives alone in a cabin on the banks of the Pelly River in the Yukon. Or almost alone. He shares his homestead with 30 dogs. The bespectacled sage claims he discovered he had a genetic predisposition towards dog mushing 16 years ago when he stepped in a pile of dog poop and didn't mind the smell. He is also one of only two drivers who have competed in every Yukon Quest.

Zen and motorcycle maintenance don't hold a candle to existentialism and dog mushing. He savours the bitter cold and hardship of his lifestyle. "I have such a heightened sense of being alive. There's so much exhilaration. I can still enjoy mushing, I haven't lost it. If I ever do, it'll be time to move onto sailing or even tiddly-winks."

He adjusts his eyeglasses, then gazes thoughtfully at his team, which stares expectantly back. They may not be aware of it, but Turner is graduating up one level in his own personal Yukon Quest. Rather than running the race just for the experience, this year he is raising funds for the Yukon Association for Special Needs People, an organization that works with the physically and mentally handicapped.

"I'm using the race as a vehicle for things beyond the race. It's a sense of giving something back somehow. I've always looked at the Quest from the beginning as being a number of levels, and this is one of the levels: to do something."

Ed Borden was here in 1986. A chemist from Kenai, Alaska, he wasn't here to win. Nor was he here simply for the experience of driving a long distance race — he had two Iditarod races under his belt already. He was there because he had to do it while he could. Borden suffers from multiple sclerosis, a disease that may never affect his life or that may permanently disable him. Borden was determined to make the most of what he had while he had it.

In 1990, when William Kleedehn steps onto this hallowed ground, he will have two things to demonstrate. He will be determined to show that just because he has only one leg, he isn't any more handicapped on the trail than anyone else. And, second, he will want to see if, as a musher from the east (Kenora, Ontario), he can compete with the driving elite of Alaska.

In 1989, Jeninne Cathers will make her mark in Quest history. She will be half of the first daughter-father team to enter the race. (Her father, Ned, is in the parking lot today, preparing for his first attempt.) The tall teenager wants to be the youngest musher to ever enter, compete and finish. Her 18th birthday, the minimum age allowed to compete, will fall on the closing day for entries that year.

Two nights before this parking lot bedlam, the order of departure had been determined at the starting banquet, where the drivers drank beer, ate food, listened to speeches and pulled numbers out of a fur hat.

Now the announcers at the start line are calling for the first sled. Gerry Riley had lifted out number one from the hat. He heads his team out of the parking lot, over the riverbank and along the ice to the starting banner.

Considered one of the toughest drivers on the racing circuit, the stocky 55-year-old commercial fisher, winner of the 1976 Iditarod, is from the old school of mushing. While others have moved to specific breeding programs, high-powered food and specialized equipment, he has continued to raise dogs the way he did while growing up in his home village in the Alaskan interior.

"I use dry dog food and give them their shots. That's high tech for me."

The Alaskan native is also considered one of the masters of subterfuge on the trail. Other drivers know it's what Riley isn't saying or doing that's important. He never really does not tell the truth about himself and his team, it just sort of comes out like a half truth. The problem is figuring out which half to believe, and when to believe it.

"You run into Gerry in the summer and he tells you about his back and how bad it is. His dogs are sick; worse than that, they're dying. He doesn't know if he's going to race this year or not," smiles Jon Gleason. "The next time you see him, in the race, you're looking at his bad back as his dying dogs leave you in the dust."

Gleason, a former professional motorcycle racer who gave up wheels in favour of dog mushing, will follow closely behind Riley. He watches Riley pull out of the parking lot, then returns to preparing his team to start his third Yukon Quest.

As Riley draws up to the starting chute, volunteers and officials step forward to assist him. It's not easy. The dogs yelp, leap and drive towards the trail ahead of them. Three or four people hang onto the neck lines, restraining them. A half dozen more anchor down the sled.

Riley walks down the team, rubbing each dog on the head, talking quietly to them, reminding them who is boss. It's like watching a coach prepare a team for the big game, trying to calm them down while keeping them pumped up. But there is more to the relationship between mushers and their dogs; it borders on something like a parent-child bond rather than just players and their mentor.

Riley turns and responds to a question or statement from the crowd pressed up against the snow fence. Most of the spectators have listened to Niggemyer's warnings and are watching from the bridge behind the starting chute, or from the riverbank. A few of those who venture onto the ice pay the price later in the morning when they drop through into ice-cold ankle-deep water near the shore line.

Somebody shouts at Riley from near the announcer's booth. He looks back at the sled, at the dogs, down the trail, then jogs back to his sled. The starter's flag goes up. The timer counts down.

"Three.

"Two.

"One.

"Go!"

The flag drops, the volunteers fall back and the team surges forward. Through the starting area, Riley rides with all his weight holding down his brake; not until he is past the crowd does he step off the brake and let the dogs have their head.

The race is on.

Some carry passengers for extra weight; others drag behind them an anchor, which can be anything from another sled to an old rubber tire, anything to slow down the teams which are fresh, strong and pumped up with the sheer joy of finally being let loose to run. All the frustrations and confusion of the parking lot are left behind in this initial burst for freedom on the trail.

At this point, the driver's job is simply to hang onto the sled and not let the dogs get out of control. Too much speed now could result in injury to driver or dogs, or could damage the sled. In addition, an out-of-control sled whipping through spectators can be dangerous. The passenger or anchor will be dropped off or cut loose once the sled passes beyond the crowds.

Behind Riley, in their predetermined order, the rest of the competitors file down from the parking lot in two-minute intervals. Forty-seven times the starting chute sequence is repeated. The barking and yowling of dogs diminish as the teams leave. Then, finally, there is silence. The crowd pauses for a moment, reluctant to leave, but they gradually start to drift away from the Chena River. Now they must rely on the media to know what's happening out there on the trail.

Lawyer-turned-professional-dog-musher Dave Monson is the 13th driver to pull out from the starting chute. The superstition surrounding the number doesn't bother him. One of the pre-race favourites, the second-place finisher of the 1987 Quest is, in fact, quite delighted with his number. The number 13 is considered a good omen in the Iditarod (a race that Monson's wife Susan Butcher has already won twice) and he is planning to make it lucky in this race also.

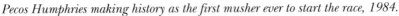

Pecos Humphries making history as the first musher ever to start the race, 1984.

A few minutes behind him is Rick Atkinson, the stubbornly dogged Scot who tried to "steal" the 1985 race but faltered in the home stretch. A documentary film about his second-place finish that year has won several major international awards. The veteran of dog driving in Antarctica is at his best in the wilderness and his 16 years of experience as a mountaineering guide cannot be discounted.

Then Jeff King sets off. Jeff, with his intense gaze that reflects a single-minded determination to win, is another pre-race favourite. A construction contractor, he is the only musher other than Turner to have raced in all the Yukon Quests so far. He has been in the thick of the fight every time but has fallen short in every race to now. The smart money rides on his sled this year. He is due.

Pecos Humphries, the long-bearded trapper from Talkeetna, Alaska, was the first musher to start the inaugural Quest in 1984. The luck of the draw at the musher's banquet that year gave him a claim to fame that no one can ever take away.

"Maybe I'll be a trivia question 10 years from now," muses Humphries, who came north in 1973 for a short stint with the United States Air Force and just never left.

Former Iowa rodeo rider and artist, Jim Reiter, sweats over whether or not he has covered all his bases. In addition to the approximately $10,000 cash each driver invests, there is a lot of physical and emotional preparation for the race. But, at the start line, what is left undone remains undone. What is forgotten, stays forgotten, and stays behind. Most of the time.

In this case, what Reiter has forgotten doesn't get left behind when he kicks off to help the dogs break the runners from the snow, it goes with him. In his pocket is the key to his truck and left stranded at the start line is his girlfriend and handler Debbie Styer. Undaunted, she starts looking for a ride to Angel Creek, the first checkpoint 75 miles away.

Ahead of the teams lies the Yukon Quest trail; 1,000 miles of narrow track cut in the snow across three major mountain ranges, through miles of thick underbrush and trees and down much of the length of the Yukon River, one of North America's great waterways.

The route to Angel Creek is, comparatively speaking, the easiest leg of the entire race, but it also can trap the unwary. The track meanders along the Chena River for about 15 miles. The ice is fairly smooth, most of it covered by a crust of snow. Other areas have been swept clear by the winds, exposing glare ice, a surface on which the dogs can find no secure footing and which is highly reflective, often preventing the driver from seeing any hazardous features.

The trail then turns off the river, following smaller streams and bush trails. Twisting and winding through the trees, it occasionally emerges to run parallel to the Chena Hot Springs Road before dropping onto the north fork of the Chena River, which takes it to Angel Creek.

This is a land greatly transformed since Jack McQuesten drove his dogs along the Tanana River in the winter of 1878 to trade for furs. That was the first recorded trip by a non-native into a country now crisscrossed by hundreds of winter dog sled and snowmachine trails.

The Quest trail was primarily a freighting trail and mail route in the early part of the 20th century. It was also the route along which Juchiro Wada — a Japanese cook and renowned long distance musher in the 1890s — set off, into the ice fog and minus 50-degree temperatures, to carry word of the 1902 gold strike.

There is a local joke in Fairbanks that the crookedest street in the city is Barnette Street. It refers to the business practices of one E.T. Barnette, the founder of Fairbanks. He had been dropped off on the Chena River at this location in 1901 because the riverboat he was on couldn't go any further upstream. Shortly after his arrival, a prospector named Felix Pedro walked into his camp and asked for supplies because he had just found gold in the adjacent hills. It was this news that sent Wada on his trip.

That journey almost ended Wada's life, not because of the hardships he faced on the trail, but because, when the stampeders arrived, they found there was lots of gold but no food to get them through the winter.

They decided at first to lynch the cook. However, Barnette was ultimately fingered as the culprit when he tried to sell them his food at inflated prices. Faced with a hungry mob just aching for a hanging, he sold them all his food at bargain rates, then temporarily skipped town on the next dog sled heading north. Wada, his necktie party cancelled by Barnette's flight, survived to mush again.

The shortest Yukon Quest ever run ended in 1986 just 20 miles from Fairbanks.

Ralph Nestor was running alongside his sled when the trail took a sharp turn to the left. The dogs made the corner and so did the sled. But Nestor was slingshotted away from the sled and kept going in a straight line, colliding headfirst with a tree. On standing up, his legs seemed a little shaky and he had some minor dizziness.

"I'll just take a bit of a break," he muttered to himself, "then I'll keep on going." Dentist and dog driver Ron Rosser was right behind Nestor. He glanced at Nestor's head. "I don't think you should keep going," he suggested to Nestor. "I can see your skull through your hair."

Nestor put his hand to his head where it landed on a cold, smooth surface. He pulled down his hand and looked at it, but there was only a little blood. Most of it had frozen on the exposed bone.

Rosser loaded the injured musher on his sled and carried him the couple of miles to the highway. A motorist took him to Fairbanks Memorial

Hospital. Nestor's Quest ended with a black eye, 72 stitches, a place in the record books and a new lesson for his students when he returned to his job as director of the travel industry management program at the University of Alaska in Fairbanks.

On the trail, it is getting close to dusk when nature calls Lorrina Mitchell. At first she figures she can ignore it, but it won't go away.

"Now this is not usually a problem in the summertime, but when you're wearing all your layers of clothes, it requires a lot more preparation…to find a convenient place to secure the team and to make sure you don't have too much company on the trail."

She picks her spot, puts the snow hook around a tree then, almost as an afterthought, ties another rope to another tree.

The first woman ever to have finished the Yukon Quest — 11th place in 1984 — she grew up surrounded by dog drivers in the northern British Columbia bush. Even her love life has been connected with mushing.

A romantic dog sled ride to an isolated cabin for the weekend was supposed to be the ultimate experience for Mitchell and her boyfriend a few years ago. The weekend turned somewhat less than romantic when the sled tipped over and the boyfriend was knocked out. Mitchell had to load him into the sled and spend the weekend trying to cure his headache. It may not have gone as planned, but the romance continued. The boyfriend was Gordie Mitchell, now her husband and handler.

Two days before the race she had put on her most alluring black evening dress and cranked up her most feminine charms for the mushers' banquet because "as of Saturday, you can't tell the girls from the boys, so tonight we're helping you out." As she wrestles with her clothes in the trees, she thinks about how much easier this might be if she were a boy.

A few moments later, her pants down around her knees, her heart isn't the only thing that comes to a halt as she hears her team start heading off down the trail. The snow hook bounces loose, but the extra snub-line, the one she tied as an afterthought, holds. She recovers her pants, her composure and her team and spends the rest of the day wondering how she would have explained this one if that extra rope hadn't held.

There is a steep embankment to climb as the drivers turn off the Chena River and into the bush. Ed Salter, one of Alaska's premiere sled dog builders, got hung up on this escarpment in 1987. His lead dogs were over the top but for some reason the team didn't want to pull the sled up. Jon Gleason gave him a hand to finish the climb, then his team started up the hill and stopped in exactly the same position.

"Dogs can be so stupid sometimes," sums up Gleason. "It's almost like it was written, 'you will get to the top and you will stop and you will not go any further no matter how much they cuss and swear.' At that particular point, all our dogs have got the same damn name: you dumb sonofabitch. I don't care whose team it is, we've all got the same dumb dogs and they all have the same name."

Getting lost is not uncommon on this part of the trail. With so many tracks cutting across the race route, a wrong turn or a missed marker is expected. Mushers often find themselves knocking on cabin doors to ask directions or sitting in gravel pits with one set of sled runner marks, their own, entering and none going out. Most often, the solution is backtracking to find out where the mistake was made. Providing you don't make another error while backtracking, it usually works. Sometimes it's sheer luck or divine providence that provides the solution.

In 1986, Harry Sutherland, a wiry ex-paratrooper-turned-carpenter-dog-driver, prayed he would find the trail soon after taking a wrong turn and, sure enough, his inspiration came from above. "I was really disoriented. I turned around. I went across a gravel pit and into the woods. I was stumbling around and pretty soon a helicopter comes over and there are a couple of TV guys from Fairbanks in it. I've got to talk to those guys. Get them to land. I'm waving at them and they come down." Sutherland's weathered face has wrinkles in it when he's relaxed. When he's angry or frustrated, the wrinkles turn into gullies. The journalists could see that Sutherland was upset. When he started running again, the helicopter hovered overhead, the reporters pointing the way back to the trail.

The first one to arrive at Angel Creek in 1988 isn't an official, a dog or a driver. As Steve and Ann Verbanec, owners of the popular weekend bar that serves as the first checkpoint, prepare for the onslaught of spectators, media, organizers, and volunteers, a small moose strolls casually into the parking lot and stands watching all the commotion.

After a few minutes it wanders over to warm itself by a campfire on the edge of the yard. Eventually, with no musher in sight yet and bored with being gawked at, the moose saunters back into the trees and disappears.

There are two schools of thought about arriving first at the first checkpoint. It may be an advantage, providing a small psychological lift similar to the kind of boost sprinters get when they know they've had a good start. Or it may be a disadvantage to have a lead at this early stage because of the feeling you get having all those other teams following along behind you, taking advantage of the work you did breaking trail.

"Dogs that go out after number one can really move it without using up a lot of energy because they chase the leading teams like a fox chases rabbits," says Pecos Humphries.

Never one to hang back and let someone else set the pace, Jeff King is the first to arrive in the late evening darkness. For King, his moustache and fur trim around his parka hood hanging with icicles, being first into Angel Creek provides an analytical satisfaction. It gives him the opportunity to get a better look at Kathy Swenson and David Monson than they will get of him.

King's stoic reaction at reaching the first checkpoint contrasts strongly with the euphoric high that Stan Bearup felt when he arrived in 1985. Bearup was in the middle of the pack, but his position in the standings wasn't that important. The fact that he had even gotten this far was reason enough to celebrate. A year earlier, the young native from North Pole, Alaska, had almost died while training for the Quest.

While he was out in the bush running his dogs, a blood vessel burst in his brain and almost killed him. Another musher came across him lying on the trail and carried him to help. "You'll be partially paralysed for the rest of your life," his doctors informed him. "Forget about the Quest. You're going to have enough trouble just walking."

Medically they may have been right, but doctors are also aware that special events or specific goals can cause people to accomplish the impossible with their health, even to the extent of cheating death. And, like most Alaskans, Bearup hated to be told he couldn't do something that he wanted to do.

The training started the day he left the hospital. His 1984 Christmas present to himself was officially filing his entry papers. When he stepped off the sled at the first checkpoint, he crossed over a psychological barrier just as great as the physical one he was on his way to conquering. Fifteen days later, he completed the race he had been told he could never run.

Angel Creek Lodge was a layover spot on the old winter road between Fairbanks and the Circle District. Today, the weatherworn log structure is home for a bevy of outdoor winter activities, including snowmobile sprints and middle distance and sprint dog sled races, as well as indoor activities like Trivial Pursuit tournaments. It didn't actually become an official checkpoint for the Yukon Quest until 1986.

For two years the Quest trail simply ran past the front door to Chena Hot Springs, 15 miles further up the valley. The hospitality at Chena was fine, but the environment left a lot to be desired.

The warm ground around the thermal springs resort kept the snow in a perpetual state of slush — half water, half snow. The dogs would rest in the slush and be soaking wet when it was time to go. The water would freeze in their fur once they left the warmth, depriving the dogs of their natural insulation against the cold. The mushers also didn't like the idea of giving mineralized water to their teams. Anything out of the ordinary introduced into their diet at this stage could make the entire team sick and end their race right there.

So the decision was made by organizers to move the checkpoint to Angel Creek. There is lots of room for the drivers to park their teams outside the lodge and the Verbanecs keep three large barrels of fresh, unmineralized water warming near a fire. Checkpoint life for the dogs has improved, but the mushers are the ones who pay the price. Angel Creek isn't what the drivers consider a peaceful checkpoint. Most of the spectators crowd into the bar at the lodge, which is also the only place where the mushers can rest.

Here they can get a good meal of stew, some pasta dishes, buns, desserts and whatever they want to drink. It's warm and they can dry any wet clothes or gear.

But it's a tough place to catch a little shut-eye. Some of the mushers try to sleep sitting upright in chairs at the tables, or leaning against the wall in a chair. Others prop themselves up in the corner or drop their head on a table while the fans party around them.

Harry Sutherland fell asleep at one of the tables in 1986, then woke up to find himself surrounded by a group of Japanese tourists who split their attention between observing him and watching the early morning cartoons on the bar television.

"I don't think they understood either me or the TV."

Frank Turner tries catching a little shut-eye under the pool table. He gets kicked occasionally by players and a beer is dumped on him. He crawls out and beds down on top of his sled. It's cold, but it's quiet and dry.

"Really can't blame them," he says. "They are a business and it is an opportunity to make some money. They try to make it comfortable, but it's not really a place where we can totally relax. A lot of us just feed and water the dogs, then keep on going."

Bob Bright couldn't sleep if he wanted to when he arrives. His stomach is tied up in knots over the condition of his sled. It has taken a beating on the trail and he isn't sure if it will survive the next stretch of trail. Titanium parts for repairs are proving to be difficult to get hold of.

Jim Reiter arrives in a buoyant mood. Everything has gone just fine. The team is healthy and happy. So is he. And nothing has been left behind. He smiles as he watches Debbie Styer walk towards him. It is nice of her to drive up here just to see how he is doing, he thinks, but he wonders why she isn't smiling. Then he puts his hands in his pockets and feels a set of keys.

Mary Sheilds is just happy to be anywhere. Whether she's on the trail or in a checkpoint, she always seems to be happy. The only woman to complete both the Iditarod and the Yukon Quest, the amiable author of books on dog mushing and life in the northern wilderness walks down her line of dogs flashing her trademark smile. She gives an affectionate rub and talks quietly to each of "her guys."

Nineteen years ago, as a Wisconsin high school student, she came north to work for the Camp Fire Girls in Alaska and fell in love with the land. When she graduated, she returned to her adventure fantasy by living in the wilderness and running dogs. Even after two decades, the thrill has not jaded.

In random order over the next several hours, the mushers pull in. Dave Monson. Kathy Swenson. Rick Atkinson.

Jim Bennett, a former teacher from Fairbanks. He took up dog mushing when he got tired of having his snowmachine break down in the bush all the time. This is his second Quest as a driver; in 1984, he was the Quest's first president of the board of directors.

Tom Randall of Whitehorse pulls in. Tom is a truck driver who at one time restricted his winter excitement to operating his snowmachine while his wife Elsie drove a few dogs. When she got sick, he had to run the dogs. His first night out with them he seemed to be taking a long time to come back home. So Elsie dragged herself out of bed and went looking for him. When she caught up, he was still mushing along the trail towards who-knows-where and loving every minute of it. He still is, six years later.

Lorrina Mitchell. Ralph Tingey. Gerald Riley. Ron Rosser.

Grandmother Lena Charley arrives, the oldest woman to ever race the Quest. At 58 years of age, having worked as a trapper and dog musher for her entire life, she feels she now has the spare time required to indulge in a leisure activity. Besides that, three of her own children and two of her grandchildren are involved in racing dogs and she doesn't want to be left out of the fun.

Not all the drivers arrive tonight. Stragglers wander in occasionally during the next morning and afternoon. The last to arrive is Mike "Rattles" Kramer.

The first 75 miles have taken their toll on his dogs; they are in no shape to tackle the next stage. After 24 hours on the trail, Kramer himself is also beat. He quits the race.

The arctic air mass is delayed in its advance to the south. The first afternoon of the race was rather pleasant, but a brisk northern wind is now sweeping in the bone-numbing cold. Up above, the stars and moon are gradually obscured by a billowing bank of clouds. There is no fresh snow falling, but the wind, gusting up to gale force, will compensate for that by drifting a lot of the old snow.

It is the worst combination of environmental conditions at the worst possible time. Above the lodge at Angel Creek looms the silhouette of the first of the three major mountain ranges that stand between the drivers and the finish.

(over) Lorrina Mitchell (back) and Don Glassburn (front) midway between Fairbanks and Chena Hot Springs, 1984.

The dreamers

The dreamers

Every once in a while, as he sits at home playing with his cats, the question filters through his mind. "Why in hell is a Mississippi boy mixed up in something like a dog race when I don't even like dogs?"

The answer is easy.

"To me a dog sled race is still just simply a dog sled race," grins Roger Williams. "It's the international and philosophical aspect of what we're doing. Sitting down with people from Alaska and the Yukon and everybody working for a common goal. That's what keeps me going. As far as the competition of the race…hell, that only lasts two weeks out of the year. The rest of it. The complexities of running an international event. The logistics. The politics.

"The different philosophies of the Canadians and Americans or the people who live in the villages versus the cities. Here in Fairbanks we think differently than, say, someone living in Maisy May or Biederman's Cabin or wherever. The only thing that brings all those people together and working for a common cause is the Yukon Quest.

"I've met a lot of people because of this that I probably would never have met — people that have made a lasting impression on me. I'll remember them for the rest of my life."

When Williams sat down in the Bull's Eye Saloon in the spring of 1983, he had no idea that it would change his life. But major changes have a way of happening to Williams when he least expects them.

For example, there was the decision to move to Alaska in the first place, in 1975. Working as a chemical engineer in Memphis, Tennessee, Roger found himself on call 24 hours a day. Responding to a phone call that was dragging him out of bed at two o'clock one morning, he commented to his wife Jocelyn, "Hey, you know, it's like I'm married to this company and I'm not really married to you. There's got to be a better way to make a living. Maybe we should move. Or change jobs."

"Why don't we move to Alaska?" she responded. So they did.

And there was the spot where Williams began his love affair with northern history, a fascination that was to mould his role in a sport about which he had, and still has, limited enthusiasm.

It was the barest beginnings of spring in 1981, during a stopover in Whitehorse, Yukon. They were camping during what felt more like a late-winter drive up the Alaska Highway, spending every night in a tent in minus 20-degree temperatures. Eventually, Jocelyn decided that being economical could take a back seat to being warm. "I want to spend the night in a hotel room," she said, "in a real bed." And Whitehorse was the next stop on the road map.

For a small city (about 20,000 inhabitants), Whitehorse is surprisingly cosmopolitan, featuring facilities that one would expect to find only in larger centres. One of those facilities is the small log building that houses the MacBride Museum.

Williams is an insatiably curious man. He loves to discover things or research them. Museums are of particular interest to him. Since both Jocelyn and Roger had had a good night's sleep, he decided to spend a couple of hours browsing through the building. He would never look at the north in quite the same way again.

"I could live in that museum. It's just packed full of a lot of good stuff. Anyone who lives in the Yukon or Alaska should go through there because there's well-preserved newspaper articles, histories of the gold rushes in the north, a lot of colourful stuff on some of the characters back then. I think it's one of the finest museums for a town that size I've ever seen."

For two days he prowled from room to room, discovering nostalgia that hearkened back to a time before airplanes, highways, radios and telephones.

He uncovered the fabled mystique of the gold that lay hidden under the ice and snow for centuries. A history measured in ounces and lives lost or ruined in its pursuit. He found a time when there were true heroes; some lauded for their feats, most unrecognized, since being a hero was just a way of life.

In his own way, he became like a dog driver, seeking the romantic fantasy of the pioneer. But rather than trying to find it on the back of a sled following the spirits of the long-dead mail drivers who preceded him, Williams sought to understand the common threads that joined the Yukon and Alaska through a shared history and the unique society which that legacy produced.

"We are really one distinctive type of people, those of us who live in the Yukon and Alaska and the Northwest Territories by choice. The only thing that really divides us are political boundaries."

Possibly it was this shared fantasy that was the basis of the friendship between Williams and his co-worker at the *Fairbanks Daily News Miner*, Leroy Shank, a recreational dog musher. On the surface, they have little in common. Williams is slender, Shank is heavyset. Williams' education comes from universities and colleges, Shank's book-learning comes mostly from having little else to do while on his trapline except read. Like most of the dog drivers who live or have lived in the bush, it is a highly developed, although unconventional, education. Williams likes cats and hates dogs; Shank loves dogs and hates cats.

To this day Williams really can't explain how Shank was able to convince him to be the handler for his dog team in the 1983 Angel Creek-Bull's Eye Saloon sled dog race. But for whatever reason, the decision to help his friend set him up for one of those unexpected moments of great change.

There were four of them at the table in the Bull's Eye Saloon following the race: Williams, Shank, Ron Rosser and Willie Libb, a Fairbanks musher who specializes in sprints and middle distance races. The beer was flowing easily and the imaginations of the drivers started to get fairly well lubricated. It started out as a casual comment, something like "God, this is a fun race. Wouldn't it be nice if they made it a little longer?"

From there it started to get longer. It went past Angel Creek to Chena Hot Springs, over the mountains to Circle Hot Springs, to Circle. Williams was enjoying the flights of fantasy, but attached no importance to them until the race hit the Yukon River and turned southeast towards the Canadian border.

"Once we got to the Yukon River, I thought, 'Well shit. We're at the Yukon River, there's a trail right there all the way into the Yukon. We could run a race, an international race and it also follows a historical trail. We could really do something that makes a statement.'"

As the bar bill got longer, so did the race. Eventually, it got all the way to Los Angeles. When Williams woke up the next morning, there was a glowing ember of an idea in his head, but his hangover took precedence for the moment and the idea was left to linger on its own for the next few months.

It wasn't until he and Shank went fishing during the summer that the spark burst into flame and he found he wasn't alone. That same ember was lying smouldering in Shank's mind as well, although for entirely different reasons.

Unlike Williams, Shank's whole life has been involved with dogs. His father raced dogs in Colorado during the summer and in the winter used them for hunting coyotes and trapping. Shank was the youngest of three children, and the only boy. They lived in a lightly populated part of the mountain state and having neighbours was more an expression of longing for company than it was reality. His father's dogs were his closest friends as he grew up.

"When I was a child everyone would ask me, 'What are you going to do when you grow up?' and I'd say, 'I'm going to live somewhere where I can have lots of dogs and be a bachelor.'"

The opportunity to do both came in 1960 when his brother-in-law called him from Fairbanks. "Hey, Leroy," he said. "You know you've always wanted to come to Alaska. I have a job for you."

"I'll be there in a week," he replied, and he was.

It was heaven for Shank. The 1960s were the heyday of big game hunting in Alaska. A lot of the interior was still relatively unexplored and Shank spent his summers collecting an array of hunting trophies and taking fishing trips. In the 1970s he started trapping in winter, but he chose a snowmachine over dogs.

The bachelor part of his ideal lifestyle ended in 1974 when he married his wife Kathleen. The dog part started in 1977 when he decided to switch from a snowmachine on his trap line to something more dependable and less susceptible to the vagaries of the climate — a dog team.

Shank had heard about a race called the Iditarod and talked to some of the mushers who competed in the Anchorage-to-Nome classic, but he swore, "I'm never going to race." "Never say never" is a rule of life that Shank had yet to learn. Five years later, in 1982, he found himself at the start line in Anchorage and two weeks after that, he crossed under the finish line. In 1983, he did it again. But, while the idea of a long distance race still attracted him, the Iditarod itself didn't exactly thrill him.

The original Iditarod rules dictated that the musher was to be totally self-sufficient and could not receive assistance while on the trail or at the checkpoints. However, in the past few years it has become the practice for the top drivers to have a handler look after the team at most checkpoints and to change sleds when the one they are using breaks or when their strategy in the race demands a different type of sled.

This was part of the inequity that Shank didn't like. The smaller kennels, like his, couldn't afford to have a handler in the checkpoints or to have more than one sled. He felt the race catered to the elite racers, the big-name competitors, and that campers like himself were treated somewhat like second-class citizens.

"I said, 'There's got to be something besides this.' I mean, there's got to be more to long distance racing or there's got to be an alternative.

"Alternative. That word kept going through my mind. And I also thought of all those people in Fairbanks who invested all their time in the Iditarod. And they have to drive 500 miles just to start. And you finish in Nome. There's no highway back. You have to fly. It's expensive. And I thought, there's got to be something from Fairbanks."

The conversation in the Bull's Eye Saloon just a month or so after Shank finished his second Iditarod suggested a route, one that was very viable.

It wasn't the first time a race between Fairbanks and Whitehorse had been talked about. By 1976, a group of mushers — including Ron Aldrich (the only musher to have driven in both the first Iditarod, in 1973, and the first Quest, in 1984), Ralph Nestor and Harry Sutherland — had become disillusioned with the Iditarod. Sitting together at Ron's homestead on Montana Creek, they discussed the concept of a race between the two cities. But when the group dissolved following the conversation, so did the idea.

In that summer of 1983, with their idea now burning strongly, Shank and Williams expanded their twosome to include Bud Smyth and writer Rod Perry, both veterans of organizing and racing in the early days of the Iditarod. They had to determine a basic premise, something that would distinguish their race from any other in existence.

"We heard from Bud how, in the early Iditarods, when you broke your sled you just fixed it," says Williams. "He said, 'Take a little baling wire along with you, a little duct tape. If your sled gets busted up, then you fix it and you keep on going.' We thought that was a real good idea; to make the race one where you had to be a survivor, a carpenter, the whole nine yards."

They approached Rosser, Libb and the other mushers who had been involved in the Bull's Eye Saloon conversation. But, for them, it had been pure fantasy. Such a race wasn't feasible.

Iditarod and Yukon Quest trails

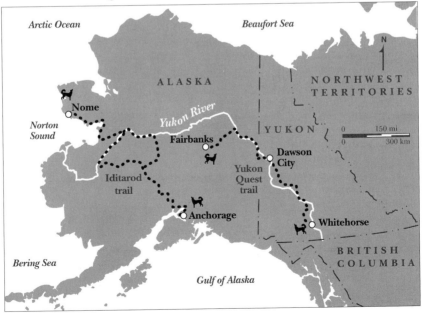

If the expertise and support to develop the idea past this point wasn't going to come from other mushers, it would have to be bought.

"We came up with a basic idea of what we wanted the race to be, then we started recruiting veterinarians, lawyers and mushers," Williams continues. "We decided to approach this the same way my grandfather would approach an attorney.

"He told me once, 'Never walk into an attorney's office and ask him what to do because he'll philosophize you into bankruptcy.' So we approached all these people and we said, 'This is what we want to do; you put it together and show us how to do it.'"

By the end of the summer, there was a definite set of rules, a specified route and even a potential starting date — February 25, 1985 — 16 months in the future.

It was time to go public. *Fairbanks Daily News Miner* sports editor Bob Eley liked the idea, but didn't think it would pass the rest of the editorial staff. "I can pass it through," he said, "but those people up there aren't really wild about dog sled races."

Eley underestimated the appeal of the idea. In its first try at publicity, the race dominated the front page of the largest newspaper in Fairbanks. He also underestimated the impact the race would have on his own life. Like almost everyone else touched by the race, he got involved, eventually becoming a board member and the president of Yukon Quest International in 1988.

The first public meeting didn't fare quite so well. Only seven people showed up. A second meeting drew 38 people, many of them reluctantly allowing themselves to be dragged along by those who were at the first meeting. The ranks of volunteers and organizers started to swell.

It was slow, but the Fairbanks end was starting to come together. However, one string still left untied was the other end of the race. It was time for the Fairbanks organizers to contact someone in Whitehorse to develop an organization to set up that half of the proposed race. Williams, Shank, Perry and Smyth headed south in October to meet their potential Canadian counterparts, Lorrina and Gordie Mitchell and the Quest's first Canadian race manager, Wendy Waters.

It had taken Lorrina Mitchell one night and the better part of a bottle of whiskey to get Waters involved in the Yukon Quest. In 1981, Waters had founded and organized the 220-mile Percy DeWolfe Race between Dawson City (also commonly known as Dawson), Yukon and Eagle, Alaska. In 1983, she had sworn off organizing races.

The first Yukon Quest would test Water's skills to the limit. But in the end, she would succeed in putting in 500 miles of trail and establishing checkpoints in a territory that was even more reluctant than Alaska to accept the Yukon Quest as a reality.

Huddled in their car somewhere along the Alaska Highway, for some reason — no one seems sure exactly why — the Fairbanks group decided to take a gamble. When they arrived in Whitehorse, they announced a new starting date — February 25, 1984.

They now had only four months to put it together. It did seem a little foolhardy. At this point they had no entries, few volunteers, no checkpoints, no trails and no trailbreakers. They just had a set of rules, a lot of work to do and a lot of faith. It was a risk, but if for some reason the race didn't go as announced — like nobody entering because of the short notice — they hoped they could still save some face if they had to postpone.

In fact, both Shank and Williams almost hoped nobody would show up to enter.

The point of no return turned up in the tall, gangly body of Murray Clayton. The commercial fisher from the coastal town of Haines stood in the back of the room at Ryan Junior High School in Fairbanks, quietly listening to the third public meeting, held in Fairbanks a week after the announcement of the starting date.

As the meeting dissolved, he pushed forward through the crowd until he reached the table at the front. Like others in the room he held out a cheque. Unlike the others, who were throwing in $100 each to help finance the venture, his cheque was for $500, the cost of entry.

"I want to be the first one to sign up and run it this year," he said. The prattle of voices around the table died away. There was silence.

Shank looked shocked for a moment. Then he reached out and took the cheque. "O.K.," he choked out the words, "it's on. This is it. We're going."

Williams felt panic well up inside himself. Hey, Murray, wait, he wanted to say. Wait until we're sure we're going to do this. But he kept his mouth shut. Whether it was the best thing or the worst thing he ever did in his life is a question for which he'll never really find an answer.

Williams' keeping his mouth closed and Shank's reaching out for Clayton's cheque that night put both of them on an emotional roller coaster that was just beginning its ride. It would disrupt their professional lives and their personal relationships with their families and friends. In some ways, seven years later, it still does, even though their involvement has been reduced significantly.

For the four months leading up to the first Yukon Quest, the organizers, and a gradually increasing number of volunteers, lived for nothing else except the race. Committees were set up to oversee the multitude of details. An executive group was established, with positions often filled for reasons beyond belief.

In one meeting, Jim Bennett stood up to make a point. He drew a circle on the blackboard to represent the financial pie that he was now going to slice into its various pieces of need. It was a good circle, almost perfectly round.

"You're president of the association," said Shank. "I can't draw a circle that good." Everyone else agreed.

The financing that Bennett started to cut up came from various and unexpected sources. One of the first was a phone call from the manager of Sampson Hardware, one of the oldest retail stores in Fairbanks. "My name is Mark Webber," said the voice on the other end. "I want to give you people some money."

Shank didn't get a speeding ticket on his way to pick up the $10,000 cheque, but he should have.

Another call came from a middle-aged widow who was scheduled to undergo serious surgery later in the week. "I read in the newspaper about your race," said Alexandria Ross. "I would like to donate $1,000." She became the first life member of Yukon Quest International, the association set up to organize and administer the race.

Not everything went smoothly. The logistics of putting together a 1,000-mile race through the wilderness exacted a toll on the endurance of the organizers. The stress ground away at the most patient of the workers and even the usually amiable Bud Smyth leaped up at one meeting screaming at

Race date is announced at first meeting of Alaskans and Yukoners.
(standing, l–r): Leroy Shank, Rod Perry, Wendy Waters
(seated, l–r): Bud Smyth, Lorrina Mitchell, Gordie Mitchell, Roger Williams

another volunteer, "Stand up, you son of a bitch! I'm going to knock your lights out."

But Williams and Shank had laid down the ground rules. The race took top priority. Regardless of emotions, personalities or philosophical clashes, the race came first and what was good for the race was all that was important.

Distance can cause great problems in communication. Trying to organize a race with the start and finish lines a thousand miles apart, and in two different countries, was often difficult. The fact that it was midwinter didn't help either.

Williams and Shank drove out of Fairbanks one morning, headed for a meeting in Whitehorse. It was cold when they started, about minus 50, and it just kept getting colder as they headed south. Eventually, the car's fan belt froze and broke, delaying them for several hours.

They arrived in Whitehorse, too late for the meeting which had ended a couple of hours earlier. Only two of the Whitehorse group were still in the hotel where the meeting had been held — Jon Rudolph of Whitehorse and Bruce Johnson, from Atlin, B.C. The two men had been sitting in the bar since the meeting had ended. Their topic of discussion had focused on the failure of Williams and Shank to make it to Whitehorse and the problems of dealing with the Alaskans via long distance. The sight of the two overdue Americans spurred them into action.

They launched themselves at Williams and Shank, pushed them against the wall, and then, uninhibited and outspoken as only an excess of drinking can make a person, they vented their feelings.

Shank, his face sombre, looked over at Williams, "God damn it, Roger," he said. "Try to make heroes out of these mushers and all the bastards can do is complain."

A trip into the Circle District, north of Fairbanks, produced another revelation. "We held a meeting in Central," remembers Shank, "and about 40 people turned up. Hell, I didn't even know that 40 people lived there."

Bit by bit, piece by piece, the organization came together. Twenty-six mushers entered the race. One thousand miles of trail were broken and marked. Seven checkpoints were established. Tons of dog food were shipped in. Aerial support was arranged and communication systems were set up.

By the time Pecos Humphries made history starting the first Quest, even the $50,000 purse for the winners (consisting of the entry fees from the mushers plus monies donated for that purpose) had been guaranteed.

For Williams and Shank, there was a moment at the start line when the noise of the crowd and the barking of the dogs seemed to fade away. Then there was a silence that only they heard. In that moment, they paused briefly to shake hands in quiet celebration.

But full realization of what they had accomplished came individually to each of the two men at different times and places along the trail.

For Shank, it came almost a week later, when he watched the leading musher, Sonny Lindner, driving his sled on the Yukon River below the spectacular rise of Eagle Bluff.

"It was in the morning and that sun was beating down there and you could see Eagle Bluff and he came around that corner through that beautiful white snow. And just as he popped around that corner, that church bell started ringing. And man! That just sent chills up my spine. I had tears in my eyes. I just said, 'Good grief.'

"And all those people were so excited because they had never seen a race before. They didn't even care who it was. They just said, 'Oh my God. Look at that. It's happening. It's him.'"

Williams' moment had to wait a little longer. He was well ahead of the teams, making sure that checkpoints were up and operating before the teams arrived. One of them, at Dawson City, was set up and organized just 10 minutes before the lead driver, Joe Runyan, arrived. It wasn't until Williams stood in Whitehorse, waiting at the finish line for the Yukon Quest's first champion to arrive, that he had a chance to consider all that had passed in the previous few months.

He thought back to one particular moment in that time, when the two of them, Williams and Shank, went to a meeting with all "the pillars of the community and we told them what we had in mind. They all stood up and laughed. They said, 'You can't do it. There's no possible way you can ever do it.'

"When Sonny crossed the finish line there in Whitehorse, we had the purse money waiting for him; everything had clicked; everything was in order. I just looked at Leroy and I could see these things in my mind where all these people were basically against us and they said, 'You can't do it. Give up before you start.'

"And when Sonny crossed that line — if nobody else ever made it across the finish line, it could be done because one guy did it. It happened to be Sonny Lindner."

(over) Jeff King chopping some frozen food for a late night snack for his dogs.

Life in a ping-pong ball

Life in a ping-pong ball

n Eagle Summit there is only Boreas, the north wind. Nothing moves without the aid or influence of the wind. It is moody, sometimes showing the harsh side of its disposition. It rears up, then crashes down, roars furiously off to the south, then turns and charges back north. It spirals, as if to burrow a hole in the earth or build a funnel to the stars.

It strips the mountain bare, exposing dark, surrealistic landscapes of weathered rock and twisted frozen vegetation, then deposits massive quantities of snow into drifts that tower into the sky.

The wind doesn't know its own strength in such rages. It tosses entire teams and sleds carelessly over cliffs or across glaciers without even expending a pittance of its power. It has substance, spitting crystals of snow that cut and sting like shards of broken glass, or settle on the skin, creating a crust of ice that pinches the eyes shut or burns into the flesh.

Or the wind can be gentle and compassionate, giving the drivers a gentle pat on the back and an encouraging push from behind.

It is best when it's at rest. The snow crystals can hang motionless in the air, a massive suspended prism through which the sunlight can create a shimmering wall of colour, like a rainbow that isn't satisfied with just arching through the air, but wants to fill the whole sky.

The wind is a musician, playing for whatever audience dares to listen. From the soft melodic hush of snow being moved over snow, it builds through a rhythmic booming of gusts to the resounding sonic whistle and howl of the gale force crescendo, or drops into motionlessness, leaving pure silence.

At such times it is like the Venus flytrap flower which uses its beauty to deceive its victims into venturing nearer, then closes the trap behind them.

The human body is not designed to resist the north wind. Moving arctic air freezes exposed skin in seconds. It drains the heat from a person in minutes. As the mushers work to stay warm, they perspire, and the moisture, freezing solid in the clothes instead of evaporating, turns the body's natural heating system into a potential liability.

The mind then sends confused warnings to the body; warnings that either panic people into making mistakes or rob them of their incentive to continue and their sensitivity to the environment around them; that encourage them to lie down for a sleep from which they may never awaken.

It is harder on the dogs; they literally freeze-dry. The dry cold absorbs the moisture they breathe out and sucks it out of their skin faster than the musher can replace it. Dehydration is a problem in any long distance dog sled race, but its effect is magnified by extreme cold and the wind.

"Mountain running is terrifying," says Lorrina Mitchell. "You have to know enough to camp down before you go over the mountain. Some people don't and they go up with half-tired dogs. All of a sudden you're above tree line and you have two options. You can turn around and go back below the tree line. Or you go straight across and you're not sure what you're going to be running into. It's almost always windy on the top of mountains...the few times it isn't, it's the nicest place in the world, but usually it's the lousiest.

"You hit that wind and your dogs start turning their back on it. If you've never experienced it before, it can be very frustrating and very frightening. You're in a situation you've never had to cope with before. All of a sudden you realize that if you don't get these dogs moving, you're going to freeze. And the dogs are going to freeze. And we're going to be in big trouble."

Angel Creek to Central

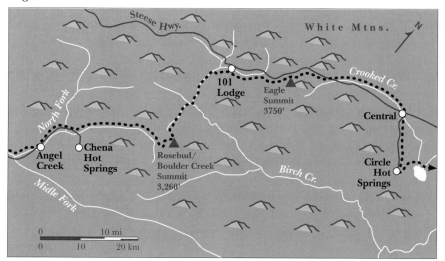

She speaks from hard-earned experience. In 1984, Mitchell had never encountered the mountain before she started crossing the White Mountains via Eagle Summit. Her previous mushing experience had been on relatively level terrain, along rivers and hilly bush trails.

Just miles from the Chena Hot Springs checkpoint, she ventured into new ground, up the steep face of Boulder Creek-Rosebud Pass. Once teams start to climb, there is little opportunity for them to rest. The ascent is not very high, but it is unbroken from bottom to top. There are no ledges or level spots to rest on.

Once on top, the teams are in the barren regions of the upper end of the tree line. The trail runs for several miles along a series of ridges. Then the team will spend many hours travelling through tundra broken only by large tussocks and the occasional spindly tree to 101 Lodge. From there the trail climbs again, away from whatever shelter may have been offered by the sparse vegetation, onto the exposed nakedness of Eagle Summit.

The snow is unpredictable up here. Some years it is a thick blanket, sometimes it barely exists. One year, the wind created drifts so high that some volunteers camped on top of one of them to help the teams climb over.

Kevin Turnbough, a former church minister who moved north because of his love for driving dogs, describes crossing Eagle Summit as being "like life inside a ping-pong ball. You can't see anything. You don't know where you are. It's noisy. It's cold. And you get banged around a lot."

In 1984, on the Boulder Creek-Rosebud Pass summit, Mitchell's team balked, her glasses slipped, fell, then vanished into the blowing snow. Blinded by her impaired sight and the blowing snow, Mitchell, sled and dogs crashed down over an embankment. Confused and lost, she bedded down. Around her, the wind raged, frustrated at not being able to tackle her directly. It threw a blanket of snow over her sleeping bag, dogs and sled.

Another musher, Jack Hayden of Lake Minchumina, Alaska, literally stumbled across her, buried in her sleeping bag beneath the snow.

Mitchell may have been able to stay warm and wait out the storm in her little snow cave, but Hayden didn't want to take the risk. He rousted her up, stirred up her dogs, tied a rope to her sled and led them down into a more sheltered area. Once they were out of the wind, he heated up some Tang and forced it down her throat until she stopped shivering. "She was definitely in trouble up there," he said. "She was definitely hypothermic."

Hayden continued his Quest and eventually finished eighth. Mitchell finished just four hours behind him.

In 1988, Ralph Tingey and Dennis Kogl stand at the bottom of the climb to Boulder Creek-Rosebud Pass watching as three teams struggle towards the top. Above them they can hear the winds howling and sense the burning cold just over the upper lip of the slope.

The arctic front has arrived as predicted.

But the winds that preceded it won't go away. Up top, out of the protection of the trees, the cold air and wind combine to push temperatures close to minus 100 degrees. Even where the two mushers stand, it is minus 25. They ponder the wisdom of pushing through without a stop.

The three drivers currently climbing — Jeff King, Jon Gleason and François Varigas — are serious contenders. If they make it through the maelstrom on top, the 1988 Yukon Quest may already be over. No one will be able to catch them.

To push now means to camp later. The two drivers talk it over briefly. Kogl, who has driven dogs for over 20 years in just about every part of the world where dog sleds can be pulled, thinks they should stay put for the moment. Tingey, a manager from Denali National Park, agrees. They decide to wait.

"We didn't want to camp up there," says Tingey. "It's a long way and there's no point in burning the dogs now. We decided to stop for a few hours."

They aren't alone. Other teams stack up behind them, and by dawn there are 18 teams backed up at the foot of the pass. Most are feeding and watering their dogs. The early arrivals have already curled up on top of their sleds in their sleeping bags. But no one dozes for long. The storm above them roars on unabated. One by one, the three ascending mushers lead their teams over the lip and out of sight.

Their disappearance puts butterflies in the stomachs of the drivers at the bottom. The waiting gets harder. Uncertainty keeps them on edge. As the hours pass, the waiting gets to some of the teams and they start packing their sleds. The three leaders can be anywhere up there; they might be hours ahead, or camped just over the top, just out of sight.

Dave Monson wants to test his team. So far, he has sat back in the pack, but now it's time to find out what his team is made of, just how well they will respond to him under duress. He is the first one to untangle himself from the crowd and head upwards, pressing his dogs all the way. By the time he reaches the winds, he knows the dogs aren't a problem, but his clothes have the potential of becoming one.

"The dogs just charged up there and I had to run with this snowsuit on. I was sweating so bad all the zippers froze. I had to pull it off and I got it down to my waist, but it would drag on the ground behind me because I couldn't get my legs out. It was like running up a 4,000-foot hill with your pants down. It was double the work to the top."

One by one, the rest of the teams follow. It is worse on top than they expect. For all his expended energy in being the first one of the waiting teams up the slope, Monson is content to sit, just down out of the wind, and wait for the others, rather than charging on ahead.

They start leapfrogging each other, taking turns breaking the windblown trails leading towards Eagle Summit. At this point, cooperation makes more sense than competition. Ahead of the pack, the three frontrunners have all run into problems.

Gleason reaches a cabin on the Steese Highway, an all-weather road which crosses the mountains in the shadow of the summit. He has four hurt dogs. One has dislocated an elbow; the other three appear to be suffering from some form of food poisoning. He settles down to wait. If the sickness passes, he'll continue. But the health of his dogs is paramount in his mind.

A year earlier, near this same spot, he was forced to scratch when one of his lead dogs, Dutch, froze his foot and the other leader, Timber, decided he had had enough of the uphill and headwinds and stopped running.

"When the bottom line is drawn, the dogs come first. Position and money aren't that vital," he says.

A few miles ahead of him, Jeff King is thawing out his left hand. It froze as he tried to catch a few hours sleep back on Birch Creek, in the flat area just past the Boulder Creek-Rosebud Pass. He is using chemical heat packs to keep his hands warm, but a mishap with a power saw during the summer damaged the nerves in his hand. When one of the packs finally cools off, he doesn't notice until it is too late. His fingers are now swollen and peeling.

"I was very naive, not thinking enough. I should have known my hand would need extra care. There's such a fine distinction between the amount of sensation I did have and the zero sensation of frostbite."

His dogs are healthy and eating well. His lead dog, Hickory, actually saves him from freezing his ears as well when his hat blows off in the wind. King anchors the team, then goes after the wayward garment. But the team breaks loose and beats him to it. When he arrives, Hickory is standing with the hat under her foot.

But the 32-year-old construction worker knows his race is over. It is a bitter conclusion for King who hasn't missed a top-five finish in his previous four years. The summit has beaten him. To continue means to risk freezing his fingers again and that could result in amputation.

There's a traditional saying that things, bad or good, happen in threes. For King, scratching is only the second of the three. Cutting his hand was the first. The third will come shortly before the 1989 Quest. His home will burn to the ground, killing his top two lead dogs. But, from that moment, his luck will turn because Jeff King is due. He will win the 1989 race.

François Varigas, transplanted from France, moved to a cabin on a small creek just outside of Dawson City because he had fallen in love with the north reading Jack London novels as a child. He has injured two wheel dogs before reaching Angel Creek, but decides to keep on running and evaluate them on the mountain. The run along Birch Creek produces a noticeable limp in the two dogs. His lead dog, Blue, also starts to hobble. When he reaches the Steese Highway, he flags down a van, loads his team into it, ties the sled to the roof and heads to Central so he can officially withdraw.

Ned Cathers looking a little frosty, 1987.

"I just decided to stop because I didn't want the dogs to pay. They were hurt. I couldn't take them to Dawson, let alone Whitehorse," he explains.

When they reach Central, the van windows are coated with ice and it smells like a doghouse. "But," says the driver, news photographer Mike Mathers, "it wasn't too bad. One of the dogs threw up, but all in all it was O.K."

The main pack of teams, leapfrogging their way through the shifting blanket of snow and headwinds, begins to crowd into 101 Lodge, the Steese Highway service station and unofficial coffee stop that provides the mushers with a brief moment's respite from the elements just before they tackle the actual summit.

Working in tandem is often a necessity for the teams on Eagle Summit. The storm in 1984 had progressively worsened until some of the slower teams were completely stopped on the leeward side of the mountain. Finally, five teams lashed themselves together and, led by Daryle Adkins, drove across. The ice built up on the dogs' eyelashes and froze them shut, blinding the leaders. But they responded perfectly to the verbal commands from Adkins who guided them flawlessly across the top.

The natural reaction of a dog suddenly blinded is to turn its back on the wind and huddle down. The performance of Adkins' dogs, in overriding their instincts and placing their trust in his word, is possibly the ultimate testimony to the bond that grows between the mushers and their

Approaching 101 Lodge.

dogs. But the strain of leading the crossing took its toll. Team and musher were all exhausted and Adkins scratched from the 1984 race the next day.

It is not uncommon, once up on the summit itself, for mushers to make mistakes. The winds and snow, dehydration and exhaustion all combine to make them inevitable. In 1986, crossing the mountain above 101 Lodge, Frank Turner lost sight of the trail and crashed down through the snow to the bottom of a steep incline. In the howling winds and darkness, he realized he had made a mistake. Later, when the weather calmed a bit and the stars and moon contributed some light, he couldn't see anything recognizable.

"No trail. No nothing. Just a big valley and mountains. I didn't know where I was. For me it ceased to be a race. That was a survival situation. I had lost my interest in the race. I was basically worried about getting out of there. I never gave up or anything, but I was pretty concerned."

He turned his dogs loose to dig themselves beds in the snow, then sat down behind his sled, sheltered from the wind. "I didn't want to commit myself any further 'cause I knew…I was conscious that I was making mistakes and, mentally, going down the hill like that was not the proper thing to do."

The dogs were depressed. "One thing that's really important for dogs is to have confidence in the person that's back there. Every time you make a mistake or get lost and you've got to turn back, the dogs know you've made a mistake and you've lost that little bit of confidence. When we were in that predicament, they didn't want to be there and got pretty despondent."

At dawn, he spotted Kathy Swenson cutting across the hill above him. Taking his cue from where she was heading, he rehitched his team and traversed the face of the hill to intersect the trail.

In 1988, it is Ralph Tingey's turn to sit on top of the summit for hours. He learned the hard way just how demoralizing it is for a dog to run into the wind and blowing snow. His lead dog, Pearls, just decides to stop running.

"She was pulling, then all of a sudden, she got bummed out. Her ears went down, her tail curled up underneath her and she got a real sad look on her face. Then she sat down and burrowed in. What can you do? Having a lead dog balk is every musher's nightmare." For Tingey, it is a temporary stop. After a few hours, he puts Pearls farther back in the team and hooks up an older leader who does the job.

The trail down follows a long steep, straight valley. The descent is over bare rock, swept clear of snow. Over top of this are build-ups of ice and small glaciers formed by overflows. When streams are no longer able to run under the ice, they are forced to find an alternate route. The water rises to above ice level, then leaks out and overflows onto the ice.

What makes the descent particularly difficult is that the teams usually have to traverse, or sidehill, their way across the ice. If they try to cross on the uphill end of the overflow, dogs and sled skid downhill. The dogs can't get a foothold and the sled's weight simply pulls them along. If they try crossing on the downhill end, the musher and sled usually end up wallowing in deep snow and the dogs are on the ice, trying to pull. The combination of ice and rock doesn't give the mushers anything to plant their brakes into to help control the descent. Some wrap chains around their runners to create more drag. Most simply take their chances and bank on their skills in the crazy ride down the backside of the mountains.

"We had to just kind of inch our way down the hill," says Swenson. "We couldn't just go straight down. I had my sled tipped sideways into the hill and I was standing on the side of my runner as it was tipped and holding onto the side rail."

It isn't until near the bottom that Swenson loses control. She swings to one side of the trail and collides with a batch of willows. The willows spring back and flip the sled completely over.

"It happened so fast. You're just kind of standing there wondering how in hell did you manage to do this. I had to think — sometimes that's hard to do when your brain is frozen — but I had to think about how I was going to tip it back over. It was a major decision at the time. So I just turned it back around and we kind of fishtailed the rest of the way down. Oh, it was nasty!"

Most drivers find their sled keeps sliding down past their lead dogs, then starts tumbling end-over-end down the mountainside, dragging the dogs along with it. When it stops rolling, the driver straightens it up and starts the whole process over again.

Dave Monson keeps letting go of his sled and having to stop to pick it up. Rick Atkinson manages to dump his sled upside down halfway down, but neither find themselves in any major difficulty.

"It was so steep," says Jim Wardlow, a Delta Junction, Alaska, carpenter. "I just rolled like a barrel while my dogs dug in and tried to hang on."

The buck brush, willows and occasional patch of soft snow absorb some of the shock of the falls, saving most of the dogs from injury. Few are hurt on the descent.

Kate Persons, who spends her vacation from her management job at a salmon hatchery in Kotzebue, Alaska, taking long distance sled dog trips, stops at the bottom of the hill. She pulls out a knife and cuts her way into her sled bag. A container of watery dog food has broken open and drenched everything inside the bag.

Then it froze solid, hermetically sealing all the contents.

The rock and roll effect of the downhill continues its beat in the small set of foothills grouped along the base of the mountains.

"We followed this kind of tailing [ridge of gravel left behind by gold dredges when they churned up the valley floor during the early and middle part of the 20th century] along a creek at the bottom," says Lorrina Mitchell. "It's all glaciered and overflowed for miles. On the glare ice, all frozen and humpy, some places you'd be going 20 miles an hour, then you'd slam into something and there's no way to stop. You got your brake down and you're still going 20 miles an hour, which isn't a lot of fun." Several times she intentionally lays the sled on its side to increase the drag and prevent collisions or just to slow down.

Then, just as suddenly as the winds, ice and rock had appeared several hours ago at the top of Boulder Creek-Rosebud Pass, they end — almost as if someone drew a line on the map and said, "Ice, wind and rock on this side. Deep snow over here."

With little warning, the teams plunge into the waist-deep snow that blankets Crooked Creek. This is a small stream that, in summer, flows gently from the bottom of the mountains toward the middle of the Circle District.

Under the freshly fallen snow, there is a trail. But it isn't visible and the markers are set a mile apart — too far apart to see from one to the next.

The teams, which had spread out a little on the summit as each encountered its own problems, bunch up again.

"Jim Wardlow and John Shandelmeier are up ahead breaking trail," Mary Sheilds informs Mitchell when she arrives. "The trail's real narrow and we can't find enough markers to know where to go."

It isn't hard to identify the route when they find it. But if they step off the packed trail, the mushers sink down to their hips and the dogs up to their ears in snow.

The mushers take turns walking in pairs ahead of the teams, breaking down the snowdrifts and beating out a path with their snowshoes. But it is slow going. And the trail is bent and twisted. It takes them to a point where they can see the buildings at Central, just a few miles away, then it takes them in another direction, just to give them another tantalizing view of their destination before another corner takes it away again.

Their experiences on top of the summit and in the lower reaches of the valleys on either side aren't without precedence. The same trails were used in the early years of the 20th century to move supplies, mail and passengers between Fairbanks and the Circle District goldfields. Not only dogs laboured with heavy loads over the mountains; horses were also used to pull sleds in winter.

Only with the building of the Steese Highway in the late 1920s was there a real road to the Circle District. Until the mid-1980s, though, the Steese was a summer-only highway. Even today it is subject to winter closures because of high winds and drifting snow.

What takes the mushers less than a day to cover in the Yukon Quest often took up to a week for the larger freight sleds. These were almost twice as long and half again as wide as the racing sleds used today. They weighed almost twice as much, and the freight was substantially heavier than the load being carried by the mushers.

Part of the old trail system is now a recreational and historical trail since, other than during the Quest, it is no longer in regular use.

Along its length were roadhouses, ranging in quality of accommodation from the log cabin luxuries of Miller's Roadhouse to beds made from spruce boughs on the dirt floors of tents. Little remains of them except their reputation as hospitable places to stop.

One of the most popular roadhouse stops was the one at Central, on the north side of the mountains. It was as renowned then for its accommodation and especially for its food, as it is today. The mushers are heading for this small community, specifically for the motel-cafe, "Crabb's Corner," which is a Quest sign-in point. (A sign-in point is not an official checkpoint or dog drop point, but is used as a means of monitoring the movement of the mushers.)

Cafe owner Jim Crabb thinks he's ready for the teams to start arriving at Central. Usually they come sporadically. One or two arrive, sign in, feed and water their dogs, have a bite to eat themselves, then push on. Neither

Chow time on the trail.

the cafe nor the parking area are terribly large. Three or four teams at a time is the most he can handle efficiently.

He's heard about the large group of teams at the foot of Rosebud yesterday, but that has happened before. The summit will sort them out, especially with this cold and the wind that is blowing up there. That will scatter them all over the face of the mountain and, he thinks, they will probably be turning up in dribs and drabs all night long.

The night starts out right. Gerald Riley and Larry "Cowboy" Smith, the taciturn Dawson City driver, pull in and talk with race marshal Jon Rudolph. In a while, Crabb expects a couple more teams. Relaxing over a cup of coffee, he glances out his window and gets the shock of his life.

What looks like a freight train is rolling down the road towards him. Coming out of the darkness, there is one light after another as far as the eye can see.

"Finally," says Mitchell, "we hit another cut that heads back towards the road and we get on the road. It was a really incredible sight to see for a while because there's all these dog teams, and we've been slogging through the snow, and as soon as they hit the road, they're loping and running-trotting fast, and they're coming down like a whole bunch of Grand Prix cars. All these teams, passing each other on the fly, and moving and cruising along down the road."

But the burst of adrenaline and high spirits is short. The mushers are momentarily relieved at finally finding a trail they can't fall off of or have to break down with their snowshoes. But at their first opportunity, upon reaching the cafe, the dogs flop over and close their eyes.

The drivers feel lead in their arms, legs and eyelids when their sleds grind to a halt. "I'm as tired now as I usually am at the end of the race," says Rick Atkinson, "and we've barely even started. It's not a race. It's a survival exercise."

Behind them, alone in a cabin below Eagle Summit, Jon Gleason watches the silhouette of a late team drive past in the darkness with desperate envy in his eyes. His dogs just aren't bouncing back. His race is over.

Above him, the wind backs off a bit, resting for a moment and allowing the stars to peek through to the earth.

(over) One of Dave Monson's dogs playing, 1988.

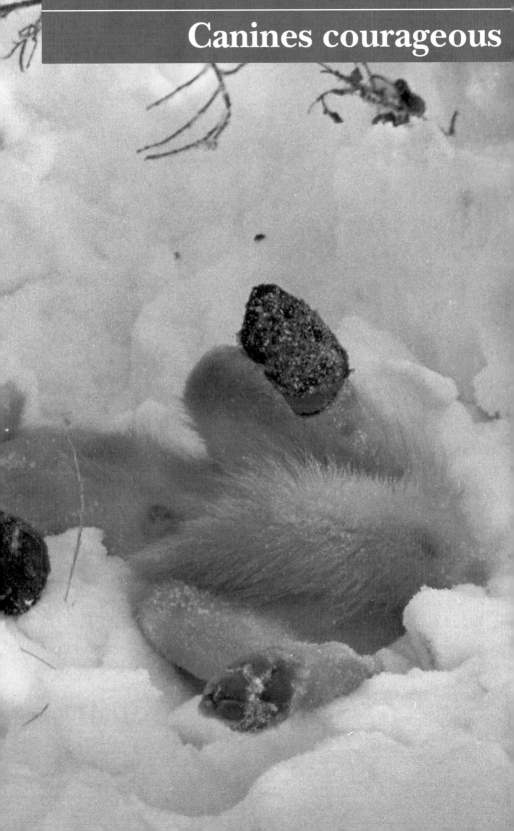

Canines courageous

Canines courageous

raw a circle around Fairbanks, Alaska. Inside it, include Manley (northwest), Nenana (south), Goldstream and the Chena Hot Springs Road (north). Inside that circle is the greatest concentration of racing dogs on the face of the earth — more than 10,000 sprinters, middle distance specialists and long distance runners. And they are unlike any other dog you will ever see.

The Alaskan breed, with its smiling blue-grey eyes, insatiable curiosity, upright tail with its flippant curl at the top, mottled coat of grey or brown and endearing toothful grin, is distinctive. Some are downright friendly, not at all your guard dog type. If you reach down to pet them, they roll over, allowing you to scratch their belly or under their chin. Or they'll give you one good sniff, and turn their backs with a disinterested air. Some are downright surly; they'd just as soon bite you as look at you.

Shyness is a dominant trait with many of the teams run by mushers from the small isolated villages of interior Alaska, and by trappers, like Don Glassburn. His dogs had been raised in the bush and had rarely encountered other human beings. When he paraded the team up to the start line in 1984, the dogs panicked at the sight of 15,000 people lining the street. His leaders tried to hide themselves behind the dogs behind them, who were making a valiant effort to crawl underneath Glassburn's sled. Glassburn spent the first few minutes of the Yukon Quest just coaxing his dogs to come out from behind him and get back in front of the sled.

The Alaskan breed bears little resemblance to the multitude of pedigrees that have combined to produce this diminutive animal. Unlike many of those purebred animals or the dogs of Jack London and Sergeant Preston, few of these racers will ever see the inside of a human home and even fewer will grow old lying at their owner's feet by the roaring fire.

They are the heart and soul of the multi-million dollar business of sled dog racing. When fitted into a harness and hooked to a tow line, they become perfectly tuned competitive racing machines. A balanced team operates almost like the pistons in an automobile engine. As tough and conditioned as the mushers may be, the mushers rank second to the true athletes who pull their sleds.

The fact that they look like dogs is almost incidental to their true purpose for being in existence. The breeding programs that created them aren't recognized by official bodies, such as the American Kennel Club or Westminster Kennel Club, which are concerned with breed appearances. In the raising of Alaskan breed dogs, function comes before appearances. They are working dogs, not house pets or showpieces, and are bred to race.

"Pedigree isn't important," says Joe Runyan, "only performance. We're a long way from an animal that can even have a pedigree that would be accepted as a purebred."

Runyan, winner of the 1985 Yukon Quest, the 1988 Alpirod (the European 1,000-mile race through Italy, Austria, Germany and France) and the 1989 Iditarod, is a methodical breeder who has no qualms about adapting new ideas from other breeding programs. His kennel has about 300 dogs, half of them puppies. Most of the pups won't be kept past their age of maturity: about six to 14 months. He will sell most to other mushers for breeding and give away the others.

Sled dog resting.

The four-legged athletes

Only the ones that show signs of what he is looking for will remain with him. The culling process for the pups is based on the method used by breeders of homing pigeons: the bird makes it home, or it doesn't. The dog meets his standards, or it doesn't.

"Everyone has their own style," Runyan says. "Some people like dogs that are fast and quick. Some like dogs that trot at moderate speed for long periods of time. Everyone looks for dogs with attitude." Most mushers believe that a dog is no better than the puppy it was. If a pup spooks easily, has mood changes without warning or picks on other dogs, it probably has problems or an attitude that won't fit in with other members of the team.

Bill Cotter looks for dogs that can quickly relate to him, then watches them with a critical eye for their gait, seeking dogs that move easily and are light on their feet. He likes happy dogs that are willing and eager to go.

He is slow at culling the pups, usually keeping all of them until they're at least a year old. Sometimes, he has discovered, slow starters turn into good dogs.

Dave Monson has a clear picture of exactly what he's looking for. "We're dealing with a working dog, with a specific function. In our case, we're working specifically with long distance racing dogs. They have to have certain physical attributes that enhance their performance: good feet, good

Curious dog, Eagle, 1984.

appetites, good trotting speed as opposed to good loping speed. They have to be hard workers. That is a function of having what we call a good head or the mental desire to perform after they're fatigued or don't particularly feel like going anymore — when they'll get up and perform out of a relationship-bonding with the musher. Not every dog has that.

"Many things can be taught to a dog, but they cannot be made faster than they naturally are and you can't teach heart. If a dog with all the physical attributes doesn't have heart, it will never be a good sled dog. The perfect dog is one whose feet are sound, who's extremely fast and who never wants to quit."

But perfection is rare and the bionic dog doesn't exist — yet. It has taken generations of dogs and years of careful mixing and matching to produce the current version of the Alaskan breed, and everyone is constantly searching for methods and dogs that can advance the process.

The toughness of the Alaskan breed comes most likely from a strain called the Yukon River village dog. They weren't the best looking, but only the strong survived in the isolated environment of the small interior villages. The best were bred with the best, producing teams that dominated the early years of sled dog racing in Alaska. Teams from Huslia, Ruby and other Yukon River villages would drive four or five hundred miles just to get to the start line of a race. Tough by nature, the village dog just got stronger from their extra work and inbreeding over the years.

As the mushers got more technical and the racing more professional, breeders began introducing specific types of dogs for specific reasons.

Siberian huskies had good feet. Malamutes were a smaller dog. Larger dogs ate more food, were generally slower and more prone to injury. "A light little dog that looks like a marathon runner is more likely to go the distance than a big Sumo wrestler dog," says Monson.

The Belgian sheep dog was introduced because they are more responsive to people and can establish a superior bond with a driver. Gordon Setters, easily trained and conditioned, were added. Even wolves were tried, but were rarely successfully bred. Greyhounds were introduced for speed and long legs.

"What we look for is a longer-legged dog," adds Monson, "because in each step, the taller dog goes maybe two inches further than the shorter-legged dog. If the dog is fast, they can move their legs fast. If you are travelling two inches further with each step, every hour you could be travelling a mile or so further. Over 10 or 12 days, that adds up."

Certain combinations of breeding worked better than others, and as the lines were inbred further, the chances of a successful hybrid dog were further enhanced. Genetic or inherited problems can be reduced as a breeding line gets older. But there were still too many unknown factors.

Certain cross-breeding that should have worked, didn't, for no apparent reason.

Breeders like Kathy and Rick Swenson have turned to science to aid them in developing a superior dog. They conduct urine tests on each dog, checking protein levels. The results tell them about certain factors, such as the lactic acid level in the dog's system. Low levels indicate that a dog has good muscles and is able to recover quickly from fatigue. "We won't breed a dog unless it's clear on all those tests that we have what we want."

Runyan is exploring the possibility of the Franconi Syndrome, apparently well documented in humans, being present in dogs. It is allegedly connected to the efficiency of the kidney in breaking down amino acids. That could be a factor in performance, particularly in reducing the time required to recover after rigorous, stressful exercise. "A dog without Franconi Syndrome can bounce back faster than one with it."

Monson does a regular blood chemistry analysis of his dogs to determine fitness levels during the training and conditioning process. "It can tell you whether the dog's fighting an infection, whether the dog is anaemic, whether they've been stressed too much and whether your feeding program is the right one for what you're trying to do."

Not all dogs are born equal. Some will become wheel dogs — the tandem of pullers who run closest to the sled. Their job is to redirect the nose of the sled so it follows the team smoothly as they corner, or to jar the sled loose when it's frozen into the snow or ice. They take a beating as the sled will often bang into them from behind when they slow down, and they absorb most of the stress on ascents when the sled drags them back.

Even though they do most of the hardest work, they are not necessarily the biggest dogs in the team. However, they are the dogs who look over their shoulder most often to see what is happening behind them since they pay the highest price when a mistake is made.

"I like a real strong dog with fairly short legs, with a low centre of gravity. On a tall dog, the tug line is at an angle, pulling its hips constantly

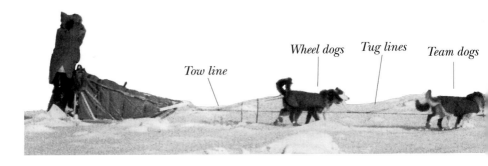

Tow line

Wheel dogs   Tug lines   Team dogs

into the ground. A smaller dog pulls off its shoulder," says Ed Salter. "I like my big dogs right ahead of the wheel dogs."

Ahead of the wheel dogs are the team dogs. Once the wheel dogs have the sled moving, the team dogs' role is to follow the example set by their leader and maintain the momentum. They just have to pull and be able to maintain a solid pace. But a team dog isn't always solely a team dog.

Extra wheelers are carried in this group so they can be rotated with the regular wheel dogs, giving them a break from the most physically demanding position. It is also the place to carry extra leaders for the varying conditions which are encountered on the trail. Sometimes a shrewd driver will hide an extremely fast leader as a team dog for most of the race, then put it up front for the final sprint.

The swing or point dogs are the two animals just behind the lead dogs. Their job is to keep everyone on track and let the leaders concentrate on leading. If the team starts to drift sideways or some of the team dogs try to take a short-cut around a corner, the swing dogs pull them back in line.

Strung out 40 feet in front of the driver are the lead dogs. On the slight shoulders of these animals rests the heavy load of determining success or failure for the entire team. "They're the dogs that provide the motivation for the other dogs," says Gerald Riley. "The other dogs are lost without their leaders."

Lena Charley puts all her faith in the animals she puts up front. "They're the ones you can trust, the ones that listen. They know their way around and they're smarter than the other dogs."

Most breeders believe that leadership is an inherited genetic trait. Therefore, male leaders are bred to female leaders. Often the newborn pup who crawls out of the litter first or bosses around the other pups is a potential leader. Then, three or four years in harness with an old leader will give the dog the training it needs to develop its natural talents.

Leaders are developed as specialists. There are "gee-haw" or command leaders. They respond without question to verbal commands from the driver. There are four basic commands: *gee* — go left; *haw* — go right;

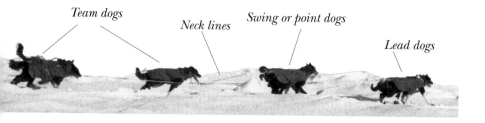

Team dogs

Neck lines

Swing or point dogs

Lead dogs

The four-legged athletes

whoa — stop; and *hike* or *mush* — go. The word "mush" is from the French word "marche," which means "go." It was the use of this word that gave the dog drivers the name "mushers." Most drivers also have their own personal commands for the dogs. It's surprising how they react to requests such as, "Get back on the goddamned trail!"

Pace leaders are fast dogs who can motivate the team to a greater speed. Storm leaders are the dogs that function well in adverse weather conditions and will head into a stiff wind without flinching. Passing leaders aren't distracted by other teams and are good at frequently passing other teams. Trail leaders can find trails which are disguised by freshly fallen or drifting snow, and can use their trail sense to find the correct route.

Trail sense is instinctive. It can mean the difference between thin ice on a river and the safest route, between being lost or running true across miles of ice or trackless tundra. "If there is a trail, but you can't see it," says Stan Bearup, "it'll find the trail. It'll sniff it out."

Some dogs can do it all. They are rare, those dogs with the physical gifts and burning desire to perform beyond expectation. Some breeders, such as the Swensons, are blessed with having bred more than one: Andy, who was up front for four Iditarod wins and Sonny Lindner's 1984 Yukon Quest win. And Mustard, who was co-lead for two Iditarod wins and spearheads Kathy Swenson's team in the 1988 Quest.

Ralph Tingey putting booties on one of his dogs, 1988.

"The dog is fast, level-headed in tough and sticky situations and can run up front all day long," she says. "I can't imagine running without a good leader. It would be disastrous."

It is the musher who must relate to each of the dogs in their respective roles, who must understand them and communicate to them what has to be done. Each dog is an individual athlete and each has its own individual personality. There are dogs that other dogs don't get along with. Some are loners; others are sociable and get along with everyone. A few are mischievous.

The musher, under race conditions, acts as a coach, stroking each one in their own particular way and making them believe that not only can they do everything they want to, but that they want to do everything they can.

The role of musher goes a great deal further than coaching at practices and game time. It is more like a parental relationship. The pup has been raised from birth by the musher. It has learned its driver's faults and strengths just as the driver has learned the dog's. For a dog who has been purchased by another musher at some point in its life, that same bonding can be achieved by the sharing of experiences and by similarities in personality.

The two learn to rely on each other, to trust each other beyond question. It is not uncommon for a musher to experience problems of one sort or another and have their team turn around or stop to find out what the problem is. Jon Rudolph once fell asleep riding on the back of his sled. When he woke up, still on the back of his sled, the team had stopped. His leaders had turned around and walked back to the sled and were sitting, watching him carefully to ensure that all was well.

Mushing lore is crammed with stories of mushers saved by teams making the right decision at the right time when the driver wasn't capable of it and of teams saved by a musher managing to convince the dogs to keep on going when everything else around them told the dogs to stop. Daryle Adkins' team on top of Eagle Summit is a prime example of the bonding between musher and dog being powerful enough for the dogs to override their natural instincts.

The mushers make great sacrifices in their lives to meld this bond. They relinquish the company of fellow human beings for the most part and live in isolation with their dogs. Their homes, while comfortable, are usually left incomplete as funds are drained away into maintaining a kennel.

Harry Sutherland has finished second and third in two Yukon Quests, and he has a third-place finish in one Iditarod. He lives with his family in the top half of a two-storey log cabin located in a scenic alpine valley. It is a perfect spot to train his team both in winter and summer, and is far enough from his nearest neighbours that they don't hear the din of the 60 dogs he has tethered in the trees behind the house.

In 1988, the top floor, where the family lives, has uncovered log walls and plywood floors. It is heated by a wood stove and there is a park-like picnic table that serves as kitchen table. There are no interior doors, just curtains hanging over the openings in the unfinished walls. The lower level has a dirt floor which serves as a playground for the multitude of puppies that roam around the yard.

The unfinished look exists because Sutherland, a carpenter by trade, pours his money and effort into being the best professional dog driver he can be. He has had some reward in recording high finishing positions in both the Iditarod and Yukon Quest as well as winning a few shorter events.

Most years his winnings won't even come close to covering his race expenses. Whatever sponsorship he can get, plus the money he earns as a carpenter, goes to cover the shortfall. But, like so many other drivers, he just can't bring himself to bail out of this money-losing proposition. It would be like giving up part of his own family.

Dave Monson could be a city-dwelling attorney, living in the "proper" suburb, driving a luxury automobile and wearing three-piece suits. Instead, he lives in a small isolated cabin in the wilderness surrounded by about 300 dogs. He dresses in coveralls or jeans and a shirt and drives an old battered pickup over the narrow ungraded dirt road that leads to civilization.

The connection between drivers and dogs becomes so complete, a driver often can't make a decision on the trail without consulting his team. After scratching from the 1985 Quest near Carmacks, 65-year-old Glenn Craig, the oldest competitor to ever enter the Yukon Quest, said, "My dogs and I got together to talk it over. We decided we were just too tired to go any further."

Having a well-dressed team is essential — well-dressed not for looks, but to protect the most vulnerable parts of the dogs. Their fur coats provide more than enough insulation against the elements over most of their bodies, but their feet are extremely susceptible to damage. And a dog with sore or bad feet can't run. A small industry has grown up around footwear for the teams.

Dog booties are made from various materials and have several functions. They prevent snow from balling up between the dogs' toes while they're running, protect them from brittle snow and sharp ice, and provide an extra layer of insulation for sore or damaged paws. Not only do the rules make it mandatory that booties are carried, it simply makes sense for the driver who wants to finish the race.

Some dogs like wearing booties, but others don't. They have developed techniques for removing booties whether they're lying down, standing up or even running. The average team will wear out, cast off, bury or eat about

1,000 booties (about 80 booties per dog) during the Yukon Quest. A favourite pastime of racing fans at the start line is picking up the booties the dogs have managed to toss getting out of the starting chute.

"I've got some that as soon as I put them on, they take them off," smiles Lorrina Mitchell. "You're going down the line, you hear zip, zip as the velcro comes open. It's the dogs taking their booties off. I have some that eat them. I've had booties regurgitated a week later. They've obviously not gone through the digestive system; they come back up and you can identify them."

Foot care is vital to the team's success. Cold temperatures or running on a poor surface or in freshly fallen snow can cause damage to paws. A cut or chafing, blisters or cracks in the pads need to be protected. Booties are the best solution; combined with foot ointments, they keep the foot warm and dry. For a dog skilled at removing booties, super glue is often used to close cuts or cracks or to attach protective pieces of cloth to the bottoms of damaged feet.

The science of developing the racing dog's diet is a never-ending search for the perfect food. Mushers have gone from traditional diets of fish, meat and fat to commercial dry foods. The manufactured food is designed to be more digestible and more nutritionally balanced and to help prevent dehydration. It also weighs less and takes up less room in the sled.

Well-dressed dogs.

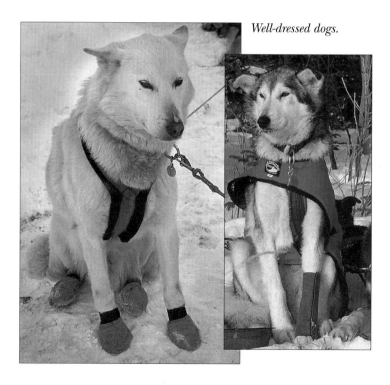

The four-legged athletes

Some mushers, like Runyan, believe that a combination of traditional meats and commercial foods is the most efficient system. During a race the average dog will consume the equivalent of almost 30 percent of its own body weight each day. The meats most commonly used are highly palatable and easily digested domestic meats. The only wild game meat used is beaver, since it is the only one that doesn't carry harmful parasites. The fat portion of the diet is provided by seal fat, corn oil, chicken fat or tallow rendered from meat scraps.

Mushers don't like to change a dog's diet during the course of the race, but sometimes they have no choice. Senley Yuill, a stocky veteran of dog driving during the early days of oil exploration in the Canadian arctic, pulled into Dawson City in 1984 and ran into a distraught Pecos Humphries. His dogs weren't eating and he was getting desperate.

"What have you got?" he asked Yuill.

"Horsemeat," Yuill replied.

"I've been using chicken; I don't have horsemeat. I'll trade you a box of chicken for a box of horsemeat." They swapped and both teams thrived on the change in their diet.

It's hard to say for sure why a dog won't eat. The reasons can range from a lovesick male pining for a female in heat, to illness, to being over-stressed, to dehydration. The methods of convincing them to eat again are just as varied.

"The average person says, 'Well, it isn't that hard to feed dogs.' Well, at home, it isn't. They should try it on the trail," laments Jon Gleason. "You could have seven different things and the dogs won't eat the first six you give to them. But if they eat the seventh, I let them eat as much as they want of that."

Sometimes it's as simple as giving them their favourite treat. Gleason's dogs respond to chicken hot dogs; Frank Turner's are fond of regular hot dogs; Jeff King's prefer ice cream. Other times, vitamin B-12 must be administered as an appetite stimulant.

The most serious reason for a dog to stop eating is dehydration. The racing animal can lose all of its body fat and half of its protein and still function. But if it loses only 20 percent of its water, it will die.

About 60 percent of the dog's weight is water. Under duress, the dog requires about a gallon of water each day to prevent dehydration. There are two ways to test for dehydration. The easiest is to pull up and pinch the skin on the back of the dog's neck. When the skin is released, it should snap back down flat quickly. If it recedes slowly or remains standing the dog is in trouble. The second method is to check the colour of the dog's urine. If it is a rusty colour, the dog isn't drinking enough.

The colder or more windy it is, the more likely dehydration will occur. Super-cooled air acts like a sponge, soaking the moisture out of the dogs.

Eventually, they stop drinking because they've lost the desire to swallow. Tired and slightly dehydrated dogs usually won't drink water straight out of a pan. The driver has to bait the animal by making the water part of the meal. But if a dog doesn't want to drink, it won't.

"I sat down once," says Harry Sutherland, "and made beaver stew for them. So they tipped the pan over, let the liquid run out and ate the meat."

When all else fails, the only solution is rest. In his first long distance race in 1987, Ralph Tingey was startled by the effect the race was having on his dogs.

"I had never seen a race-tired dog. I had never seen a dog refuse food. Refuse water. I had no idea what was happening." It took 24 hours of rest before he felt he could continue.

Snack time on the trail, 1986.

As the drivers get more experienced, they develop their own methods of judging when the dogs are rested enough to continue. Sutherland uses his team as an alarm clock for himself.

"I pull off the trail, feed the team, then I crawl on top of my sled for some sleep. Teams will go by us and neither I nor the dogs will wake up. But when they're ready to go, they'll wake up and they'll start to yelp and bark at the other teams when they go by. That wakes me up and I know they've had enough rest, so off we go.

Personality conflicts can cause problems. If a dog gets ornery and doesn't seem to want to get along with its partner in the harness, the musher will adjust the spacing on the tug line so that the dog runs alone. The other dogs will often help their teammate make an attitude adjustment by ganging up on it until the antisocial behaviour disappears.

Males trying to mount females in heat can also disrupt the rhythm of a team. Several teams have had to wait for a few hours at checkpoints or stopped along the trail when the musher fails to notice that a male has moved into a position to take advantage of the female. Once started, the act can't be stopped and the team can't run until it is completed. Two or more males jockeying for the same advantage can result in fights. The driver's only solution is to find a place in the team where the female can do her fair share of the pulling without disrupting the rest of the dogs.

Sonny Lindner's team taking a break, 1984.

Viruses, such as doggie flu, can stop a team in its tracks. They spread rapidly, causing vomiting, lethargy and diarrhoea. Collisions with trees or stepping into cracks can sprain wrists, dislocate shoulders or break legs. Fights can result in disabling cuts to paws, mouths, necks and legs.

Heat stress can cause dogs to lose their coordination, vomit and get diarrhoea. This usually happens when a dog's natural cooling system can't keep up to the heat generated by running under a warm sun, even if the surrounding air is sub-zero.

A musher can either try to nurse an infirm dog back to health with antibiotics or haul it on the sled, rather than making it run. Injured or sick dogs are usually dropped at the next checkpoint. Since a maximum of only four dogs can be dropped from each team during the Quest, it's in the musher's best interest to ensure the dogs are capable of completing the distance before they even start. Dropped dogs are shipped out and kennelled in the city where the race ends, to await the arrival of the rest of their team.

Some dogs do die. Gastric torsion, or a twisted stomach, can kill them. Burst blood vessels in their brains claim others. Dehydration is often the catalyst that precipitates a fatal health condition. But the mortality rate of race dogs is no higher than it is for the dog who lives a sedentary lifestyle.

Because of the bond that exists between driver and dog, the death of a team member can seriously affect the musher. Nick Erickson spent several hours alone on the ice of the Yukon River in 1984, hugging one of his dogs that had just died. Kevin Turnbough came across him, started a fire to warm him up, fed him and was able to convince him to continue mushing. Both mushers finished the race.

Lorrina Mitchell scratched in 1987 when she was psychologically demoralized by the loss of a dog. Don Donaldson does the same in 1988 as will Tom Randall in 1989.

"When you get right down to it," says Mitchell, "the care of the animal and the individual's welfare transcends all the other bullshit."

"Our dogs are beautiful animals," said Joe Runyan in his banquet address to the mushers in 1986. "They are to mushers what horses are to the Arabians and the Plains Indians. The winning or losing does not matter...we want to preserve the integrity of the animals throughout this race."

(over) The Circle City checkpoint.

Circle route

Circle route

entral is not an official Yukon Quest checkpoint — yet. But, as a result of the residents' determination to make their small community something special for the drivers, it has gained honorary status as an official sign-in stop. Their efforts have paid off. There are few sights along the trail that are as welcome for both musher and dogs as the Crabb's Corner Café, especially after a day and night spent bucking the wind on Eagle Summit and burrowing through the snow along Crooked Creek.

There's room for the dogs to curl up and get a snooze — plenty of water, heated for food or cool for drinking. When the mushers finish tending their teams, they wander inside for a hot meal, a cold beer and a place to sleep. Since it's also a motel, there are rooms here with beds, but not everyone stays awake long enough to get to them.

Lorrina Mitchell needs some sleep. Suffering from exhaustion and mild hypothermia, she knows that, if she continues the way she is, she will become her own worst enemy further down the trail.

"But I was so hyper I couldn't sleep. I asked Jim Crabb for a hot buttered rum with a double shot of rum. I don't drink alcohol on the trail, but I thought I've got to mellow out and get some rest. About the time that thing hit bottom, I fell asleep in the hallway beside the bathroom. Nobody wanted to sleep there. It was too noisy. Too busy. People walking back and forth. But it was a big wide hallway, so I just curled up against the wall and never heard a thing."

Food and drinks are on the house for the drivers, and that's a rule strictly enforced.

Jon Rudolph remembers an argument he got into during his second Quest in 1986 when he decided to stay at Crabb's for an extra day. He wandered into the bar and sat down to buy himself a beer. "You're a musher," said the bartender when Rudolph put his money on the bar. "You don't buy nothing here." Rudolph explained he was only staying because he really didn't feel like leaving, not because he had to. So he wanted to pay for his beer.

"I don't care if you're staying a week," responded the bartender. "You're not buying anything here." Rudolph is back in Central this year, but as race marshal rather than a competitor. He will return as race marshal again in 1989 and 1990.

The community was originally a roadhouse called Windy Jim's on the Circle-Fairbanks trail in the early 1900s. One of the better and bigger lodges on the trail, it offered meals and rooms for travellers and miners, along with stable facilities for horses and kennels for dog teams. It was a hub for trails to the various regions of the Circle gold-mining district and eventually became known as Central House. When the Steese Highway, the "Road to the Midnight Sun," was completed, it went right past the front doorstep of the lodge.

The highway brought a change in the focus of the district. Circle City (also known as Circle), north of Central, had been the district's main supply depot because of its proximity to barge traffic on the Yukon River. But the road provided a connection via Fairbanks with the Alaska Railway and the south coast. Central profited greatly from its location on the highway and now boasts a school, a highway maintenance camp, a post office and various service facilities for the local miners, woodcutters and trappers as well as tourists and travellers.

The hospitality extends far beyond the walls of Crabb's Corner. In 1984, when Wilson Sam, the big, amiable trapper from Huslia, lost his bag of dog booties in the storm on top of Eagle Summit, two women in Central heard

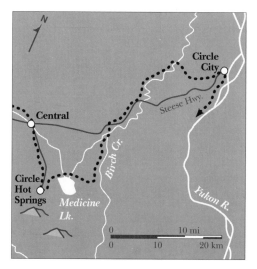

Central to Circle City

the news and went to work. They, and Sam, knew the rules. Mushers had to carry a minimum number of booties for their dogs.

Jill Ruzniak and Connie Catt fired up their sewing machines and by the time Sam arrived, they had produced 85 booties for him and he was able to continue. His lost booties were later found on the mountain and turned in at Central by another musher.

Wilson Sam had a completely individual approach to long distance sled dog racing. He ran the 1984 Yukon Quest almost as a public relations exercise. He spent as much time stopping to socialize with spectators and pose for photographs as he did actually mushing. His entire philosophy was summed up when he arrived in Chena Hot Springs. Jumping off his sled, he enveloped Roger Williams in a huge bear hug and loudly declared, "God damn. I'm having a good time!"

After the ferocity of the weather on Eagle Summit, the trail through the Circle District is almost like a holiday for the drivers. From Central, they follow the road for about 15 miles to Circle Hot Springs. Then they swing north, heading for about 40 miles along the narrow, twisting Birch Creek, then overland for another 40 miles on old mining and mail route roads to Circle City and the Yukon River.

Wilson Sam having a good time, 1984.

"It's definitely much more restful than what you encounter on either side," says Mitchell. "It's an easy piece of trail. It's pleasant and you can just motor along and not have to worry too much."

One by one, the mushers hit the road, to cover the short distance to Circle Hot Springs. Bob Bright heads out, but there is much speculation on whether or not he will run for much longer. His titanium sled has been badly battered on the descent from Eagle Summit and the runners on the bottom have an unnatural clatter to them as he moves along the road. He searches in Central, but is unable to find anything to repair the damage. He will try again at the Hot Springs.

Bright's high technology sled is a source of constant curiosity among the mushers, who are generally sceptical about anything new and untried. The basket sled works well on hard-packed trails, but tends to bog down in deep snow and isn't really practical for long distance races. The drivers stayed with them until Alaskan sled designer Tim White finally perfected his toboggan sled in the early 1980s and Rick Swenson proved it was a superior distance sled by driving it to victory in the Iditarod.

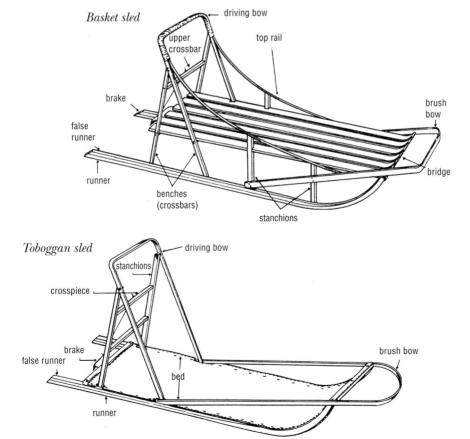

The major advantage of the toboggan sled is that it's easier to repair than the basket sled. This is vital on the Yukon Quest since the rules dictate that the mushers finish with the same sled they started with. White's toboggan sled has been improved over the years and most of the drivers now use the basket sled solely for sprint, or short distance, racing.

The heavier construction of the toboggan sled is also an advantage in the long distance mushing game. "You've got to build in such durability on the Quest," says Ed Salter, a sled-builder for 12 years, "for two reasons. One, you can't change sleds. And two, is the fact that you carry such heavy loads."

The sleds are built using Alaskan birch, white ash, hickory, oak or maple for the wooden parts, such as the stanchions, driving bows, runners or brush bows. The bed of the sled is constructed of high density plastic which can be cut three-quarters of the way through its thickness without breaking. But it's not perfect, as Harry Sutherland will find out in 1989 when he knocks a hole the size of a basketball in the bottom of his sled.

The same plastic is on the bottom of the runners and protects them from being damaged by the trail surface. On a snow surface, a set of runner bottoms can last two to three hundred miles. But mix in a little gravel and most drivers will be changing the plastic every 30 miles or so.

The colour of the plastic tells the musher which plastic should be used in the different conditions. Orange is best for warm weather. Black is better for cold. White is a compromise that's durable in both warm and cold, but isn't as good in either as the recommended colour of plastic.

There was a short-lived experiment using lightweight aircraft alloys instead of wood and plastic. The alloy was very strong and mushers liked the lightness of the sled. But when damage did occur, it was difficult to repair on the trail. So far, the mushers prefer to stick to wood and plastic sleds.

Repairs on the trail are makeshift and depend on ingenuity. In 1987, Karin Schmidt used a hockey stick splint to repair a broken stanchion. She used surgical tape to hold the splint in place. Ty Duggar used radiator hose clamps to repair one of his runners, along with a combination of glue and tape.

The ultimate repair kit for any dog sled is bailing wire and duct tape. Combining those two items with a few extra bolts, some extra strips of runner plastic and a small hand drill, the musher can make repairs right on the trail. Sometimes the repaired piece is better than the piece that broke.

"I broke one runner which my wife, Shari, fixed in Dawson City," says Ralph Tingey. "She reinforced it with another piece of plastic sandwiched in and lots of bolts and we're still running that sled just that way. Her repair job was probably stronger than the original."

Just 15 miles down the road from Central, Circle Hot Springs has long been a lure for those who enjoy the healing warmth of the geothermal waters. Bill Cotter made a point of going for a swim in the pool in 1984 after battling his way across Eagle Summit. "It felt pretty good after the night before."

Kathy Swenson found it tough to leave once she arrived in 1986. She spent 16 hours, having a Jacuzzi, a shower and a sleep. When she woke up, her husband Rick had only two questions, "What the hell are you doing?" and "Are you on a camping trip or in a race?"

Since the first day that gold was mined in the Circle District in the early 1900s, the local residents and visitors have used the springs to soak their tired arms, legs and backs. Almost all the mines in the area were underground. In the early days, the air in the small, cramped mining shafts below ground was choked with fumes from the coal oil lamps used for light. Above ground miners fought clouds of mosquitoes in summer and sub-zero temperatures in winter. The hot water not only took the ache out of the miners' bones and the itch out of their bug bites, it also heated the cabins they stayed in while at the springs. It was almost unbearable luxury, being able to sit inside a warm cabin without having to cut wood for a fire.

The local Indians had known about the mineral springs long before they were "discovered" by prospector Billy Greets in 1897 and homesteaded by Frank Leach in the early 1900s. It was Leach who saw the commercial

Jon Rudolph replacing a sled runner.

potential of the springs and built a hotel there in the 1930s. He also envisioned that aviation would play a major role in the development of the Alaskan interior and, in 1924, built the first airstrip north of Anchorage.

What Leach probably never foresaw was the existence of the Yukon Quest Air Corps. From an airstrip very close to that original site, the planes used for the Yukon Quest do a lot of their flying. In the first couple of years, the Quest had to rely solely on the generosity of a few small regional airlines to supply aircraft, and the donation of time and planes by private fliers.

In 1987, the United States Air Force started to take an interest in the event. Part of their training is low-level aerial reconnaissance, and spotting mushers for the Yukon Quest was a perfect exercise for them. While individual volunteer pilots are still a big part of the Quest, assistance from civil air patrols and flying clubs is making the job of spotting a little easier.

The business of spotting mushers from the air isn't as easy as it sounds. Identifying the individuals is important to help the race officials understand what is happening out on the trail and whether anyone is in need of assistance. The aircraft generally fly about 500 feet above the ground, tipping left, then right and following around the corners in the trail on the ground. Passengers are glued to every window, seeking out spots where teams could be stopped or watching the track where they should be running.

When a musher is spotted, it's not always possible to identify who it is on the first pass. Often a second pass is required and, occasionally, a third if

Circle Hot Springs checkpoint, 1987.

there's something that may indicate a problem. The excitement of spotting mushers is contagious and it's hard for someone to ignore it if they're in the aircraft with the officials.

Roger Williams, Jocelyn Williams and race marshal Carl Huntington were flying with pilot Les Bradley during the first Quest, looking for mushers on the trail out of Dawson.

"Jocelyn has the best eyes of anybody in the world," said Roger, "and all of a sudden she sees a musher. Everybody, including Les, leans over and we're looking at this musher, trying to figure out who it is and I kind of look up, and there's this big hill coming at us. I reach out and tap Carl 'cause Les is really into this spotting. And Carl looks, and he grabs Les and says, 'Let us do the looking. You do the flying.'"

On the ground, the mushers drive comfortably, knowing that someone is up there looking over them. However, the planes can also be a source of irritation.

Lorrina Mitchell, once again answering the call of nature in 1988, steps off the trail for a minute when a plane flies overhead. Then it turns back and passes over again. While the view from the sides is blocked by the bush, the view from the top isn't. A routine double-check for the spotters turns into an agonizing eternity for Mitchell. "Five minutes is a long time when you're waiting for an airplane to go away so you can look after your personal problems."

In 1987, spotters saw Ron Rosser, the tall red-headed dentist from Fort Yukon, jumping up and down behind his sled. They turned back for another look — he was still jumping. And he was still going up and down on the third fly-past. But since they couldn't see anything specifically wrong, the plane flew to the next checkpoint. A few hours later Rosser pulled in. "What the hell were you doing out there?" asked Williams. "The first time you guys passed," he replied, "I pulled down my pants and mooned you. Then I couldn't get my pants back up. My suspenders got tangled and I was trying to get them unsnagged."

"But those guys (the pilots) should be decorated," says Williams. "They don't have to be out there. They don't get paid. They risk their lives, just like the mushers risk theirs. And they do it just because they enjoy it."

For the moment, there are few planes patrolling the trail. The race has come to a temporary halt at Circle Hot Springs.

The resort hotel looks and feels like a carnival is about to start. Festooned in brightly coloured dog harnesses and clothing hung out to dry, the rooms populated by a crowd of freshly showered, lightly sleeping mushers, there is an air of excitement and expectation.

They wait for the ringing of the telephone — ironically one of the things the drivers live in the bush to avoid.

Somewhere ahead of the drivers, two trailbreakers on snowmachines are making one more pass over the trail to Circle City. The storm on Eagle Summit last night hadn't ignored the Circle District. A layer of freshly fallen and windblown snow covers the area. The trailbreakers are knocking down the drifts and re-setting the markers along the route.

When they get to the other end, they will call. Every time a fork or knife is dropped on the floor in the restaurant, ears perk and backs straighten up. Even the deepest sleeper becomes instantly alert. Then, realizing it's not the phone, they settle down again. The game of "hurry up and wait" is on. The only questions are, how long will it last and who will be the first to go?

The two trailbreakers are a critical link in the chain of dedicated volunteers whose job it is to ensure that there's a safe and dependable trail through 1,000 miles of wilderness. For the past two months, over a hundred men, women and machines from every community along the route have spent their weekends beating a path through the bush.

They must evaluate each section of the trail and mark it appropriately. Straight trails are marked with single markers. Corners are indicated by two markers close together on the side to which the team must turn. Once around the corner, the teams pass through a set of markers, one on each side of the trail, that tells them they've made the correct turn. Two markers forming an "X" warn of potential danger. At places like Eagle Summit, tripods are built to tower above the snow drifts and guide the drivers in white-out conditions. Trail markers are usually narrow slats of wood, about four feet tall, with reflective circular discs on the tops.

Over 6,000 markers are used each year and accurate maps are kept so the mushers can be briefed on the trail and trail conditions at each checkpoint. On the Alaskan side, the markers are mass-produced by the inmates at the Fairbanks Correctional Center. On the Yukon side, the inmates at the Whitehorse Correctional Centre do their part.

The path through the bush is created using axes, swede saws, chainsaws and fires. The trailbreakers' accommodations consist of wall tents and trappers' cabins. The days are long, cold and lonely. The snow is packed under the treads of snowmachines; when the snow is too deep for snowmachines, they use snowshoes.

Once open, a trail usually doesn't stay open. Snowfalls and winds can close it back in almost as fast as the trailbreakers open it. So, once they've opened it, they often have to turn around and go over it again, all the time battling the same elements and dangerous terrain the mushers will face when they come. Yet, like the mushers, they keep returning to do it again, year after year.

Breaking trail, like mushing, can become an obsession with some people. Last year, five Whitehorse businesspeople took holidays and, rather than fly south to sunshine, palm trees and sandy beaches like many northerners do in winter, they had their own Yukon Quest. Starting a day ahead of the mushers, they drove their snowmachines from Whitehorse to Fairbanks just to make sure that everything was in order along the way. They had already been on their snowmachines breaking the trail from Whitehorse to Carmacks for two months prior to the trip.

The phone finally rings.

"It's open now," comes the word from the two ice-covered and exhausted trailbreakers in Circle City.

David Sawatzky, who got started in dog mushing when he bought a dog for his son five years ago, is the first one to take the plunge. An hour later, Vern Halter takes the bait. Then the exodus starts.

"The exit was incredible," says Jack Niggemyer. "It looked like a second, mass start to the race."

In the middle of the pack is David Monson, who had been the first to arrive at the hot springs. "There's no point in wasting the dogs by jumping out in front of everyone else on bad trails," he casually comments to curious reporters. "I might as well wait until others go over them and the trails harden up a little."

Behind the main pack that heads out linger the "campers" — mushers who are in the race for the experience and adventure, who entertain no

Jon Gleason (r) checks in at Circle Hot Springs, 1987.

fantasies of coming from behind to win in the end. Their moment of personal triumph will come when they cross the finish line, no matter how far behind the leaders they may be.

A few teams pull in as the last of the main pack trundles off down the trail. One team is bedded down at Central and still a couple more are plugging their way over a now passive Eagle Summit.

One, who had arrived with the leaders, but will travel no farther, is Steve Mullen. "I can't hang onto my sled," he says quietly. His screwdriver slipped while he was fixing his sled and plunged through the palm of his hand. "It's a bummer," he says, contemplating his bandaged hand. "My dogs were just starting to do good."

In 1986, Connie Frerichs dumped her sled and twisted her knee as she tried to negotiate a sharp turn just a few yards from the checkpoint. She was packed to the hotel on a stretcher while her team was parked for the last time that year by her handlers. The seven-year veteran of driving dogs was back to complete her second Quest in 1987.

She will return again with her daughter, Terri, in 1990, as the first-ever mother-daughter pair to run the race. Both will finish as part of the "significant seven." This will be the group of mushers who will be so far behind the leaders that they decide to hold their own race within the race.

The next checkpoint is Circle City, home of the Perry Davis Pain Killer thermometer. This environmental device consists of four bottles set outside a window during winter. Looking out the window, a person can see just how cold it is outside. If the first bottle, containing mercury, freezes, it isn't too

Senley Yuill approaches trailbreaker Bill Chisholm near Whitehorse, 1984

bad. If the second, whiskey, freezes, it isn't great, but it is bearable. The third bottle holds kerosene. If that hardens, one should hesitate before heading out. But if the fourth bottle, containing Perry Davis Pain Killer, becomes solidified, throw another log on the fire and stay home.

It isn't frozen-Pain-Killer-cold this year, but it was in 1987. Jon Rudolph and Harry Sutherland travelled together through this area that year. The temperatures hovered around minus 50 and a constant north wind hammered at them. "Geez, it was cold. We had to stop about every hour and light a fire, we were so bloody cold. We'd stay there for an hour, then get going again. It was bloody miserable," remembers Rudolph.

The race slowed to a crawl, from fire to fire, as the drivers and dogs battled dehydration and frozen feet. At one point Jeff King turned to Ed Salter, whose team was trudging along behind him.

"Have you ever seen a dog team go four miles an hour before?" asked King. Salter shook his head. Then it got even slower for him as his leaders started to balk against the cold. Eventually, Salter's team stopped altogether and he had to turn back to the previous checkpoint for a longer rest to get them back on their feet.

Kathy Swenson remembers stopping to build a small fire for herself on Birch Creek last year. It was so cold, the ice under the fire wouldn't melt even with the heat from the flame. She soon found herself sharing it with Bill Cotter, King and Monson, who just couldn't go past a fire without stopping.

The fire is the musher's second-best friend (after the dogs). Techniques for building one range from neatly piling the wood and striking a match, to dumping kerosene on a pile of driftwood on the riverbank. Bill Cotter's bonfire building has become legendary.

"My philosophy is that if you're carrying a lot of gear and food, you're better off building fires than carrying a stove."

Cotter doesn't waste time building small fires. He drags out entire trees and piles them on the flames. They serve two purposes for him. They heat his dog food for him and they substitute for his sleeping bag. He rarely uses a sleeping bag to keep warm, even when it is 60 below.

"I don't like using sleeping bags. I would just wrap a blanket around myself and fall asleep in front of the fire." That way, he reasons, when he wakes up, he will already be cold. He won't have to crawl out of a warm sleeping bag into cold air. He can warm himself up again by dragging out more trees and rebuilding the fire.

Cotter is one of the few drivers left who uses a fire to heat his food. Most of the drivers now use alcohol stoves (small round containers using a fibreglass wick soaked in alcohol) or campstoves (which use white naphtha gas). The step from using an open fire to cook, to using a stove, has reduced the time required to feed a team from about two hours to under 40 minutes.

In 1990, Jeff King will find himself on the verge of a tongue-in-cheek breakthrough in improving the campstove for the racing musher. Many mushers use headlamps, which are small, but extremely powerful flashlights that can be worn on their head. They are powered by a battery pack, usually worn under the coat. Their purpose is to provide the musher with light while they are travelling in the dark.

King will have a headlamp developed with a light bulb that is so hot it will keep melting the lamp lens. He will suggest marketing it as a combination campstove-headlamp.

Headlamps are essential tonight. A cloud cover hangs over the Circle District and driving in the trees makes it seem even darker. The dogs find the newly broken track with ease, however, and the drivers sit back on their small foldout chairs attached to the rear end of the sled. While they can watch the dogs illuminated by their lamps and dodge any overhanging

Campstove getting fired up, headlamps in place, 1986.

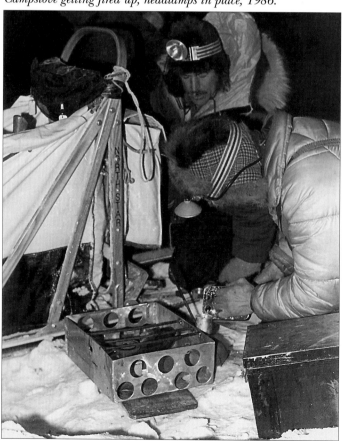

branches that threaten to sweep them off the sled, their vision doesn't go any farther. The light is devoured by the night.

Speed and distance become impossible to judge since there are no visible landmarks by which mushers can judge their progress. They know approximately how long it will take to reach Circle City, so they estimate their trip and schedule stops according to their watches.

At the end of the trail from Circle Hot Springs is the sparsely populated Circle City. Established in 1893, Circle City — the first major gold camp in interior Alaska — got its name when its founders erroneously believed it to be on the Arctic Circle. By 1896, it boasted of being the world's largest log cabin city. It had an opera house, a hospital, a library, countless saloons, hotels and gambling halls, stores and trading posts, a U.S. Customs station and the first official post office north of Juneau. It even had its own newspaper in 1898.

But time hasn't been kind to Circle City. The gold started to run out after only a few years and the gold seekers left soon after. The Steese Highway arrived and, instead of bringing people into the dying community, it served as an easy road out. The bustling metropolis became a shell of its former self. Now there's only one store, one restaurant, a small post office and a school to service the 70 or so residents who are left. Not even the original historical site of this hand-hewn log community remains, having been swept away by the Yukon River.

The residents, while few in number, turn out in force to make sure they provide the best service possible. The effort they put in is phenomenal. There is a constant flow of hot food for everyone, and there is always someone on hand when the mushers arrive to officially greet them and check them in.

Housewife and mother, Mary Dopler, is one of the checkers. Her dedication to the Quest results in her working nonstop for 48 hours at a time, until she's forced to take a break because her eyes are too glazed to see and her hands shake too much to hold anything. But the breaks are just brief enough for her to get a second wind and start over again. For a week, she will greet mushers with her ever-present smile.

"It's like a job," she smiles. "You shouldn't do it if you don't enjoy it."

It is the 200 or so people like Dopler along the trail that cause Leroy Shank to shake his head in disbelief.

"You couldn't pay people to work like that," he says. "Nobody working for wages would work that hard."

The community hall has been the checkpoint since the first Quest. It has been, and still is, home to the handlers, media, officials, the curious and the teams for the time they spend in Circle. It should feel good, like an old often-used shoe, but it doesn't. Not knowing what is happening out there, but knowing what could be going wrong, keeps everyone on edge.

"At night you start thinking about all the worst things that can possibly happen. You've got to try and rationalize by remembering there are 30 to 40 other teams out there, not just one. And they'll all help each other if there's any problem," says Gordie Mitchell.

Shari Tingey, who is handling for her husband Ralph, is particularly irked by the lack of news while the teams are actually on the trail, between areas where they can be spotted. She accepts that there are times where there can't be news, but when it is possible and it doesn't arrive, it irritates her.

"I think as an observer, one of the interesting differences is having been at both ends of the pack. This time Ralph is close to the front, but the first year, he was two and a half days behind. And there's no one there. Nobody knows where those guys are, and I've seen it in the faces of the people, all the handlers whose mushers are way back in the pack. They have no idea where those guys are and they are just as concerned as the handlers for the people who are up front.

"There's all the interest in the front of the pack, and I can understand that. But they don't keep real good track of the back. They never knew where Ralph was that first year. They had him off by days. They had him all sorts of strange places that he never was. I never knew when he was going to show up."

There is a false sense of confidence and security in the community hall as the handlers and families pick at food, talk about everything but dogs or talk dogs to the exclusion of all else.

The daylight fades and night settles in outside the hall. Then, finally, Sawatzky appears out of the dark. The checkers go out to greet him, and the nerves of the waiting handlers, whose mushers are still out there somewhere, wind up even tighter. Their eyes keep seeking the spot in the darkness where headlamps should appear. Occasionally someone wanders up the road, trying to see deeper into the night. At last, more headlamps appear, followed quietly by dogs, sleds and mushers.

Yet, while the waiting is hard, arrival more often results not in relief, but in frustration. Only in Dawson City can the handlers or family actually assist the musher. Here in Circle City, they can only watch, supply information and advice, and hope for the best.

"It's a real thin thread on the emotions out there," says Shari Tingey. "It's just a real thin thread because they are so tired. You can offer all sorts of advice, but they've got to be in the right mental state to pick up on it. The longer someone has raced and the better the racer they are, the more they'll pick up on you. You see them mentally fall off. You say something right to them, you see them mentally build up again. You say something wrong, they fall off again. You watch them go out the window and there's just no coming back."

But John Shandelmeier suggests that just the fact that there's some support for you outside of your immediate family of dogs helps, "Even if all they can do is look at you, it helps."

Ned Cathers draws up, nursing a few minor bruises on his shins. He ran through some knee-deep overflow earlier in the day, then stopped to build a fire and dry out. To speed the process, he banged the dull end of his axe head against his legs to knock the ice off.

Canadian musher Adolphus Capot-Blanc just nips by American driver Cliff Cadzow at the final corner to edge into the checkpoint ahead of him. "We race at times," smiles Cadzow. "We even raced to see who would get into bed first last night. Adolphus won that too."

Bob Bright clatters into the checkpoint and announces his decision to quit the race. His sled runner is cracked and the plastic runner-bottom just won't stay attached. "The sled can't be fixed. I tried to find some parts, but they're not available."

Failure with this sled doesn't dampen his enthusiasm for the race or for trying to use new technology for long distance racing. Next year he will turn up with a new sled: a torpedo-shaped device with an innovative brush bow, built out of kevlar. That sled will not complete the Quest either.

Circle City is the last place that the handlers and families will have a chance to see the mushers before reaching Dawson City, 280 miles farther down the trail — another reason why the handlers and families don't really feel comfortable here. The checkpoint at Eagle, about halfway to Dawson, is accessible only by airplane, dog sled or snowmachine in winter.

The drivers' time here isn't spent idly. With the first long totally isolated stretch of the trail facing them, they check and double-check to ensure that everything is in order. They drag sleds into the community hall to repair them. The walls are hung with drying dog gear and clothes. Dog food is cooking in a dozen different pots while the teams lay in an open field across the road from the community hall. Mushers are sprawled across beds in the back room, sitting on bundles of hay or spread-eagled on the floor trying to get a little sleep.

The volunteers treat the mushers to the last luxury they will see for a while. Their food is heated for them on small stoves and if it gets cold while they're eating, they can always zap it in the microwave. In 1984, held up by strong winds, Kevin Turnbough summed up the mushers' feelings about this checkpoint, "If I have to be stuck somewhere, it may as well be somewhere with a microwave."

Just down the road and over the bank through a patch of willows, shrouded in mist and drifting snow, the Yukon River awaits them with cold anticipation.

(over) Kevin Turnbough camps at Circle Hot Springs, 1984.

Canyons of ice

Canyons of ice

The Yukon River meanders for almost 2,000 miles bordered on both banks by pre-Cambrian mountains that predate life on earth. In some places the river runs deep, fast and narrow. In other areas the valley spreads out for miles and the river seems to be able to fill most of the basin.

It is the source of water. Rain clouds build over top of it, but few dare to unload their burden within its realm. Rainfall is sparse in the Yukon River watershed, which covers almost a third of Alaska and more than two-thirds of the Yukon. Even during the prehistoric ice ages, low precipitation along its length kept most of it ice free while glaciers covered the rest of the northern hemisphere.

In the summer, dry means warm. In winter, it means cold. While the summers are the hottest of most northern regions and often rank as summertime hot spots for North America, it is in the Yukon River basin that the coldest temperatures of the 1989 Alaska Aurora High will be reported, including the lowest temperature ever recorded in North America.

Communities along the river normally spend at least four months of each year in sub-zero temperatures. The long duration of winter numbs a person to the environment. After a couple of months, 40 below is like 30 below — only colder. Just as people shelter themselves in houses during the winter and dogs grow extra quantities of fur, the land protects itself from the cold as well. The mountains are insulated under a blanket of snow; the river shields itself with a shell of ice.

If the river would freeze in one level, unbroken sheet of ice, like a skating rink, it would be a simple matter to run the dog teams. But the face of the Yukon is not so predictable. Ice comes in its own collection of wrinkles, scars and character lines.

It can be glare ice, flat and featureless, where distance is deceptive and the surface is too sheer for dogs to grip and pull effectively and where there is nothing to stop a sled from weaving uncontrollably from side to side.

It can be pack ice. As the river freezes, cakes of ice are carried by the current until they snag on a sandbar, a log jam or a solid band of ice. Then they refreeze in jumbled heaps. Some of the pieces are as big as small cabins; others are slender, razor-edged blades of ice that stick straight up like knives.

Overflow ice (water from streams running into the river) forms a jagged fan shape when frozen or a steaming, seeping slush when not. Black ice windows (areas of ice that are so transparent the dark water below can be seen) could be five feet thick or too weak to travel on.

At any point along the river, the water level occasionally rises and the current eats away at the ice, reducing it to an unsafe thinness that could collapse under the sled. According to Frank Turner, conditions under any given section of ice can change within four or five hours.

When the river freezes, the ice is initially at one level. Then, below the ice, the water level drops as its glacial sources in the mountains also freeze. Canyons of ice are formed when the ice, no longer supported by the water, collapses in the middle. There are cracks, formed by changing surface pressures, that are small enough to trap a dog's foot or large enough to swallow the entire dog. Some areas never freeze shut for one reason or another. They can be identified by a stationary fog during the day or the roar of the river current at night.

All of these hazards may be exposed by the north wind or disguised under dry, sand-like snow that is so coarse it can cut the dogs' feet and tear up the plastic runner-bottoms. On this treacherous surface, the Yukon Quest becomes like no other race on earth.

Circle City to Eagle

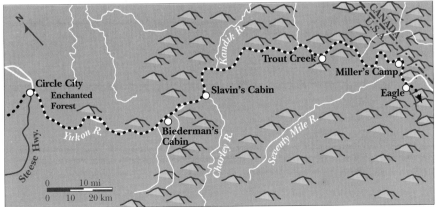

"The river itself was real jumbled ice and we had to run right on the bank," said Ed Salter in 1987. "It was just hundreds of miles of sidehills. And it was pretty tough, real hard on the teams."

Jim Reiter will remember the river by the ache in his ankles that he gets from leaning so hard, for so long, as he rides his sled along the sides. "It all depends on the ice conditions," he says. "They put the trail in then the river drops over the next two weeks or so. Even when they broke the trail, the ice couldn't have been that stable so they really never did get out onto the river itself. I'd rather run the sidehills anyway than take a chance of getting wet."

Even after the trail has been set, the river surface can change. In 1986, Sonny Lindner was among a group of mushers who spent the night looking for the trail. "We kept zig-zagging from one side of the river to the other. Two of the markers on the trail went right up to open leads on the river." During the night, the river had risen and eroded away the ice the mushers had crossed over just a few minutes earlier.

The mushers linger in Circle City, preparing physically and psychologically for the first long haul on the Yukon Quest — 180 miles upriver to Eagle. It is just a short section of one of the world's longest rivers and it occasionally provides evidence of thousands of years of river travel by people, but its recorded history is one of the shortest of the world's great waterways.

The Gwich'in people called it Yu Choo, "big river" or "the greatest river," and it was the last major river in North America to be explored by Europeans. The Russians found the mouth of the river in 1834. It wasn't until later that the river was mapped.

In the 1880s, prospectors, disillusioned by the dwindling number of valuable mineral finds further south, made their way into the Yukon River watershed. Small communities started popping up around areas where gold was found: Forty Mile in 1886, Circle in 1892, Dawson City in 1896.

The Yukon River was the highway connecting the interior goldfields of Alaska with the fabled Klondike in the central Yukon. It was the history of gold discoveries in the north, and the postal service they spawned, that caught the imagination of Roger Williams in Whitehorse in 1981.

The mail carriers were the most frequent users of the trails on the river and they kept them clearly marked and broken. Their massive freight sleds were pulled by eight to 10 large powerful dogs, about twice the size of today's racing dog, hitched in single file. Occasionally, the mail carriers took passengers, but the passengers didn't just ride. They had to run alongside, riding only when they needed a rest, to keep the sled as light as possible for the dogs.

It was a livelihood filled with risk. In 1901, a mail carrier waited patiently for an overdue sled to arrive at one cabin. (Cabins were built the length of the river to provide shelter.) Finally, he headed upriver, thinking he might meet the delayed team. All he found was a hole in the ice with a fur hat lying beside it.

The last carriers on this stretch of the river were Adolphe and Charlie Biederman, who handled the mail between Circle City and Eagle in the 1930s. They were mail carriers not to be trifled with. Despite the fact the round trip took eight days, the mail always got through precisely on schedule, regardless of the weather or ice conditions.

But their time was running out. The airplane was becoming the mail carrier of the future for the remote communities and, in 1940, the Biedermans lost their contract to Wien Air Alaska. That gradually became the fate of dog sled mail carriers over the next two decades. The final dog sled mail driver in Alaska retired in 1963.

For Ralph Tingey, an avid student of history, there is a feeling of déjà vu. "I drove past rock walls I'd seen in a 1920 photo of an old-time mail carrier on the Yukon River."

Overnight, the arctic air mass has faltered. The cold is being gradually broken down by a slightly warmer block of air, pushing temperatures up to about minus 10.

David Sawatzky tucks the last of his gear inside the sled bag and pulls the zipper tight. The dogs shiver with excitement and pull at their harness collars. They are ready to go and are looking forward to getting back on the trail, but there is none of the frantic excitement and lunging that took place in the starting chute in Fairbanks.

Sawatzky steps onto the runners at the back of the sled. "Hike!" he shouts. A jarring yank by the dogs, a push from the driver and the sled jerks loose from the hard-packed snow and moves past the other teams who perk up at the sudden activity. First into the checkpoint, he is the first to leave.

Gerald Riley doesn't look like he is in a rush, but he is next out an hour later. "My strategy is to stay light, travel fast and draw out the leaders." Within four hours, 14 drivers have pulled out of Circle City.

Bruce Lee isn't looking forward to the canyons of ice. "There's no life on the river in winter," he says. "It's just a frozen path with willow and spruce trees along the bank. It's the same scenery in one stretch as it is around the next corner. The dogs get bored. The pace slows down and they trudge along until they get to an open stretch where they can see something different. Then they perk up."

Race judge Ed Foran is more concerned with the logistical problems a stretch of trail like this could bring. "It is long and will separate teams. It's not racing from checkpoint to checkpoint anymore. Some of the teams just hanging on with the front runners will start to fade away." The gap between the teams in front and back can stretch from hours to days and keeping track of all the teams will become more difficult.

While the trail skirts the river for the first couple of miles, it swings inland through the Enchanted Forest before finally dropping onto the ice for the duration of the way. The short overland section earned that name in 1986.

That year, the teams battled their way through a snowstorm that just wouldn't stop, forcing the drivers to break trail almost the entire 1,000 miles from Fairbanks to Whitehorse. Every day for two weeks, the snow fell so heavily that the trail filled in almost as fast as each individual sled could break its way through.

Jeff King, with bloodstained ice hanging from his moustache (the blood came from the ice cutting into his upper lip) stumbled around feeding his dogs on the trail. "It's no longer the team that has the fastest dogs," he said to reporters. "It's by no means a race anymore. That ended when we hit the snow. We just went 25 miles and it's like we went 80."

For the first few miles out of Circle, the snowbound mushers also had to contend with a trail that the trailbreakers had somehow managed to snake through the trees. It became painfully obvious that a six-foot-long snowmachine could go places that a dog team stretched out over 40 feet couldn't.

"We called that section the Enchanted Forest because it's almost impossible to drive dogs in there and live through the experience," said Joe May. The 50-year-old former 1980 Iditarod champion had been lucky — only his sled bag had been damaged. King had splintered parts of his sled as he dodged around stumps and tried to squeeze between trees on the narrow trail.

Harry Sutherland lost it on a sharp turn. His sled spun, then jammed sideways across the trail. Jon Rudolph was right behind him and couldn't get his dogs past the jackknifed team. "There was a stump caught between his brake and runner. We needed a saw to cut the sled out."

Frank Turner couldn't believe how tight the corners were. "If you've got 10 or 12 dogs, the corners are too tough, too sharp. Your team almost starts coming back on itself. That's where you start getting dogs hung up on the neckline and you start getting injuries. I don't know how else I can describe it. It's just a very narrow trail with trees all over the place. It wasn't made for teams to go through. There were trees literally stuck in the middle of the trail and you had no way around them."

Bruce Johnson talked about U-turns so tight at the end, he could reach over and pat his lead dog on the head as it came up the other side of the bend. "It's a wonder there haven't been any dogs killed." A few dogs were hurt, and one was actually knocked unconscious in a collision with a tree.

Since that year, the trail has been gradually improved, but it still features areas that make the teams work for any ground they may gain. And the hazards don't end after exiting the trees.

Ed Borden took it easy in 1986 going through the trees and reached the river ice without too much damage. He made a short stop to feed the dogs, then kept on driving. The trail was rough; it was tossing the sled back and forth as the team passed through an area of rugged pack ice. Borden, balancing on the runners, went to step out to steady the sled and found his knee crushed between the 300-pound sled and a block of ice.

Some knocks hurt at first, without being serious. Borden gritted his teeth and waited for the agony to subside. But it didn't. He noticed the leg starting to get cold below the knee, and the pain was starting to physically wear him out. He dug in his brake, stopping the team, then hobbled forward to turn the team around to return to Circle City. Heading back, his hands started to swell, then to freeze.

When Don Glassburn met Borden's team, six hours later, just seven miles from Circle, Borden was semiconscious. His arm was wrapped around the driving bow of his sled, but the rest of his body was dragging in the snow behind.

Glassburn loaded the injured musher onto his sled, tied the confused and frightened dogs to the back, then backtracked to a cabin occupied by Doug Dill. Dill piled Borden onto his snowmachine and headed for town.

Jack Hayden leaving Circle City, 1984.

The checkers at Circle City were startled to see a snowmobile come out of the darkness shortly after midnight.

"I need help," said Dill. "I have a musher with a broken leg in the sled."

"Sorry for the rough ride," he apologized to the injured musher.

"Hey, I don't even remember," mumbled Borden.

The next day Borden scratched. It was his final race. His smashed knee on the Yukon River was the second major crash within a couple of months for the musher who lived with the reality he might not be able to race again. Multiple sclerosis can be aggravated by physical trauma and within two years he was bedridden by the disease.

A little farther up the river, Dean Siebold and his team hit a thin patch of ice in 1987 and dropped into three feet of water — not enough to drown them, but sufficient to be a threat at minus 50 degrees. As Siebold dried himself by a fire, the dogs dried themselves off by rolling in the snow. Snow in extremely cold temperatures tends to be very dry and acts like a sponge.

Ed Borden getting treatment at Circle City, 1986.

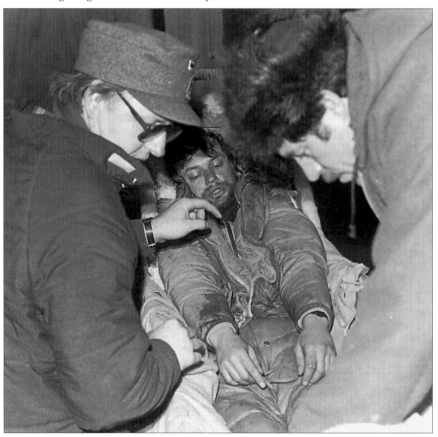

The long hours and rough trails start to wear out the drivers by this point in the race. Sleep becomes a rare commodity and whatever shut-eye the mushers can grab is welcome, but sometimes those moments can come at the most inopportune times.

"I know one night I wanted to sleep," remembers Ed Salter, "and I didn't want to lie down. The thought of lying down in that temperature just didn't sit right even though I was really tired and I was almost sleeping standing up. I just grabbed the handlebar and figured if I fell asleep I'd fall over on my dogs."

Ralph Tingey isn't in the habit of falling asleep on his sled, but there's one incident from the 1987 race he won't forget — or remember.

"I fell asleep on the sled and I must have been asleep for a while. When I camped the next day with Dean Siebold he said, 'Boy, wasn't that stretch of the Yukon back there horrible with that ice kind of sloping into that huge open hole?' I said, 'Dean, I fell asleep on the sled yesterday. What hole?' He says, 'There was this great big hole, with the river boiling through it, and there was all this side ice and it was really hard to negotiate.' I said, 'Oh.'"

Now, with the arctic air mass collapsing around them, the warmer temperatures slow down the pace. The days are too warm for the dogs with their fur coats and the drivers travel mainly in the cooler night hours.

"I couldn't believe just how beautiful it was driving on the Yukon River with just polypropylene gloves in the moonlight, in the northern lights, in February," says Vern Halter.

David Sawatzky can't maintain his lead on the river. Kathy Swenson, Dave Monson and Bruce Lee pull ahead of him. Gerald Riley, the self-avowed hater of trailbreaking, is running his own distinct race a short distance behind them. While the others are systematically running four hours on and four hours off, Riley is blasting along nonstop for 12 to 16 hours, then resting for 12 to 16 hours. But he refuses to pull up with the leaders, instead allowing them to set the pace and break the trail.

Some of the drivers will camp on the river all the way to Eagle, but most will stop at one or more of the cabins along the way. A few, like Ron Rosser, will stop at some of the lesser-used locations. In 1986, he overnighted in a cabin owned by a German woodcarver, ate a meal of cookies and home-made beer at a small place occupied by a French-Canadian woman and visited a hermit who lived in a teepee.

It was that year that all the mushers were forced off the ice and into the cabins along the river. Not much had gone right for the teams from the moment they left the starting chute. The snow had fallen relentlessly. The temperatures stayed cold. A blinding headwind was being funnelled down the river valley. A dozen drivers shared the lead, alternating the first-place position.

Before the 1986 Yukon Quest was over, the drivers, many of them veterans of the Alaska mushing circuit, would call it one of the toughest races ever run.

Jon Rudolph remembers the time spent in the canyons that year. His voice sounds old as he recalls it: age not measured in years but by the experience of having been there. "People were falling off their sleds, they were so tired, but we kept going. No one wanted to be left out there. It was blowing so hard I couldn't see my own hands on the driving bow. We all moved like a train following a string of lights at night. When the leaders stopped, we all stopped. When the first light started moving again, we'd all get going again."

The 1987 Quest featured a bitter cold that took its toll on the teams as temperatures got stuck around minus 50. Jon Gleason's hands and face were dry and splitting from frostbite. "I took off from Slavin's Cabin and I got cold. I mean really cold." (Slavin's Cabin, about halfway between Circle and Eagle, is named after former British Empire heavyweight boxing champion Frank Slavin, who was supposed to have lived there. Slavin quit the ring after he had been denied an opportunity to fight for the world championship in the 1890s and headed north to the Klondike. Arriving too late to stake a gold claim, he made a living with exhibition boxing bouts, as a bouncer in the dance halls and cutting firewood during the summer to sell in the winter. This cabin was located on one of his wood lots.)

Gleason pulled off the trail again a few miles farther down at Biederman's Cabin. (In the 1930s, this cabin was the summer home for the mail-carrying Biederman family. It was abandoned after they lost their mail contract in the 1940s.) Inside the cabin, he felt the pins and needles of warm blood revitalizing the nerves in his frozen parts. The weird thing was that his tongue hurt too. "I was eating these M&Ms and it was 50 below. I'm just shoving them into my mouth. I was so damn tired I should never have done that. I should have put them in my pocket, warmed them up, then ate them. I'm at Biederman's and my tongue starts to hurt. I'm trying to figure out, 'Geez, how come my tongue hurts? I haven't drank any hot soup or coffee.' All of a sudden I realize I've been eating all those M&Ms and froze my damn tongue."

To live on the Yukon River is to step back in time to an era when people didn't lock their doors, when a stranger was someone who used your cabin while you were gone and left you a fresh pile of split firewood as payment.

Swiss architect Peter Thomann, who will run the 1990 Yukon Quest, will be astounded at the inhabitants of the cabins who open their doors, sit back, and let the mushers take complete possession of their home. "Sometimes they don't even know who we are. I'm amazed that sort of thing can happen."

The chili at Slavin's Cabin, staffed today by people from the National Parks Service, is second to none. They also offer hot coffee, stew, hot soup and freshly baked bread for the drivers, and water for the dogs.

Biederman's Cabin is abandoned for most of the year, but each February Mark and Laurie Richards travel 50 miles by dog sled from their own wilderness home to set up and operate a ham radio station there for the Quest organization. They provide food and shelter for the teams, then radio forward to the next checkpoint to let them know who's in and how they're doing.

For the first few years of the Quest it was occupied by a fellow called Woody Wilson. After offering hospitality for the first two years he was there, Wilson tried to capitalize on the mushers passing by in 1987. He set up a bed-and-breakfast for the teams. A room was $40 for the night. A bowl of soup was $5 and a bun was $3.50. Cash only please, no cheques or credit cards accepted. The mushers don't carry a lot of cash on the river and all passed him by. In 1988, Wilson is gone and the cabin abandoned once again — except for the Richards family.

Mike Sager's place at Trout Creek, about 40 miles from Eagle, is another regular stop. He's a fisher, trapper and carver. The bannisters on his staircase to the second floor are hand-carved from top to bottom. Here, the coffee's always on. The drivers are welcome to floor space if they want to sleep, and if they want conversation, Sager can't be described as the quiet type either.

"What an interesting guy," said Leroy Shank in 1987. "We were up most of the night talking with him. It was one of the most enjoyable parts of that section of trail."

Trout Creek is also the site of the most infamous outhouse on the trail. The outhouse is perched on the edge of a cliff, about 20 feet above the spot where the teams rest their dogs. At one time, the embankment in front of the outhouse must have been wide enough for a footpath, since the door looks out over the camping area below in the creek valley.

But the bank has eroded and the front door of the outhouse has disappeared. The only way into the small log-walled structure is through a hole in the back wall. The occupant then sits in full view of the other mushers. Not only can it be somewhat indiscreet, but it can also be downright embarrassing. David Sawatzky lost his balance in 1987 while crawling in from the back, fell out the front door and rolled down the embankment into the camping area.

Cabin fever has also reared its bizarre head. Isolation and low light levels in winter have odd effects on individuals and it's one of the reasons people do strange things after living for extended periods in the north.

In 1986, Ron Rosser and Frank Turner pulled into a cabin a few miles from Eagle about eight at night. There was one occupant, "a big, big man, about 230 pounds. Darrel was his name," said Turner. "He had hot chocolate for us and really made us feel welcome."

The two drivers pulled out again close to midnight, but the trail was blown in and the snow kept falling. They decided to turn back to the cabin to wait for some daylight to tackle the trail.

"We got back to the cabin, and all of a sudden," says Turner, "this guy just flips out. He wasn't going to let us back into the cabin. He started calling us all these names I've never heard before. I guess he had this macho thing that once we were gone, there was no turning back.

"That's the only person I ever had any trouble with. Everyone else along the river is so happy to see you. They don't see a lot of people for a lot of months every year...and it's a really big thing for them."

Led by Kathy Swenson, the front teams start to open a gap between themselves and the rest of the pack. Swenson, Monson, Lee, Riley and Sawatzky start a push towards Eagle from Trout Creek. The heat has made the trail punchy, or soft, causing the dogs' feet to punch down into the snow, but the trail is faster than the crystallized snow of the previous two years.

The warmer temperatures also make cooking dog food a little easier. In 1987, Swenson boiled some dog food for her team, but before the dogs could completely devour the hot food, it had frozen in the bottom of the pan.

In addition to marking the route and packing the trail, the trailbreakers have also provided some other aids along the river over the years, some of which have more value for the drivers than others.

Senley Yuill and Bill Cotter both remember a small sign on a portage just outside of Eagle in 1984. It had the standard crossed trail markers to warn the teams, but there was also a small sign nailed to a tree just a little further on. Just past the sign on the tree was a 15-foot embankment that dropped steeply down to the river.

"By the time you got to the sign to read it, half of your team was over the bank," said Yuill. "The sign said, 'Check bank before going over,' but by then you were going whether you wanted to or not."

Ahead of the teams, where the town of Eagle is perched on a level gravel bench above the Yukon, the residents watch and wait. With the exception of occasional static-filled reports from ham radio stations, there is only speculation about who is in front and when they will arrive.

The entire village of Eagle is involved in the Quest, either as volunteers or as supporters who come out at the ringing of the church bell to greet the teams, no matter what hour of the day or night. Only once will the bell not greet every musher who arrives. In 1990, the rope will be found frozen to the side of the church.

When access from the "outside" (the rest of the world outside the Yukon-Alaska area) is limited to those who travel the river, or land on the small airstrip, every visitor to the town is a welcome one. There is a special heart that the inhabitants of this collection of historical log cabins — hung with moose and caribou antlers and hides, and modern structures — put into their Quest participation.

The people who live here are a distinctively independent breed. They are here because they like the feeling of being distant from the giant urban centres and the society such metropolises spawn. It is about as far from the bright city lights as you can possibly get. The residents are rebels in their own right and are proud of their history of fighting government bureaucracy. Battling the government is almost an obsessive pastime in Eagle. Rarely does a year go by without a major dispute over one issue or another. They share a strong identity with the drivers on the river. Both groups are doing what they choose to do rather than something they have to do.

For most of the winter, the weather here stinks. "The people at Eagle have a most commanding view of the river," describes present-day resident Hudson Stuck, "but they pay for it." The wind normally whistles relentlessly

Outside the Eagle checkpoint.

around the snow-encrusted collection of new and old buildings, and the mercury usually drops to the bottom of the thermometer and stays there for the winter.

But for some reason, this year it's different. Checkpoint worker John Borg is surprised at the light wind and warm temperatures. "This is the warmest Quest since the beginning. Usually, every year the mushers arrive with or ahead of a big snow. It'll be a pleasant change this year."

The residents take turns watching the foot of Eagle Bluff, watching at night for a telltale headlamp or during the day for anything that would change the whiteness of the snow around the base of Eagle Bluff. It is around the base of this massive buttress of rock, that juts out into the river about a half-mile downstream from the town, that the first musher will appear.

Standing and watching the river, volunteer Serge Waller is looking forward to the arrival of the first driver. For him, the Quest is an indicator of the end of winter and the coming of spring. "The Quest is a break in the monotony. Everyone looks forward to it and pitches in." Even the children share spotting duties.

Dusk is coming and still there's no sign. Radio signals from Mike Sager's place at Trout Creek, Biederman's or even from Dick Cook, just a few miles out of town at Miller's Camp, are being jammed by the effects of the aurora borealis on the atmosphere. But an incoming pilot reports seeing teams closing in on Eagle, well past Miller's Camp.

The gathering darkness is suddenly pierced by a small, sudden, sharp spot of light on the river. "Team on the ice," shouts a voice. Another light,

Inside the Eagle checkpoint.

just minutes behind the first, appears in the distance. The church bell starts to clang and a crowd begins to gather near the small schoolhouse where the checkpoint is located. The light vanishes momentarily.

Whoever it is has reached the end of the trail on the ice and is now entering the trees. Now the light can be seen intermittently through the trees as the team creeps closer until the whole team is illuminated by the spotlight shining from the front of the schoolhouse.

The smiling, tired eyes of Kathy Swenson drink in the scene of the applauding spectators. Her dogs stand wagging their tails, their tongues hanging out.

"How was it?" asks one bystander, as the checkers identify the mandatory items (snowshoes, axe, sleeping bag, dog booties, map, compass and promotional material) in the sled and the veterinarians look over her dogs.

"Not bad," she replies. "Yesterday I spun around on the ice in a circle for about 10 minutes while the wind blew. Trail's pretty punchy."

Dave Monson's is the second headlamp. "We're a happy bunch of campers." He smiles in response to a deluge of questions about his strategy. "We only fight about who is the first to leave the campsite."

More lights on the river and more teams stream steadily into Eagle through the night. Some teams recently found overflow on the ice just outside of town and are soaked. Frank Turner has gone for a wild ride just a couple of miles out when his team smelled a wolf on the wind and bolted for a short distance. Gerald Riley pulls in silently, then parks his team in an isolated area away from the other drivers. His dogs look rested.

He is the subject of silent scrutiny from the other drivers. "He often travels just out of sight behind us and when he pulls in front, he turns out his headlamp so we can't see where he is," mutters Swenson. Riley simply smiles when he hears suggestions that he's playing head games.

"Keeping other mushers guessing is one way a fast team can pull ahead of other teams of comparable abilities," he states.

In previous years, the trail beyond Eagle to Dawson City has continued along the Yukon River. But there is too much open water and rotten ice there this year. The trail has been rerouted overland. It goes up the mountain behind Eagle towards American Summit, on top of the Dawson Range, then down the Fortymile River back to the Yukon River for the final miles into Dawson.

There is relief that they are finally free of the canyons of ice. But there is apprehension, too. The route over American Summit is unknown to any of the drivers, and trail conditions and prevailing winds are major unknowns. The memories of their most recent experiences above tree line, three days ago on Eagle Summit, are still fresh in their minds.

(over) Team leaving Eagle, Alaska. Eagle Bluff is in the background.

Seeing things

Seeing things

Broken. Alone on the trail. Days behind everyone else. His fingers and face frozen, ice preventing him from even untying his boots and no longer capable of motivating himself or his team, Michael Schwandt sank defeated into the snow on the Yukon River. He had long ago lost contact with any other stragglers in the 1986 Yukon Quest. His first shot at long distance racing now had the potential of turning into tragedy. He lay back and looked desperately to the heavens for divine inspiration.

The northern lights were there, dancing and weaving between stars, hiding behind mountains, then launching themselves across the sky in multicoloured waves, drowning out the brightness of the stars themselves. A beautiful fantasy was played out across the universe above the motionless musher.

The very air sang to him, with the crackling hum of the northern lights, with the haunting whispers of winds shifting the snow softly across the ice. And when they stilled, in his mind he could hear the trees in the forest take a deep silent breath in anticipation of what would be coming up next. He could smell the crispness of the cold in the air. It pierced cleanly and deep into his sinuses. Then he smelled the distinctive tang of dog breath as his team, lying beside him, watched their driver intently.

The assault on his senses penetrated into his world of dark despair and rejuvenated Michael Schwandt. He struggled to his feet. The dogs stood up, their tails wagging.

His fingers and face never really thawed out. He was always alone on the trail. He never stopped being tired, but he never gave up. Michael Schwandt completed the 1986 Quest, the toughest race ever run, arriving almost five days after the winner. He was on the trail nearly three weeks.

For each driver the northern lights have a different meaning. For Schwandt, the lights turned potential disaster into personal triumph.

Lorrina Mitchell views them as being astral companions that watch over the teams as they travel.

"They seem like another living thing because they have motion and light. You're out there alone, and all of a sudden, it's all right. You don't even feel the 40 below any more. You just say, 'Isn't that beautiful,' and when you see a falling star, that's really exciting."

Jeninne Cathers echoes that sentiment. "Even when there's no one around, you get the feeling you're among friends."

Bill Cotter relates to them as part of the total experience of the trail. He specifically remembers a camp in the 1984 Quest he shared with Sonny Lindner, Jeff King and Joe Runyan. The four of them had lost the trail in the dark and decided to camp under an embankment, out of the wind.

"The stars were out. The northern lights were out dancing. We had a big bonfire and everybody hauled wood, fed the dogs and tried to keep warm all night. We talked about where we thought the trail was, how the dogs were doing. We swapped stories. It was one of the most fun times I ever had on the trail."

The northern lights are just part of the overpowering proximity of nature that captured Frank Turner's imagination.

"There's been times when you're out there and you're just by yourself. It almost becomes like a religious or spiritual experience, with the northern

Eagle to Dawson City

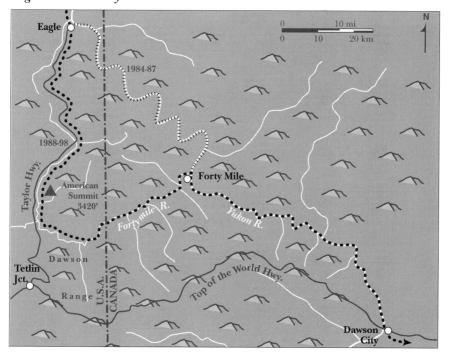

lights. A lot of people get religion out there. Not the church kind. I don't mean religion in that way. But it really is spiritual because you're so close to nature. You're so close to a total sense of being alive; there's nothing that transcends that. It's just an incredible, incredible feeling."

Not all the light shows are provided by nature. The drivers, after four or five sleepless days and nights on the trail, can provide much of their own inspiration and entertainment.

"Lots of hallucinations," says Jon Rudolph, sitting in his office two years after running his last Quest. He mimics the exhausted driver on the sled: "There's a checkpoint coming up. It's there. Yeah. It's there! It's coming up...there's no light there. It's not a light. What the hell was that?"

And again, reflecting from his chair, no longer on the trail. "It's scary... You say to yourself, 'I've got to get back to reality. I'm here on a dog team. How are the dogs doing? They're just going down the trail. There's nothing going on here; it's all in your head.' Then, just when you're back down again, you look up and you start drifting away again."

John Schandelmeier looks into the sky and sees only headlamps dancing in the dark. "You see all sorts of things when you're running on empty."

Ed Salter did a nosedive off his sled into the snow when he spotted a bear right beside his head. "It was just shadow. I started to laugh. Bears hibernate in winter." Marc Boily, an experienced long distance driver with three Iditarods and one Quest under his belt, watched the trees move, marching alongside the river. Dave Monson hears people singing and yelling. At night, patches of willow trees turn into herds of caribou. Stationary tree stumps become wolves racing alongside the trail.

Trail briefing in Eagle for Sonny Lindner (l) from Leo Oleson (r), 1984.

Jon Gleason suddenly came under attack from a wave of flying swords and spears. "I'm ducking and weaving and bopping and I end up falling off the dang dog sled." Another time he spotted his daughter Shayne riding on the back of Snowball, one of his dogs. "What are you doing out here?" he asked. "You're supposed to be home with your mother."

Confusion can result when the musher suddenly sees his dogs facing the sled and running backwards down the trail. The heart can momentarily stop when they vanish into black holes in the ice, only to miraculously reappear on the other side, running as if nothing had happened.

In 1984, Harry Sutherland spotted someone sitting on his brush bow. "This guy was in a T-shirt and he was riding in front of my sled, smoking a cigar, drinking a Coke and blowing smoke rings at me. There he was, then he'd go away when I realized it was a hallucination, then he'd come back again." Occasionally, his passenger would ask a question about the dogs, about philosophy, whatever. And Sutherland would respond. It wasn't his only vision on the trail, but the fact that he answered made it memorable.

Frank Turner once saw Jon Rudolph standing by his sled puffing on a pipe, but there were no sled tracks in the snow leading out to the sled and Rudolph, in reality, was miles away. Besides that, he doesn't smoke a pipe.

Not all drivers are subject to the scenarios the exhausted mind can conjure, but they are all aware of it. Joe Runyan uses a disciplined feeding-running schedule to keep his mind occupied and prevent himself from falling victim to the phenomenon. He even wears two watches, in case one breaks, to ensure he doesn't break from the pattern.

Lorrina Mitchell changes booties frequently, stops a little more than usual and feeds the dogs. While travelling, she mentally redesigns the kitchen pantry in her new house or resolves never to put herself through this kind of stupidity again. Next year, just short races. When that line of daydreaming runs dry, she sings to the dogs:

Mush along little doggies
Mush along there well
'Cause it's your misfortune
And none of my own
You know that you have to
Mush a thousand miles home.

The average dog team will trot between six and 10 miles per hour. It's not the kind of speed where the mushers need to focus solely on steering, so they have to do something. A few, like Mitchell, sing to their teams. Others chat incessantly to them. "John Schandelmeier talks to his dogs," says Gleason. "You can hear him coming a mile away."

The biggest thrill for people like Senley Yuill is to sit on the back of the sled in silence and listen to the music in the patter of the paws on the crisp snow, the muffled thunder of the runners on the snow and the panting of the dogs. "It's so peaceful a sound, like a quiet chair. It's got to be the most peaceful way to travel on earth."

It is into this world of inspirational light-shows, half-true fantasies and peaceful tranquillity that Dave Monson enters when he hitches up under a partially full moon and pulls out of Eagle in the early hours of the morning. Bruce Lee and Kathy Swenson are just minutes behind.

On this portion of the trail everyone is a rookie. None of the drivers have ever run up the Taylor Highway (a summer-only road into Eagle), to American Summit and over the top of the Dawson range of mountains. The ascent is a constant steady grind of 15 miles up the side of a sheltered valley. On top, they pass over a seven-mile stretch from one tree line to the other before starting to descend to the Taylor Highway. The top, according to the trailbreakers, is notorious for winds and whiteouts. The snow is hard-packed by the wind and there are lots of drifts.

"It was every bit as wicked as Eagle Summit," says Jim Reiter. "I could see the country, and where the wind had blown, the drifts that were in there. And it's a long way across. At least on Eagle Summit, you could crawl your way across if you had to. This one here, you could wander around up there for a long time."

The wind has done its work on the few trees that survive up that high. Over the years they have twisted and contorted themselves into the shapes that best protect against the harsh environment. In the light from the drivers' headlamps, the hoarfrost-covered branches look as if someone had shattered the fragile darkness into a thousand cracks — deformed, pure-white spider webs spread over a velvet-black background.

"You swear that these things come alive," describes Turner, "that they've got their own life when nobody else is around. They're only frozen when somebody's there to look at them."

Monson pulls up from the Taylor Highway and breaks onto the open summit. There is no wind tonight. There are no clouds in the sky. He shuts off his headlamp and lets his leaders take command. All around him he can see the wilderness surrealistically illuminated by the pale reflections of the stars and moon off the snow.

"It was so beautiful. The stars and moon were out. You were up on these vistas that you could see forever. You could see the teams way behind you, and you could look ahead and see where you needed to go. And the team was travelling along really well. And you were just enjoying the fact that you were out here in the wilderness doing something you had prepared yourself for all year."

It doesn't take long for Monson and the other leaders to clear the top and start down. And it isn't far past the tree line where the trail turns sharply off the Taylor Highway and drops onto the Fortymile River. The trail snakes through narrow canyons in the river's upper reaches before widening into a substantial valley which takes them back to the Yukon River just 50 miles from the Dawson City checkpoint.

Several cabins line the narrow concourse. One of them, owned by 1985 Quest veteran Dave Likins, has a lamp in the window to signal the drivers that they can stop here to feed their dogs, have a coffee, a bite to eat or just warm up.

Monson pulls up for a rest. Somewhere along the summit he has twisted his arm and he is finding it hard to hang onto the sled. Likins helps him wrap a bandage around it. Swenson turns up 20 minutes later; Bruce Lee is a half hour behind her. The three of them park, waiting for daylight and watching the trail behind. Around them, beneath the snow, lay the remains of the first of the major gold rushes that opened up the interior of Alaska and the Yukon.

It was in 1886 that two brothers, Frank and Henry Madison, ventured up the river and discovered gold. They called the river the Fortymile because it was believed to have been that far from Fort Reliance, a trading post farther up the Yukon River, near the site of what would become Dawson City. The town that grew to service the rush of miners to the area took on the same name as the river, though written as two words, Forty Mile. Eventually, it included a trading post, storage sheds, an opera house, six saloons and a multitude of sod-roof cabins, located where the Fortymile met the Yukon River.

In addition to being the first of the gold rushes, it was also the most important in the development of the unique mining techniques and technology that came to be used in the north. It was here that the miners first encountered the difficulties of digging into permafrost — muck and

Gerald Riley crossing American Summit, 1988.

gravel permanently frozen as hard as rock. They solved the problem by building fires at the bottom of their mine shafts, then excavating the melted materials, mainly in the form of a soupy mud. The knowledge acquired in Forty Mile was effectively applied later in the Klondike, Circle District, Fairbanks and Nome gold strikes.

When gold was discovered upstream in 1896, in the Klondike River valley, most of the miners left Forty Mile. But a few remained to scrape a living from the ground, and it wasn't until 1958 that the original townsite was totally abandoned. Modern mining techniques revived interest in the area in the 1970s and there are still several individual operators, like Likins, profitably working the old river bed and the bench claims on the hills above.

Dawn comes. The three leaders can see a storm developing on the mountain behind them. As Monson and Swenson pack up to leave, Gerry Riley rolls through the yard, gives them a quick look and keeps on going. His brief appearance rattles the two drivers.

"At that point," says Monson, "it was kind of scary because I didn't know why his dogs were doing so good. The reason they were doing so good was because he was compelling a superior performance from them."

A game of cat-and-mouse starts to develop among the front four teams. They drive, then stop and wait to see who will take the initiative. Monson is the first to cross the border into Canada, 30 miles from the Likins cabin. Swenson is a few hundred yards behind. Riley and Lee are about two miles back of her.

Above and behind them, a wind starts to blow on top of the summit. "It was all windblown. Nothing on top so you can't stop, and it was getting windy," describes Reiter. "Storm was coming. Tom Randall was right behind me and he ran through part of it. He had to hole up right after he got across."

The storm creates an even greater disparity between the teams up front and the rest of the pack, which, until now, has managed to stay relatively close. Hampered by the winds and not knowing exactly where to look for the trail in the reduced visibility, the teams on the summit slow down. But they do not have to war with the weather as they did on Eagle Summit.

The four teams up front stop to see if there is anyone else in the hunt. "We stayed there for five hours and nobody else showed up," says Monson. "So at that point we'd already had a five-hour rest and took off before anyone else turned up. That established the front pack right there. There were four teams. Those were the people you were going to compete against."

"We've been together long enough to know what the others can do," summarizes Lee. "Now we take a hard look at our strong and weak points and try to figure out a plan that will eventually put us in front." But Lee knows his limitations. Looking at the other three teams, he smiles. "I'm keeping up. But I'm just travelling in their wake."

They pull out and, a few hours later, drop onto the Yukon River and turn south towards Dawson. This is Percy DeWolfe country.

DeWolfe was a legendary mail carrier who ran this trail by dog sled between Eagle and Dawson for three decades. He was honoured in two countries for his single-minded determination that a job worth doing was worth doing well.

Nicknamed the "Iron Man of the Yukon," DeWolfe once broke through the ice just below the mouth of the Fortymile. He jumped free of the sled, then, realizing he couldn't save the team, leaped back and grabbed the mail bag. Throwing the mail onto the ice, he launched himself to safety just as the dogs and sled vanished under the black surface of the water beneath the ice. Picking himself up, he retrieved the mail and continued on foot the final 70 miles to Eagle.

None of the front four lose their teams through the ice at the mouth of the Fortymile, but in 1989, all six lead teams will break through in separate incidents and find themselves partially immersed in the river.

Jeff King will sink to his armpits. "I was hanging onto my sled with one hand and paddling with the other. I couldn't touch bottom." He will pull himself out along the gang line, then help the dogs pull the sled free. There is a trapper's cabin close by that he'll head to after getting on secure ice. "My clothes froze up. I couldn't bend at the middle when I got there."

Gerry Riley will be standing on the trail close to where Kate Persons breaks through. "When she went through I grabbed her leader and gave the hardest pull I could. But the ice just kept breaking." With Riley pulling and Persons windmilling her legs on top of the broken ice and water, they will shift the sled to firmer footings. "She couldn't get her mukluks off," says Riley, "so I yanked and yanked and yanked. When we got them off I put one of her feet in my coat next to my skin to warm it up."

Breaking through isn't the only way the Yukon River threatens to swallow teams. Open leads (open water) also pose a threat, especially at night. Crossing a glaciated section just outside of Dawson City in 1985, Bill Cotter could hear a loud roar similar to the thunder created by falling water at Niagara Falls, but he couldn't see anything in the dark. He turned his headlamp on and found his dogs trotting complacently just inches away from an open hole in the ice through which the river water was boiling up.

The biggest problem with open leads that can't be bypassed by going overland is that the trail to go past them is often put on a sidehill just above them. The trailbreaker sets the track 15 feet up from the hole, but as each team passes, the sleds cut the track a little lower down the hill and closer to the water. By the time the slowest teams approach, the trail can be right on the hole's edge. Only by tipping the sled and using the edge of the runner to direct the sled uphill can the driver avert disaster.

In 1984, Frank Turner didn't have any trouble with water, but encountered problems with all the things that had floated in it before it froze. He bruised his hip in a collision with a log sticking out of the ice, and broke his glasses and damaged part of his sled banging against pack ice. Then he discovered his headlamp wasn't working and he was running out of dog booties.

"So what I would do is, as I went along, I would pick up dog booties along the way. Well, it was getting dark and I could see on the trail, there was a bootie up there. It was on the right side of the sled. So I slung my sled over to the side and I went down to pick it up…and it wasn't a bootie after all. It was a piece of dog shit. I said to myself, 'This has got to be the absolute end. There's nothing else that can possibly happen to me now.'"

The environment along the river is reminiscent of Eagle Summit and is just as unpredictable. While John Mitchell complains about the heat in 1985 — "It was so hot it was like being in Hawaii. Every time I stopped to rest, my dogs dug caves in the snow to try and cool off." — Jon Rudolph remembers the snow storm in 1986.

"You couldn't see the next guy in front or behind you. You couldn't even see your dogs. But I knew there was a team less than 20 seconds ahead of me. His runner marks and everything else were completely wiped out. You'd all stop and someone changed the lead and you're supposed to get going. And you're yelling at the guy in front of you and he's sound asleep standing there. You had to go by and give him a kick and he'd wake up and off we'd go."

High clouds and light south winds are keeping temperatures just below freezing this year: perfect driving weather for teams who seek a fast time. On the river, the front four drivers are using the packed trails to manoeuvre for a psychological advantage.

Monson continues to lead until about 15 miles from Dawson when he stops to feed his dogs. Swenson and Lee have dropped back far enough that the bends in the river hide them from sight. Riley is right behind. He pulls over and feeds his team as well. "How far is Dawson?" asks Riley.

"I don't really know," replies Monson. The two watch their dogs chew for a moment.

"Tell you what," suggests Riley. "I'll take over the lead and break trail for a while." Tired of being tailgated, Monson agrees. He had offered Riley the lead before, but breaking trail isn't the older musher's favourite task and he declined.

Riley feels that now might be the time to deflate Monson a little by beating him into Dawson City and winning the four ounces of gold that awaits the first arrival at the halfway point of the race. Riley takes off and quickly opens a substantial gap, but as he vanishes from sight a mile or so ahead, Monson has a change of heart. "I've been breaking trail now for 200 miles, why should I let him get into Dawson ahead of me?"

Riley continues to drive his team, confident he is on his way to an advantage. Monson gradually accelerates his pace, picking it up bit by bit. The difference between them starts to shrink. A couple of miles outside of Dawson, passing Moosehide village, his quarry comes within sight.

"He saw that I was catching him and that's when he really started kicking in, running and kicking and really trying to get his dogs going. But by that point my dogs were in a speed and it was faster than he was going. Finally, I caught him, gave the dogs the command to pass and really picked them up then and just thumped away from him just to get rid of him. I think for him that was probably the most demoralizing point of the race, because until then it had been his impression that he was faster than me."

Monson cuts it close. The welcoming wail of the Dawson City Fire Department siren greets him just eight minutes ahead of Riley. He is still in front of the two-storey visitor information centre, where the checkpoint is located, when Riley arrives.

The late charge, while successful, has both Monson and Riley concerned. The dogs look tired as they patiently wait for the formalities to end so they can find some straw and go to sleep. Even though they have a 36-hour stop awaiting them, it will only be when they get back on the trail that the question of how fast their teams can bounce back will be answered.

"I hope four ounces of gold doesn't end up costing me $20,000," says Monson. "That last push took something out of my dogs." The gold wasn't the reason for the finishing kick, he explains. "Coming in first was a question of honour."

Swenson pulls in two hours later. Her dogs look perky as they lope up the bank off the river. "I didn't want to get suckered into racing, so I stopped on the river to rest my dogs when Monson and Riley took off," she smiles confidently. "Now my dogs are fine and theirs are so tired they practically had to walk to town."

Bruce Lee's reason for falling back is sitting in his sled basket. One of his dogs injured a foot about 30 miles out of Dawson City. The extra weight and reduced pulling power has slowed Lee down. He is an hour behind Swenson, his dogs are sick, and he looks depressed.

Behind them, Rick Atkinson and David Sawatzky have closed the gap a little, but aren't really within striking distance. It appears, barring any unforeseen catastrophe, that only three contenders remain in the race. These three are sleeping in Dawson City while the rest of the field struggles on, stretched out back along the river and through the mountains past Eagle where six teams have still to arrive.

(over) A dog hitches a ride to Dawson City, past an almost-buried sign.

Paris of the north

Paris of the north

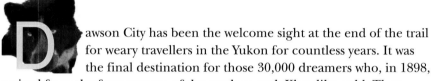

awson City has been the welcome sight at the end of the trail for weary travellers in the Yukon for countless years. It was the final destination for those 30,000 dreamers who, in 1898, arrived from the four corners of the earth to seek Klondike gold. They laboured by foot over the coastal mountains and sailed in handbuilt boats and rafts across lakes and down rivers to catch a glimpse of the distinctive gravel scar on the mountainside above the city that became known as the Paris of the North: the largest metropolis on the North American continent north of San Francisco and west of Winnipeg.

The scar itself is the result of an ancient landslide which carried down a substantial portion of the mountainside to cover a large part of the moose pasture which eventually became Dawson City. It is part of local lore that a village and its inhabitants were buried by the slide.

At its peak, Dawson City had a waterfront crowded with warehouses, streets packed with a bevy of saloons and dance halls, a hospital, several churches, a police detachment, an opera house, a multitude of restaurants, hotels and barbershops, and no shortage of brothels. But even as it grew, it was dying. Like any gold rush boom town, it was destined to disappear when the gold was gone.

Close to 1,000 permanent residents now occupy the townsite which stands at the confluence of one of the world's greatest rivers (the Yukon) and one of its most famous (the Klondike).

The dog mushers, nearing the end of almost two full days spent driving through the snow from Eagle, are thankful to arrive. From the Yukon River, they climb up the bank to the city by the ice bridge — a strip of the river that has been reinforced by freezing extra water on top of the ice to support the weight of heavy vehicles — then run along Front Street to check in at the visitor information centre.

Once checked in, they turn around and return to the river, crossing over to a government campground on the opposite bank. In the summer, it is home to tourists' tents, trailers, campers and recreation vehicles. In winter, it's empty except when the Yukon Quest is in town.

And at that time, winterized Dawson warms up. The inhabitants, who hibernate indoors for much of the cold period, roll out to greet the teams. They open their homes and their hearts, as well as Diamond Tooth Gerties, at one time, Canada's only legal gambling casino. These visitors are only here until the lure of gold, this time at the finish line in Whitehorse, takes them away again. But while the teams are here, it's a good excuse to hold a party and the residents are determined to enjoy themselves.

Dawson stands apart from the other checkpoints on the Quest for two reasons. First, it is the site of a mandatory 36-hour rest period for the teams. Other than a veterinarians' check at the last checkpoint before the finish line, it is the only required stop in the race. And second, this is the only spot on the entire trail where the mushers are permitted outside help in tending to the dogs and repairing their sled or equipment.

It's a nice feeling to arrive in the campground on the Yukon River. "Your handler takes over," said Jon Rudolph, "and you just dissolve from the race for 10 or 12 hours. You usually don't sleep very good. You go to sleep, but you're tense all the time. You wake up asking, 'Where are the

Grabbing a moment's sleep, 1986.

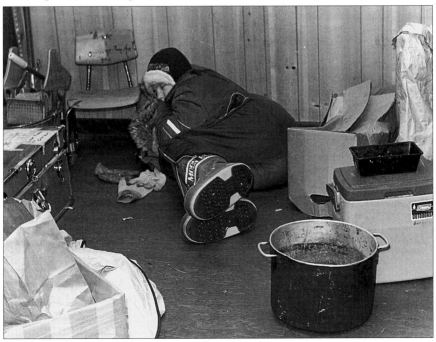

dogs?' 'What am I doing in bed?' and 'Where am I?' Then you realize you're on your break and you don't really have to worry."

Just simple everyday activities, like taking a bath or doing laundry, become almost unbelievable luxuries. "This is pretty comfortable. I mean, THIS IS NICE. And you start thinking about all the horror shows that have happened out on the trail and the misery you went through. You don't really look forward to getting back out there again."

"The 36 hours in Dawson is the fastest 36 hours you'll ever spend in your entire life," says Lorrina Mitchell. "You spend half the time sleeping and the other half is spent checking your dogs, giving your handler orders, working on the sled, lightening up your load. I always start the race with everything and the kitchen sink in the sled. Then, as the race progresses, you see what extra weight you can drop."

Jim Reiter won't even see his dogs from the moment he arrives until the moment he leaves. "Debbie met me and just took over the dogs. Says to me, 'I don't want to see you over at the dog yard until you're ready to go. Just stay away from them. They're tired of looking at you. You're tired of looking at them. Just let me baby them a little bit.' I slept quite a bit. Walked around town, visited, had a beer and went shopping for things that I'd either lost on the trail or had decided I needed."

Dawson is where the frustration of not being able to do anything and the nightmare of waiting ends for the handlers. For the first time since the race started, they can actively get involved. And for the next 36 hours they know exactly where their drivers are and what they are doing.

While Dave Monson rests, his handler, Nate Gray, manages only 20 minutes of sleep, and he pays a price for it. "I fell asleep on a tree stump with my coat sleeve pushed up and my foot a little too close to the fire." His leg is burned and his wrist freezes. For the 36-hour layover, Gray repairs equipment, mends the sled, applies foot medicine to the dogs (and puts the same stuff on his burned leg), walks them so they won't stiffen up too much, feeds them and waters them.

It is a thankless job for the 20-year-old native of Connecticut, who flew north four months earlier specifically to do it. It isn't the money that keeps him going; he makes only $50 per week plus room and board. It's a lust for adventure and a love for the dogs. When the racing season is over he will either return home, his desire for excitement satisfied, or he will stay in Alaska, another cheechako (newcomer from the "outside") who, feeling the south too crowded and overdeveloped, is forever enchanted by the wide open spaces and pure air.

"Mushers trust handlers with their lives and their dogs," said Bob English, a veteran of the 1984 Quest and a handler for Frank Turner in 1985. "They also depend on them mentally for a hug or a kick in the rear, whatever is needed."

"Handling lets me travel and spend the winter out in the bush without having to invest money in a dog team myself," explains Rick Atkinson's handler, Don Schmuckal.

Gordie Mitchell has finally had it with long distance racing. Lorrina Mitchell takes more than two days to make the trip from Eagle, almost a half-day slower than the average time over that distance. She has no real problems, the team is simply moving slower than she expected. But the emotional stress is finally too much for him. The fun is gone and the waiting game has turned into a nightmare of not being able to sleep or eat because the worry keeps his stomach upset and his imagination racing.

Gordie announces Lorrina's retirement to her when she arrives. "This is the last time we're going to do this," he states. She nods in agreement. This will be her final long distance race, but it's not over yet. She heads for bed while Gordie takes the team into the dog lot for their rest.

Mary Sheilds also trots in after an extended time on the trail. She'll finish this one, but this is it. While dog mushing will still be the centrepiece of her life, she won't race the thousand-milers any more.

There are still a few teams out on the trail. Tom Randall hasn't made it in yet and hasn't been seen by anyone for the past 18 hours. His wife and handler, Elsie Wain, is playing it cool on the outside, but it's just a facade.

Sled repair shop in Dawson City, 1987.

"The only thing I'm worried about is if something happened," she says. "I mean, we're sitting around laughing and joking about them partying on the trail, but it would be awful if he was hurt...I vary between that fear and the urge to kill him when he gets here." Randall is spotted a few hours later, mushing along slowly but in no trouble, just a few miles out of Dawson.

While most of the worrying is done at the checkpoint in town and much of the work is done over at the dog lot across the river, there is one more spot where the handlers will spend a fair amount of their time.

A small workshop in the middle of town is turned into a dog sled hospital. Here the handlers replace parts that were broken and temporarily repaired on the trail. One sled gets a new brush bow. Another needs several bolts replaced that broke due to a slight flaw in the sled design. Broken stanchions, ripped sled bags and damaged or heavily worn runners are the most prevalent problems.

With dogs and sleds being tended to, the drivers have an opportunity to take care of themselves for a change. The race wreaks havoc with their bodies as they struggle through snow drifts, fight with the sleds on sidehills or run into open water. The mushers perspire and their clothes get wet from the inside. The snow and water soak them from outside.

They are seldom, if ever, dry in the sub-zero temperatures and frigid winds. Thin sheets of ice form between layers of clothes and the insulating qualities of the material are lost. Denied the warmth of the clothing, the body gradually loses its ability to heat itself. The cold penetrates so deeply that neither hot food nor fire can relieve the aching bones.

It's common knowledge that most of the body's heat is lost through the extremities such as the hands, head and feet. The feet are the most vulnerable and a great deal of attention has been paid to taking care of them on the trail.

Some mushers wear mukluks with a foam insert. Dry, they are warm and comfortable, even at 60 below. Wet, the musher's toes and heels can freeze in minutes. Mukluks are also soft and provide no protection against bangs and bruises from kicking or stepping on chunks of ice or tree stumps.

"Bunny boots," heavily insulated waterproof rubber and canvas boots with a steel shank supported sole, are still the most popular with the drivers. They are warm at any temperature, provide sufficient protection and function equally well in wet and dry conditions. Yet, they are the root of a lot of problems. Feet perspire, and the boots that won't let water in also won't let it out. The feet stay constantly wet, turning into prunes, then becoming hamburger.

The constant standing, walking and running also exacts a toll. Pain is the price the driver must pay to have warm feet.

"My feet hurt so much," says Senley Yuill in 1984. "I don't know if they're cold or not."

"You lose the feeling in them," says Mitchell. "You know they're not frozen. They're just desensitized."

Jon Gleason started out with mukluks in 1987, but when they got wet he switched to bunny boots. "Every bit of skin on the bottom of my feet — all that callus you build up over 40 years — came off. I had brand new feet, like the day I was born. It was like walking on hot coals all the time."

Dave Monson has a trick, learned from a mountain climber in Alaska, to give his feet some relief. "If you take off your bunny boots every night and stick your feet in the snow for 10 minutes, it slams your pores shut and helps your feet. Keeps them from becoming tender. And your feet are so hot, they don't really freeze no matter how cold it is. You don't want to meditate for four hours, but you can certainly stand it for 10 minutes."

Cold-weather head gear usually consists of hats made from wolf, fox or beaver pelts, since there are few insulators that can compare with the natural hide of an animal. The fur is inside the hat with a woollen felt on the outside. The hat has a flap that can be folded down in cooler weather to cover the back of the neck and the ears. When it's very windy or extremely cold, the mushers pull up the hood of their parka with fur trim around the facial opening. A light cotton or wool toque suffices during warm spells.

The mushers' mitts are usually made with fur backs and thick leather palms. Inside the mitts, they wear a light glove that enables them to keep their fingers relatively warm, yet flexible enough to feed the dogs and work

Hot feet in the cold snow, cure for bad feet.

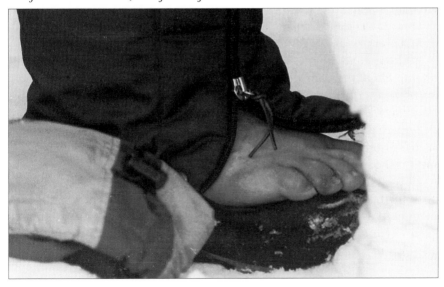

on the trail. The danger of forgetting their big mitts when they've reached the point of exhaustion is solved by use of an "idiot-string" attached to both gloves and looped around the individual's neck.

Just as there has been an evolution towards high efficiency in dog breeding, camping equipment and sleds, there has been progress in the clothes worn by the drivers. Working on improving the insulating quality and the practicality of the clothes is the goal of Shari Tingey, one of just a few clothing designers and manufacturers who are working in the field of producing custom winter wear for drivers.

After designing skiing and mountaineering clothes for 18 years in Wyoming, she found a new challenge when her husband, Ralph, moved to Alaska and started running dogs. The clothes she had designed for his mountaineering activities just didn't work for his activities as a dog musher. Just the flexibility required in the pants to enable him to bend over while tending to the dogs or to push off from the back of the sled was something she had never had to plan for previously.

So out came the drawing board and the sewing machine. "My love was always to make clothes that just really worked well for whatever situation you were going to be in, rather than designing a general all-purpose jacket. Nothing I'd done before suited Ralph for running dogs. Then a few people came when they learned I made clothes and asked me to make coats for these long distance races and that sort of got my interest going."

At that time most mushers wore a material called Venteel, a tight-woven cotton material. It was tough, but it absorbed water and perspiration and eventually lost its insulating qualities. Mushers like wool too, which stays warm when wet, but it is extremely heavy. Snowmobile suits are another option, but they are only good for short stays in the cold. Down parkas are effective when dry, but lose their warmth when wet. Frank Turner discovered another shortcoming of the down parka in 1984 when he tried drying his out over his campstove.

"The shell in my jacket was really wet from perspiration and we camped off the side of the trail. We didn't light a fire. I just had my stove so I hung my jacket over the back of my sled and the snowshoes I stuck in the ground. I put my MSR stove under the parka and we were sitting and talking on the sled, when all of a sudden I heard this 'Whoomp!' We looked around and there's nothing but feathers floating through the air. I found out down is a very combustible material. I've never used down since."

Tingey and other designers turned to artificial materials like Gortex, Thinsulate and Thermalite. They were lighter, windproof, just as warm and more practical. The designers also stuck to the concept of ensuring each piece of clothing was as uncomplicated as they could make it.

"You're talking about 65 below, high winds and the individual inside that parka is sweating because they're working hard. You want this stuff to work. You've got to make it the simplest thing you can come up with. You've got to get rid of anything that can screw up."

But like anything else in a period of rapid technological change, each suit that came off her sewing machine was different from the one that preceded it. And each driver had personal preferences. "I started out with the zippers changing four or five times. Then some people didn't want zippers. Gators inside the legs for mushers who use bunny boots rather than mukluks, snap-on hoods, hoods permanently attached. I'd say the first 15 coats I made changed every single time."

For Tingey, what started out as a quest for the perfect winter suit, turned into the evolution of two winter suits in one, a bib-style pair of pants (which allows for bending over to feed the dogs) and a long parka over top.

Her husband, Ralph, tends to feel the cold, but wearing both pieces of her coat, he can sleep on top of the snow without a sleeping bag and not get a chill. Dennis Kogl, on the other hand, usually wears only one of the pieces because he doesn't get cold.

For the drivers, clothes are not just a form of protection from the environment, they are often the butt of off-beat humour. Bruce Johnson and Jon Rudolph spent a few slap-happy hours parked below the Black Hills south of Dawson City in 1985, talking about Joe May, who was one of the first to wear the new high-tech mushing suits.

"Did you see Joe," said Johnson, "with his clean red suit at the start line? Yesterday I looked at it and it's all covered with dog shit. It's got burn holes in it from the fires and it's all ripped up."

Then they laughed so hard that Johnson's hat fell off his head and landed in the dog food. He retrieved the dripping headgear from the pot and replaced it on his head. Then they started to laugh again at the liquid freezing in icicles hanging from his hat around his head.

The musher's stomach takes the worst abuse of any part of the body: not because the drivers eat bad food, but because they just don't eat enough. Most of them carry freeze-dried foods that are easily and quickly cooked in boiling water. Pizza or hot dogs warmed up in a fry pan over the stove or fire are big favourites. Food with fats in them, like salami sausages, or with sugar for instant energy, like honey or chocolate, are popular snack items. Turkey, chicken and beans are avoided in warm weather because of the danger of salmonella.

Rookie mushers will suffer the most. In their first few races, they tend to lose a lot of weight on the trail, but when they have less waistline and more races under their belt, the diet starts to improve.

Harry Sutherland is one of the veterans of the racing circuit. He eats "surf and turf" (lobster tails and steak) on the trail although it is fairly primitive — there's no wine or silverware. Compare that to the unappetizing bags of brown "glop" that Eric Buetow, 1986 president of

Yukon Quest International, dropped into pots of boiling water during his first Quest in 1985. Nobody ever found out for sure exactly what he was eating since no one else wanted to eat it.

Sometimes fast food outlets come in handy. Frank Turner left his pre-cooked and prepackaged human food for the 1984 race on his front porch when he drove off to Fairbanks, so he had to find a substitute, quickly.

"So I went to Burger King, explained the situation, and the manager said, 'Come back in an hour.' I went back and he had 25 patties stacked there. I said, 'This is great, but do you think I can get some buns too?' And he said, 'Your dogs eat buns too?' They had the pickle on them and everything and all the way to the first checkpoint I had these frozen burgers just clanging around against each other. I finally cleaned them out because I couldn't eat them anymore. Once they got frozen, they just weren't any good."

Constantly perspiring and exhaling moisture into the cold, dry air, while not drinking regularly or enough, can dehydrate a musher. The first symptoms of dehydration are a loss of concentration and the tendency to get chills easily. As with their dogs, mushers can check for dehydration easily enough by checking the colour of their own urine. If it's a rusty colour, it's time to be concerned about drinking habits.

"I can remember saying to Sonny Lindner, 'God, I'm so cold. What's the temperature?'" said Harry Sutherland, in 1986. "And he says, 'It's 34 degrees. Plus 34 degrees.' Why am I so cold? Then I remember I've got a half-gallon thermos that I've been carrying for 24 hours. I haven't taken a drink in 24 hours. You're always checking the dogs' urine; every time the dog takes a leak you're looking to see what colour its urine is so you can tell

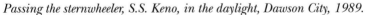

Passing the sternwheeler, S.S. Keno, in the daylight, Dawson City, 1989.

how much water it needs. And I got to looking at my own and I'm worse than the dogs."

Water and coffee are the two prime sources of liquid. Gatorade or Jolt (drinks with caffeine in it) is used to give a shot of instant energy and to replace fluids. While a beer or two at the checkpoints isn't uncommon, alcohol is rare.

Kathy Swenson carries a small bottle of liqueur to give her coffee a little bite and Lorrina Mitchell admits to carrying a small flask "to help me shut down when I'm overtired. One sip of alcohol will relax all the nerves in my body so I can go to sleep."

Driving the team isn't just a matter of sitting back on the runners and letting the dogs do all the work. The mushers, like the dogs, are constantly working and need to have the ability to bounce back after a week or so of pushing themselves to the limit. It takes powerful arms to handle the three- to four-hundred pound sled while it's moving across a sidehill or skidding off a packed trail into deep snow. A strong back is needed for the lifting and for the hours that are spent bent over feeding the dogs or tending to their feet.

A well-conditioned heart and cardiovascular system are vital. Something as simple as having a cold wind blow in your face can raise blood pressure significantly. Any emergency situation, such as the team refusing to run in the face of a storm or getting away from the driver, causes extreme physical and emotional stress.

The mushers' legs are usually very solid. The drivers use them to lift heavy loads or pump constantly to assist the team from the back of the sled. Some, like Joe Runyan, will run virtually the entire race behind the sled. He attributes a great percentage of his success to his superior physical condition.

"Anything you can do to get yourself in better condition before the race, you should do. It makes you more alert, helps you make better decisions. Every factor helps. If you can run up a hill, that's one less hill your dogs have to carry you up. The big factors are good dogs, good preparation and strategy. But when it comes down to the minutes and seconds, being in shape helps. If you're in shape and you're running against someone who isn't, you have the edge. And they know it."

The sound of dogs waking up and barking to stretch their vocal cords echoes across the river as the dusk of early evening starts to gather. Evening comes early during the northern winter, just as morning comes late. During winter, daylight doesn't arrive until around 10 a.m. and it's already fading when two o'clock in the afternoon rolls around.

As mushers appear on the ice strolling casually from the city to the campground, the barking grows even more intense. It's time to go and the dogs know it.

The order of departure may be different than the order of arrival. The last musher to leave Fairbanks departed from the start line almost 90 minutes behind the first one. That time difference is corrected during the Dawson City layover.

For the last musher to leave Fairbanks, their stay in Dawson will be exactly 36 hours. For the first driver to leave the starting chute, Gerry Riley this year, the stop will actually be about thirty-seven and a half hours.

The length of time the mushers enjoy in Dawson City is almost a cruel torture imposed by the organizers. It is just long enough for the mushers to get a real taste of the creature comforts they forswore to run the race and consider not going back out there to the discomfort of the trail. It is short enough for them to look forward to continuing. But, whatever their sentiments, when their time arrives, only sickness or injury will prevent them from going.

Monson and Swenson are professional dog mushers. Like professional baseball players or professional hockey players, they make their living by going back out there. Victory increases the value of their teams and enhances their winning reputation for endorsement purposes. The prize money more than covers the bills. But the Mitchells, Tingeys, Turners, Reiters and Randalls of dog mushing aren't professional. They will lose nothing by not returning to the trail. Just the fact they have made it this far is testimony to their exceptional devotion and talent.

Ralph Tingey leaving Dawson City, 1988.

For them, there is only the knowledge that reaching the finish line will be a personal triumph. They may not be this year's champion and will probably not even recover the cost of competing with whatever prize money they may pick up, but they will have done their best, for themselves and their dogs. It is enough. When their time comes, they will drag themselves across the river, load their sleds and pull out.

Dave Monson looks rested as he packs his sled. A good sleep does wonders for a musher's confidence. Recalling how down he felt about his dogs upon arrival, he has a pretty positive attitude about them now. He will be the first one out but Swenson, who is working around her sled, and Riley, who hasn't turned up yet, will follow close behind.

"I don't think anyone else will be fast enough to keep up to us," he says with a smile. "I expect that Kathy and Gerry will catch me when I stop for a break."

Being the first isn't necessarily an advantage. There are still almost 500 miles to the finish line in Whitehorse and plenty of time to make mistakes. In fact, it is almost as if there is a hex upon drivers who leave Dawson City first. So far, the first team out of Dawson has never won the Yukon Quest.

Joe Runyan led the way out in 1984, but finished fourth. Rick Atkinson left Dawson with a seemingly insurmountable 12-hour lead in 1985, but ended up second. Sonny Lindner started breaking the trail out in 1986, but was the fourth driver to reach the finish line. Kathy Swenson was first out last year and she also came up short at the end, finishing fourth.

Right on schedule, with the light of the stars and a new moon reflecting off the crystalline surface of the river, Monson pulls his snow hook and "hikes" the dogs. Riley is due up next, but experiences some checkpoint jitters. He oversleeps and arrives just a few moments before his time to go. There are problems packing his sled. His headlamp refuses to work for a while, he misplaces a harness, then a pouch on his sled breaks. Finally, he leaves, 30 minutes behind schedule. Swenson, who has been in the campground for a few hours now, watches and waits patiently, then she too is gone.

Bruce Lee peers into the eerie light of the river and watches as Swenson fades into a spectral shadow, made real only by the narrow beam of her headlamp bobbing along the ice. He has another two hours to wait.

"They're going to be tough to catch," he sighs. "It could happen if the weather turns bad or they take a wrong turn or something. However..." Lee knows, as does everyone else, that anything can still happen to change the outcome.

The teams are like pieces on a thousand-mile chessboard; every time a piece is moved or put into play, the whole game can change.

(over) The climb to King Solomon Dome.

Over the top

Over the top

t was the squeaking of a dog sled runner on the dry snow that
inspired northern journalist Elmer "Stroller" White to write
his infamous newspaper story about the Dawson City ice
worm plague in the winter of 1900-1901.

The story, printed worldwide, informed the "outside" that extremely
low temperatures combined with a heavy fall of blue snow had resulted in
thousands of ice worms leaving their burrows in the mountain glaciers
surrounding Dawson to bask in the cold.

The problem, continued White's article, was that basking ice worms
tend to chirp constantly and the incessant noise was keeping the
unfortunate people of Dawson awake at night. Unless warmer temperatures
drove them back into their natural habitat, drastic steps would have to be
taken to control the beasts.

If an ice worm control program was ever initiated it was never
recorded, but the ice worm became an instant part of northern legend.
And if there was such a control program, it was apparently to collect them
and use them for "Ice Worm Cocktails." This is a clear alcohol-based drink
that has a long white worm in the bottom. It is not very appetizing to look
at, but in truth, is usually just a piece of spaghetti with eyes painted on it.
Such is the substance of legends.

Whether or not the ice worm really exists is a matter of somewhat
dubious speculation. The United States Department of Agriculture does
have a file on it, but the prime source of information was the author of the
newspaper article. Research is hard to get due to the fact that ice worms
come out only when blue snow falls and the temperature falls below minus
70. But if the ice worm does exist, it will probably be found on the Dome.

King Solomon Dome is one of the tallest mountains in the Klondike
region and the highest point on the Yukon Quest trail. From its summit

radiate the six creeks that were the focal point of the Klondike gold rush. Its name was given to it by disgruntled miners who searched its slopes fruitlessly for the mother lode from which all the placer gold in the creeks must have come. They never located the lode and mockingly named the prominent landmark after the forever-lost central African gold mines of King Solomon.

If anything could lure an ice worm from its home, short of blue snow and minus 70 temperatures, it would be the squeak of sled runners on snow as the teams pass over the moon-like landscape above the treeline. An ice worm probably wouldn't come as a surprise, as strange things often happen to teams while they're on or around King Solomon Dome.

Don Glassburn met the ghost of Solomon Dome in the 1987 race to Fairbanks. Tired and cold, he stopped to build a fire and feed the dogs. While perking up a pot of coffee, he debated whether or not he should continue down the trail right away or get some sleep.

Dawson City to Maisy May

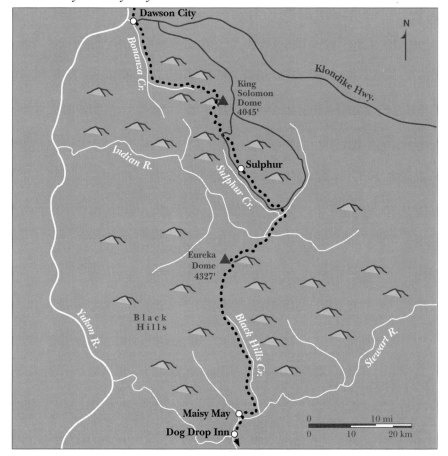

A man suddenly appeared out of nowhere and told him it was 35 miles to Dawson; it was worthwhile getting a rest. Glassburn didn't question the man, who wasn't dressed for the cold and simply vanished the same way he came. He settled down to get some sleep.

Another team came by. "What are you stopping here for?" the driver asked Glassburn. "It's only 15 miles to Dawson." Since it was so close it was worth a last push for the night. Glassburn got up, hitched up the team and headed out. "The ghost was right. It turned out to be 35 miles."

Frank Turner misses a turn in the dark when his dogs make a sharp right onto a road and he doesn't catch the trail marker. "There's this steep, icy road with some sled marks on it. I thought, 'Well. O.K. This must be the way' and I got up there and we're going by this mine site. There are lights and everything and I thought, 'This doesn't look like the trail to me.' But there were those sled runner tracks in front of me. I kept on going.

"I never knew in Dawson that they have an underground mine in the side of a hill. It's up on the Dome. It's this big hole and the whole team started to go down it. I was freaking out because we're on ice and the brake won't dig in properly. And they're freaked out because of this big hole and they just keep heading into it. Finally I get us stopped, turned around and out of there."

Later, no one else on the Quest admits to having knowledge of the mine or its location. Turner never finds out who, if anyone, made the tracks going into the mine.

Leaving Dawson and the river behind, the 1988 trail climbs over a series of ridges overlooking the gold-bearing creeks and then follows them for a short distance until it reaches the foot of the Dome.

There it connects with a series of switchbacks, trails that cross from one side of the hill to the other along a slightly inclined trail. At each end the U-turn takes the musher a little higher on the hill, then they head across the hill towards the next U-turn. It is slow going up the side of the Dome. The area, from the point where they leave the river to the top of the Dome, is crisscrossed with mining roads and the remains of old cabins.

It appears to the drivers that wherever they can see the highest and steepest hill, that's where they'll find the trail.

Charlie Boulding, originally from North Carolina's Blue Ridge Mountains and now living in Nenana, Alaska, will decide in the 1990 race that he has the perfect explanation for the trail missing the smaller, more easily climbed hills.

"The trailbreakers get lost, and when they get lost, they do the same thing I do when I get lost. They go to the top of the biggest hill and take a look around."

The climb to the summit is considered to be one of the more difficult ascents on the trail. Switchbacks can be extremely wearing on a team; the corners are steep and dogs and musher must work hard to get up and around. Then, looking back along the hillside, they are demoralized by the realization that they travelled that far along the trail and worked that hard to gain only a few feet in elevation.

Looking up, the drivers can only see trees. Occasionally, a gap in the forest gives them a view of the sky and false hope that they've finally reached the top. Then they turn the corner and it's just another switchback that seems to stretch forever across the face of the mountain.

It can grate on even the steeliest of nerves, driving mushers like Jon Rudolph in 1987 to ride up the hill screaming at the top of his lungs, "This is the stupidest thing I've ever done! I want out of here!"

Lena Charley puts out a supreme effort to conquer the climb and never stops working all the way from the bottom to the top. "I had to push the sled all the time. It was dangerous because the sled was so heavy that when I went up steep slopes it would start to come back down on me."

Falling off the trail can also be a pain. It's hard enough when a musher pulls over on the side of the trail to rest and feed the dogs. They usually pull into soft snow and it takes a terrific effort to get back onto the packed

*Climbing King
Solomon Dome.*

trail. Slipping off the trail on level ground is also cause for extra work. But when they fall off the trail on an incline, the sled usually tips over into the snow on the downhill side. Then they have to unload all the gear, dog food and camping equipment, pack it up above the trail and stack it there, lug the sled uphill back onto the trail, and reload everything.

If one team falls off the trail, it creates a huge hole at the side of the track. Each team that follows usually falls into the hollow, creating an even larger trap for the next team to deal with.

Harry Sutherland and Sonny Lindner were battling their way from one hole to another on the way up the Dome in 1984. They both managed to fall into every one. Right in front of them, Mary Sheilds was doing the same.

"We would help Mary out of the hole," Sutherland said, "then Sonny and I would fall into the hole she made and we would have to dig ourselves out while she went on ahead down the trail."

Finally, Sutherland and Lindner got past Sheilds when she took a break, then they fell into another hole. They dug themselves out, and heard Sheilds coming down the trail behind them.

"Let's get the hell outa here," said Sutherland, and they did before she could arrive.

This is the final mountain barrier on the trail and traversing the summit has the potential for disaster. If the moon had a climate, this is probably what it would be like: barren, lifeless, windy and cold. As on the Eagle and American summits, a stiff breeze creates minor problems this year.

Vern Halter, the Alaskan lawyer who will win the Quest in 1990, is tipped over a bank by the wind. Turner, who is close behind, starts down the hill towards him to help. Looking back, he sees a gust of wind rock his sled over onto one runner, threatening to send it and his dogs crashing down on top of Halter's team below.

"Vern, I've got to get out of here," Turner shouts as he retreats to his sled. "This is not a good place to stay."

Most years, the Dome has been kind to the mushers. In 1984 and 1985, it provided them with calm, safe passage. In 1986, it burdened them with lots of fresh snow. The strong winds made their appearance in 1987, along with drifting snow and extreme cold.

Bill Cotter smiles when he thinks of the Dome summit that year. In the midst of a blizzard and minus 40 temperatures, he had a birthday party and ended up spending the night with Kathy Swenson.

Cotter, Swenson, Jeff King, François Varigas, Dave Monson and Jon Gleason pulled into the leeward side of a shallow cliff for protection from the storm. Somewhere in the discussion, two facts emerged: nobody wanted to go any farther that night, and Cotter had turned 41 two days earlier.

"We were all stuck there in the storm so we decided, as long as we're stuck, we might as well enjoy it," remembers Monson. "So everybody got out their treats, like barbecued chicken wings or ribs or roast beef or cake or whatever you had and we had a birthday party."

The food was turned over to Swenson who turned it into "something delicious," as Cotter puts it.

"She's a helluva good cook," says Gleason. "I think she gets more pleasure out of cooking than she does driving dogs."

Swenson and Monson had already formed an informal partnership on the trail because of her culinary talents. At one point, Monson had pulled out to pass Swenson who had stopped for a rest.

"It's a trap she laid for me. I was passing her on the trail when I smelled Beef Wellington. My dogs wanted to go on, but my stomach forced me off the trail. We've been travelling together ever since. She cooks and I change the runners."

Even as the six sat around the fire enjoying the birthday dinner, Swenson was eyeballing the sleeping tent that Cotter had rigged on the side of his sled. It was a big, black bivouac bag that used the sled as a tent pole and anchored to the ground. She contemplated the howling winds and swirling snow.

"Do you think there's room for two in that thing?" she asked Cotter.

"Yup," he replied, "there's lots of room."

"Well," suggested Swenson as she gathered up her sleeping bag, "it's the least I can do for a man on his birthday."

The two of them bedded down in their respective sleeping bags, sheltered in Cotter's tent from the wind and insulated from the ground by a caribou mat.

"It was," Cotter says, "one of the most wonderful birthdays I've ever had, and I don't even think anyone sang 'Happy Birthday.'"

By morning, the snow, pierced here and there by breathing holes, was all that could be seen of the camp. It was only when they collided with a couple of buried sleds and woke up a few dogs and drivers that Marc Boiley, Ralph Tingey and John Shandelmeier even realized there was somebody there in the early morning light.

"They were camped right on the top of the mountain, in the middle of the trail, all sprawled out," described Tingey. "We crunched a few thermos bottles when we went by.

"We renamed the Dome, 'Sleeping Bag Hill,'" smiled Shandelmeier.

When it's clear up top, with no wind or snow to obscure the view, a musher can pause and look behind to watch the other teams snaking their way up the side of the mountain. It will be like that in 1989 and 1990.

Switchbacks don't seem so bad when you're going down them. The descent down the back side of the Dome is almost effortless. The work and the screaming to get to the top of the Dome just about wore Rudolph out in 1987. By the time he had crossed the top and started heading down the back side, he was so worn out he fell asleep on the back of his sled. When he woke up, the dogs were barrelling full speed down the side of the mountain. On one side of the trail the steep bank went straight up; on the other, it dropped straight down. He grabbed the sled to save himself and dug in the brake to slow the team down.

"If you're trying to kill yourself," he muttered to himself, "you're going about doing it the right way."

Lorrina Mitchell had been in a car crash just a few months before the 1984 Quest. It left her with a fear of going downhill fast. Travelling that year with Senley Yuill and Ron "Old Potato Nose" Aldrich (when his nose freezes it swells up, looking like a potato), she relied on their knowledge of the area to prepare her for the big hill on the back side of the Dome. Every time she reached a descent, she asked Yuill, "Is this the bad one?" and every time he would respond, "No, this one isn't too bad. I don't think we have to rough walk [wrap chains around the runners to slow the sled] yet." When she reached the bottom, she realized he had duped her.

"But it worked, didn't it?" she said. "I really give him credit. Senley has to be one of the coolest cucumbers I ever met."

The end of the switchbacks brings the teams through the ruins of Sulphur (an abandoned gold mining town named after the mineral springs near by) then down Sulphur Creek. At the bottom of the creek, the drivers rumble over the Indian River flats, then climb up to skirt the side of Eureka Dome.

If the trail went over the top of Eureka, it would be the highest point on the Quest course, but it only goes most of the way up before turning down the other side. It then runs through the rolling forested slopes of the Black Hills, along trapping trails and down Black Hills Creek.

The area is still heavily worked by a variety of modern placer mining techniques. Roads, old and new, run in every direction, and mining camps, some abandoned and others just shut down for the winter months, are scattered throughout. Beyond that is the unofficial checkpoint at Maisy May, on the banks of the Stewart River.

The heavy traffic through the area can often obliterate the trails or wipe out the markers. In 1984, Wilson Sam lost the trail in the Black Hills, then went through some overflow and got soaking wet. Finally, getting totally confused, he found himself in a dead-end canyon. He turned his team around and spotted a sign nailed to a tree at the end of the canyon. "Bad Luck Gulch," it read.

"They don't know the half of it," he muttered in reply. A couple of hours later he found a trail marker and continued on his way to Whitehorse.

On this side of the mountain, just a few miles into the longest stretch between checkpoints (300 miles from Dawson to Carmacks) drivers are truly isolated when it comes to helping their dog teams. There are no veterinary facilities and no way to call for help when a dog goes down. It is knowledge, ingenuity, quick action and desperation that mean the difference between life and death for the dogs.

Ed Salter and Jeff King were breaking trail in 1987, snowshoeing ahead of their teams. Behind them were the dogs and sleds and right at the back was Rick Atkinson, who was trying to keep all three teams — his own, King's and Salter's — in order.

King's team bunched up, then stretched out again. The tow line got wrapped around one dog's neck, then the dog lost its footing, was dragged and was gradually being strangled by the line. Unaware of the problem behind them, King and Salter continued on. Finally, stopping for a breather, King glanced back over his shoulder.

"What the hell is Rick doing?"

Salter looked back. Behind them, Atkinson had left his spot at the back and was digging frantically in the snow beside King's team. He grabbed one dog that was standing in his way and threw it aside.

"What the hell...?" exclaimed King.

He started back towards the teams just as Atkinson reached into the snow and pulled out a dog, limp and apparently lifeless. He unwrapped the tow line from its neck, then forced the mouth open. Lifting the eyelids he saw the eyes rolled back, showing only the whites. The tongue was discoloured and the animal wasn't breathing.

Atkinson remembered that when he had attended agricultural college in Scotland, he had been told to breathe down an animal's nostrils when giving mouth-to-muzzle resuscitation. Maybe that worked for cows and sheep, Atkinson wasn't sure. He had never had to do it before and he didn't do it properly this time. Instead, he leaned over and blew hard, directly into the dog's mouth. He breathed again and again. He looked up at King and said, "I think we lost him." But he gave it one more try.

The eyes of the dog rolled like a couple of pinball machines. It gave a little start, then coughed and started to breathe.

"I didn't walk up to the team thinking I'd do that," said Atkinson. "But until I got the dog sorted out, I didn't realize he was out of it. I did what came naturally to help. It's no big deal, it's just luck. Lucky for Jeff really."

There was silence. The three teams stood immobile, the falling snow disturbed only by the weak wagging of the dog's tail. Years of life and death experience in the arctic had not prepared any of them, human or beast, for what they had just witnessed.

Necessity broke the spell. They had to keep moving or risk becoming snowbound. King loaded the dog onto his sled and the three drivers resumed breaking their way through the snow. As they continued driving, one surprising consideration occurred to Atkinson — that he might actually end up regretting his actions if King and his miracle dog went on to beat him across the finish line.

It was a prophetic thought. King did finish ahead of Atkinson in 1987 and the revived dog was in harness at the end, but the big Scot never regretted it for one moment.

One year later, less dramatic but no less effective, is Dennis Kogl's cure for one of David Sawatzky's lead dogs. The animal simply lays down in the middle of the trail and won't get up. Sawatzky loads it into his sled and it just flops over, eyes cloudy, displaying no interest in food or water.

After carrying the animal for 30 miles, Sawatzky starts to worry. If he has to carry it all the way to Carmacks, it will exhaust the rest of the team. When he comes across Kogl, he asks the veteran for advice.

"This dog had a dump lately?" inquires Kogl.

Nope. Not since getting a pill in Dawson City to stop a brief bout of diarrhoea. Kogl runs his hand over the dog's stomach. It is hard as a rock, the intestines are distended. The anti-diarrhoea pill has done its job, maybe too well.

"I think I can take care of this," Kogl announces as he turns to his campstove over which he is heating water for dog food. He pulls a rubber tube out of the sled, cuts off the ends, inserts it into the dog's rectum and pours warm water down it. Pulling out the tube, he lays the dog on the snow, where it rests spread-eagled with a perplexed look on its face.

"Will this take long?" asks Sawatzky. Kogl doesn't respond.

There is no need to. It doesn't take long. The dog has one bowel movement, crawls a few feet and has another. Then it stands up, gives a shake and looks back at the mushers, its pride dented but not broken. There is no fairytale ending for this dog, however. Sawatzky has burned out his team by battling with the leaders through the early stages of the race and he scratches in Carmacks two days later.

Many miles ahead of them, Monson is breaking trail by himself. Riley and Swenson tarry a short distance behind him. With any luck, they hope, he will wear himself down. Bruce Lee has fallen well off the pace and now drops to fifth as a charging Rick Atkinson catches up to him.

"I may have taken too much out of my team on the way to Dawson. They don't seem to be getting their speed back," explains Lee.

Maisy May is a musher's favourite as a stopping place. Harry Sutherland rates it as one of the high points along the trail.

"I'm reminded of the Bible passage about the widows who gave out of their poverty. Those people live simply and you get some donuts, granola, homemade bread, coffee. That's what they have to offer and that, to them, is probably worth more than 30 steaks to someone else. They're doing the most they can do and I really appreciate the people at Maisy May."

In fact, the Bible analogy is very appropriate. The tenants of the cabins, which were originally built as a hay farm in 1897, are Mike and Vicki Fletcher, members of a Christian religious commune affiliated with the Living Word Ministry. They have been part of the Yukon Quest since it first appeared in their front yard in 1984.

Race judge Ed Foran and marshal Jon Rudolph arrive by plane, which lands on skis on the river ice. Both of them know Maisy May hospitality from having raced the Quest in previous years. "It's a real neat stop," mumbles Foran through a mouthful of coffee and donuts. "It's a welcome break. Everybody's exhausted when they hit Maisy May."

However, 1988 is the swan song for the Fletchers. They will leave the Yukon in late 1988 and in future years their place will be filled by volunteers flown in to run a ham radio base.

The trail, along which Monson leads the Quest into Maisy May, runs across part of the 100 acres of cleared land the Fletchers cultivate in summer. Then it twists around some fences, past a few abandoned buildings, then between the barn and blacksmith shop to arrive at the two-storey main cabin.

In daylight, there isn't much problem negotiating the track across the property. But at night it can be confusing since there are several other tracks crossing the marked trail.

"It's quite a big area," smiles Mitchell. "It's quite easy to get turned around and forget where you put your dog team."

Maisy May, 1988.

Swenson is starting to get impatient. She finally overtakes Riley just five miles from Maisy May, pulls away from him and follows Monson in an hour later. Monson simply smiles when she suggests his dogs look tired from breaking trail.

"We're fine. You just can't get up a lot of speed when you're breaking trail."

Riley breezes in. His dogs' feet look sore, but their tails are up and they appear rested.

"I didn't want to push too hard to get here," he says. "But I did want to make sure I was in a position where Monson can't get a jump on me in Carmacks."

The spot where Swenson passes Riley is just about the same spot that Jon Rudolph and Harry Sutherland passed a gang of teams camped out in 1986.

"How come you guys are camped here?" asked Rudolph. "Maisy May's only about five miles farther down."

"Oh no," replied Bruce Johnson. "It's still a long way from here."

Sutherland and Rudolph looked at the group as they huddled around a bonfire trying to keep warm in the minus 40-degree temperature, then at each other. It didn't look like too much fun. Besides, there was a warm bed just a few miles down the trail. They kept on going.

It wasn't until the next morning that they heard anything more from the drivers camped with Johnson. Sonny Lindner had been one of the campers and now he stormed into the room where Rudolph and Sutherland were sleeping and started kicking Sutherland's bed.

"Come on you sonofabitch," Lindner snarled. "No way you're going to sleep. We spend the night out at 40 below and you're here. No way you're sleeping. Get up." The other drivers joined in, making so much commotion that sleep was impossible.

In 1988, Atkinson has become a new factor in the chase to the finish line. He is still five hours behind Monson, but his time from Dawson is the fastest so far.

"My dogs won't have had as much rest as Monson's or Swenson's when we leave here, but we'll be with them. Especially if there's trail to break. Nothing is impossible as long as the leaders are in sight," he says, noting with satisfaction that the three teams ahead of him are still parked in the yard when he arrives at Maisy May.

Behind them, teams are stretched out for 200 miles. Fourteen teams are somewhere in the mountains and hills between Dawson and Maisy May. Eight are still waiting in Dawson for their departure time. Seven are either on American Summit or running the Yukon River, heading upstream from Eagle.

The number of casualties continues to climb. Adolphus Capot-Blanc's dogs have a flu of some sort and he decides they have had enough. The jovial trapper from northern British Columbia, called the trail jester for his endless sense of humour, will return in 1990 but he won't finish that race either. However, he will gain his place in the history of the race by being of such service to the people along the trail that the mushers will award him one of the most coveted prizes next to the winner's paycheque: the Sportsmanship Award.

Clifton Cadzow had burned up the trail from Eagle, and burned out his team. His leaders were getting rebellious and balked at following his commands. "I pushed them too hard over American Summit in the heat of the day and now they're not with me. If I go on, I could ruin them forever. At this point they don't trust me any more." He scratches at Dawson City.

Minutes are now becoming crucial and while it's not yet time to reveal their grand strategy for victory, the frontrunners are starting to play games with each other.

The drivers behind the team breaking trail have an opportunity to study the leader. The team directly in front has to concentrate on locating the trail. With no sled runners to follow and markers knocked over or buried, Monson has worked a little harder than he wanted to. It has worn him down.

"The problem was, I was the first one on the trail. There's nothing and nobody ahead of me so I had to make sure I was right. It took an awful lot of concentration."

He has to sleep, but while his eyes are shut, he doesn't want Swenson — whom he considers his prime competition at this time — to sneak out of Maisy May and build any kind of a lead. He watches for his moment, then lays down on top of her coat and dozes off. If she has any clandestine plans for leaving, she will wake him up when she pulls her coat out.

But she doesn't pull it out. And he doesn't sleep very well anyway. He can't relax, wondering why she doesn't even try. Maybe her team is stronger than he thinks. Maybe Riley's isn't as slow as pre-race evaluations had indicated.

Riley is really starting to get on his nerves. For a guy who wasn't supposed to be a threat, he is proving damned hard to shake. Atkinson is moving fast too. Too fast maybe, or is he showing what his team is capable of doing?

The eyes are closed. The body apparently at rest. But behind the eyelids, the brain keeps ticking.

(over) Sonny Lindner's team, 1984.

Cat trains

Cat trains

The race route is called the Gold Trail because it passes through the site of almost every major gold discovery in the Yukon River watershed. It must seem ironic to race organizers that the price of gold has been a thorn in the side of the mushers since the race's inception.

It was pure coincidence: in the early 1980s, the value of gold took off in meteoric style, climbing from $32 per ounce to over $800 before dropping back to settle at about $400. The increased price and demand for gold generated interest in previously mined regions that could still be productive with improved techniques and equipment.

Access to some of the goldfields is through marshy areas that are impassable for heavy equipment in summer. The solution is to travel over those roads in late winter and early spring, when the ground is still frozen and capable of supporting heavy loads. Cat trains — convoys of trucks and trailers pulled or led by bulldozers (originally named Caterpillar, after the company that made them) that push the snow aside to permit passage — have become a common sight on back roads and bush trails in late February and early March.

One of their regular routes is along an old road that parallels Scroggie Creek, a minor, short-lived gold producing area in 1898. The road is primarily used to gain access to the Black Hills area north of the Stewart River from the Pelly River, almost 90 miles south of Maisy May.

When the organizers of the Quest laid out their trail in 1984, using the long-abandoned stagecoach road between Dawson City and Whitehorse, the 90-mile road along Scroggie Creek was part of the route. It was about that same time the gold miners decided to use the same route to reach their gold claims.

Neither group knew what the other planned and for the first four years of the race, the two have literally met head-to-head. They will continue to confront each other for the next two years while the Quest organization attempts to find or develop an alternative trail that will avoid the conflict.

Jon Rudolph is in Maisy May to let the mushers know that the cat trains started to move the day before.

"You may run into a cat train," he says to the lead group of mushers. "We don't know when they're moving, and there's nothing we can do about it." There are already 10 miles of exposed gravel on the trail that they spotted while flying in.

How long the teams will spend on the cat-train road depends on where they are positioned in the race. The front runners run along the plowed road for between four to 15 miles. The campers at the back face up to 70 miles on exposed gravel and rock. Almost all will meet heavy equipment of one sort or another along the way.

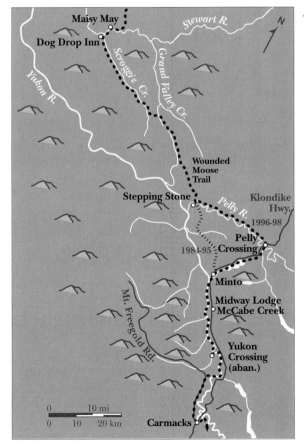

Maisy May to Carmacks

When Jeff King said in 1984, "Anything a stagecoach can get over, my team can get over," he, like the organizers, envisioned a wide, snow-covered throughway cut through the woods. No one had any idea of the chaos of ice, rock and dirt the teams would encounter along the Scroggie Creek road.

Leroy Shank was driving along quite comfortably in 1987, pushing through a series of small creeks and ravines, when he came across a Caterpillar parked on a patch of gravel. Passing it, he found himself running along a wide dirt trail. "I realized this was the infamous mining cat-train road. The worst thing was that it wasn't like frozen dirt. It was mud. The dogs were walking in mud up to their knees. Booties were worthless. This stuff was like glue and just pulled them off."

After a few hours of this, he stopped to wait for nightfall. By the time he was ready to go, it was snowing slightly and the air was cooler. The mud had started to freeze up and get hard. "It helped a little, but it wasn't good going by any means." The cat blades not only push aside the snow, they also bust up massive boulders into jagged chunks and churn up broken shards of shale. Lorrina Mitchell finds the surface is especially bad this year.

"They'd taken most of the snow off and the musher had to walk an awful lot of that because it would take the weight off the sled and help prevent wearing out your dogs and your runner plastic. I hit some really bad stuff that just got stuck in the runner and opened it up like a razor blade."

Jim Reiter changes five sets of runners and endless numbers of booties when he travels over 70 miles on the mud and rocks. "The further back in the race you were, it got progressively worse. It took an awful lot out of the dogs."

Dogs suffer sprained knees and wrists. One of Kathy Swenson's cuts his foot on a piece of shale and the wound becomes infected before she reaches Carmacks. She is forced to drop the dog at the checkpoint there.

Each driver has their way of dealing with the cat-train trail. The front runners get there as early as possible so they will run over as little of it as possible. The drivers in the middle of the pack have to run over a little more so they try different ways of coping.

Ralph Tingey tilts his sled and rides on one runner to reduce the drag on the dogs and minimize the damage to the runners.

Vince Stack, who ran his first Quest in 1987 with the goal of finishing it without turning into a wreck, just cursed it from one end to the other. It didn't improve the running surface, but it made him feel better.

Most merely resign themselves to the fact that the trail is better suited for trucks than it is for dogs and they will just have to endure the inconvenience.

Few drivers will ever forget the harrowing experience of encountering the equipment itself.

Mitchell turns a corner and her leaders come muzzle-to-blade with "the biggest piece of equipment I've ever seen. This thing was literally right across the road. It had one side of its blade stuck into the mountain and the other end hanging off the road and there was no way around it. I made sure they saw me before they ran over my dog team." She squeezes past when the cat skinner (bulldozer driver) is able to pull off to one side a few yards further down the road.

Hans Oettli, a heavy equipment mechanic from Switzerland, experienced a little déjà vu in 1987 when his team encountered the cats. The last time he had been on that particular stretch of road, he had been operating a piece of equipment at least as large as the one he now faced. There was no place for the cat skinner to move off the road so he turned the cat slightly, swinging the blade out from the side of the hill and opening a passage for the dogs.

Oettli drove his team into the gap and stopped in the narrow area between the cat treads and the mountain. The dogs were intimidated by the heat, noise and size of the machine.

"My dogs had never seen a piece of equipment like that. You usually don't see that on a trail in wintertime. They went in with one command. They looked a little nervous. I'm sure they didn't like it." The cat skinner then swung the blade back into the hill behind the team and moved the back end out to open an exit for them. "I operate cats once in a while. I know how much precision you have in turning a track. I just hoped he was a good operator."

The verbal exchanges between the drivers and the heavy equipment operators range from friendly and sympathetic to unfortunate harshness. The cat skinners are the victims of the drivers' frustration even though their presence on the road is the result of decisions beyond their control. (Mining company executives decide when to start moving along the road.) Most of them insist they try to accommodate the mushers as much as possible and minimize their effect on the race while, at the same time, trying to do their job.

The Yukon mushers who are in the construction and heavy equipment business know several of the drivers personally. Jon Rudolph jumped up on the running board of one truck in 1987 and stuck his head in the window.

"Jon," exclaimed the startled driver, "what the hell you doing out here?"

"I'm in the Yukon Quest."

"God, I didn't know you were in the race. Sonofabitch, we haven't seen any other dog teams. You must be in the lead!"

"Yeh, I know that. But not for long. The rest of them are just back a couple of miles. They'll be coming along pretty quick. Say, could you guys pull over for a while so we can get by?"

"Sure. No problem."

Looking back on that day a couple of years later, Rudolph concludes that despite everything, "they were really pleasant to deal with, and they went out of their way to try and make things as easy as possible for us."

Jim Reiter has a slightly different view of the cat skinners and truck drivers. He knows what he wants to tell them as he struggles over the miles of shale and muck, but he can't find any of them.

"By the time we got through, the operators made themselves real scarce. I imagine after about the fourth or fifth guy gave his opinion about what they were doing on the trail, they didn't want to talk to us anymore. We saw a lot of equipment parked along the road, but we didn't see anyone around it."

Parked equipment was a blessing for Shank in 1987. Wet and tired, he came upon a truck parked on the side of the road. He stopped the team, gave some snacks to the dogs, then tried the door of the truck. It was open.

He crawled inside. There he fired up his stove, hung his wet gloves on the sun visor and his parka over the back of the seat and cooked up a Cajun meal of red beans and rice. Dry, rested and fed, he climbed out and continued on his way.

"I looked for registration papers. I thought, 'Well, I'm going to thank this guy, whoever he is.' But I never found any."

Dragging the sled over the road is one of the more frustrating hardships the drivers encounter in their thousand miles, but it wasn't the cat trains or their legacy that forced a group of six drivers out of the 1987 race in this area. It was snow, far too much snow.

A storm rolled in behind the front pack of mushers, dumping over four feet of snow into the Scroggie Creek area in 24 hours. The leaders just caught the leading edge of the storm. Those behind had to battle blustering winds and swirling snow at the outer reaches of it. But right in the middle of the storm were the six teams bringing up the rear.

These trailing teams had all fallen behind for various reasons: Jim Reiter and Craig Wolter just had slow teams; Kelly Wages had broken through the ice earlier; Larry Grout, a former professional downhill ski racer and rodeo bull rider with a fast team, had been delayed when he stopped to help Wages; Ty Duggar's sled had needed constant repair; and Hans Oettli's team had been fighting a dog flu for the past 200 miles.

When the drivers started that morning, the sun was shining and the trail hard-packed and fast up to where the gravel started. Three hours later, Oettli couldn't see his lead dog, 40 feet ahead of him, because of the snow. The cat-train road, cut down to the bare earth with three-foot embankments on either side, was barely discernible as the snow quickly filled it. Trees, overburdened with snow, leaned over like drunks, then snapped off and fell across the trail.

Duggar and Oettli took three hours to travel three miles before stopping to rest. Grout, Reiter and Wolter caught up to them and then pushed past, but only for a few hundred yards. They stopped and debated the situation.

There wasn't enough food to get to the next checkpoint if the storm covered the rest of the trail. A food drop (additional food flown in by airplane) along the way would automatically disqualify them. It was suggested that all their food be concentrated on two sleds, which would continue ahead while the others turned back.

In the end, it was decided that they would all turn back and return to Stepping Stone (a popular stopping point for the mushers, located on the Pelly River). On the way down, they met Wages and he joined the retreat.

In hindsight, agree the drivers, they made the right decision. They had no way of determining how extensive the storm was or how far they would have had to travel to get clear of the snow. In fact, it was over 100 miles

Stepping Stone, 1989.

before their next opportunity to get off the trail and every inch of the way was buried under the snow. It would have been impossible to make it with their limited supply of food.

But the decision to stop racing and scratch is one that the driver finds difficult to justify, no matter how right it may be. "A lot of those things go through your head," says Reiter. "There is a lot at stake in this. You probably had a lot of support from friends, the community, sponsors and stuff...did I wimp out and take the easy way out when the going got tough or should I have kept going? Did we quit too soon? We just didn't know, that was the thing.

"I honestly believe that anybody who starts this race doesn't think they can't finish. That's simply the furthest thing from your mind. The only question really is, in what position will you finish? It's ingrained in your mind, 'there's no problem finishing.' Then, I was completely taken aback when all of a sudden I couldn't go anywhere any more."

Even a year later, Oettli still has doubts. "It's kind of hard to explain that afterwards, you know. I'll never really get over the idea that I should have kept trying. I always think there should be a way. Some people just have bad luck, I guess."

The reasons a musher has for scratching vary from individual to individual, but the most common cause seems to be an overwhelming concern for their dogs.

In 1984, Bob English broke into tears and cried when scratching in Dawson City after contemplating the toll the trail was taking on his dogs. In 1987, Jon Gleason endured frozen fingers, a frostbitten face and exhaustion to the point of losing control, but when he discovered his dog, Dutch, had frozen his foot, he withdrew immediately, just 100 miles from the finish line.

In 1988, while the cat-train road is getting longer for the lingerers, the road to the finish line is getting shorter for the leaders. Swenson is riding hard on Monson's heels as he enters the yard at Stepping Stone, just seven miles down the Wounded Moose Trail from the end of the cat-train road.

Race judge Ed Foran, watching them roll in, is impressed with the quick time they have made since leaving Dawson. "It looks like, when they're not camped, they must be going 10 miles per hour, which is really fast for this stage of the race."

There are beds at Stepping Stone, but this is not the place to be caught napping. In previous years, owners Lou and Carol Johnson had set up cabins for the mushers to sleep in. But as the race matured and became more competitive, fewer of the drivers took advantage of the sleeping facilities. Yet, at other times, the opportunity to rest in the cabins at Stepping Stone can be used strategically. It's a guessing game to try and figure out who is in which cabin and how long they plan to stay.

"By the third race, they didn't want to tell anyone how long they were going to stay," smiles Lou Johnson. "It got very confusing sometimes. Trying to sort out who's where, what cabins are being used and trying to keep it all secret."

None of the drivers want to lose track of their competition by this stage in the race and, rather than use the cabins, they sleep on the kitchen floor or in the workshop, so nobody can sneak away undetected. It gets a little crowded at times, with a dozen or so drivers sprawled out over the floor.

Stepping Stone is a place where races can be won or lost. This is where, for some reason, otherwise race-wise drivers make major mistakes. In 1987, François Varigas picked this stretch of trail to try and blow the race wide open.

The tall, bearded musher from France opened up the throttle and arrived in Stepping Stone a good hour ahead of his competition. He stopped for an hour, then kept on driving. But it was premature and two days later Varigas lay inside a cabin while outside his team refused to move any farther without more rest. He realized he could not win. "They're depressed," he said, "and so am I." They did finish eventually though.

Harry Sutherland lured Sonny Lindner out of a warm cabin at Stepping Stone into a cold campsite on the Pelly River in 1986. Sutherland stopped long enough to peer in the window at the coffee and donuts piled on the table, then considered the minus 40 temperatures and drifting snow.

"I knew that every one of the sonofabitches coming behind me is going to stop here. I looked and going out there was a freshly broken trail. I just looked around and said, 'let's go.' I don't think they even knew I was there."

The broken trail only lasted for a mile or so before dead-ending into waist-deep snow. When Lindner arrived at Stepping Stone, he only stopped for a few minutes. The fact that Sutherland hadn't stopped bothered him. He took off from Stepping Stone and found Sutherland camped at the end of the broken trail. He also got bogged down in the snow. The two of them spent an uncomfortable night in the cold night air, while behind them the other drivers snoozed happily on the warm kitchen floor.

By morning, those who had stayed at Stepping Stone had caught up to the two drivers. Their gamble had failed to pay off. The trail they thought would give them a big lead had fooled them and the night spent in the cold took its toll. If either one of them had asked Lou Johnson, he would have told them the trail was only a mile until it hit deep snow. It was a mistake that contributed to keeping them out of the winner's circle that year.

This year, the trail is unencumbered by the heavy snows of the previous two races. Across the Pelly River and past Stepping Stone the trail continues to follow the old stagecoach road built in 1902. The stages rolled over this extremely hilly route until the Klondike Highway between the two cities was completed in the late 1950s. At a point near Minto the teams leave the stagecoach road and move over to run alongside the Klondike Highway.

The trail doesn't actually go into Minto, which used to be home to a village and a wood camp for the riverboats. But passing close should give even the most exhausted team an extra reason for trotting past this spot as fast as possible.

Minto is the multiple murder capital of the Yukon. The first murder was a sensational triple killing at a place called Hoochekoo Bluff, just a few miles from Minto, in the winter of 1898-99. The last occurred in the early 1960s, an apparent triple murder-suicide that was never really resolved since no cause of death was ever determined for two of the victims. Six months later, the woman who discovered the bodies was herself shot to death. Shortly after, the final inhabitants of Minto packed up and moved out.

All that remains at Minto now are a few derelict cabins and an emergency air strip. There are some permanent residents farther down the river, mostly trappers.

The trail bypasses Minto, then turns out to run alongside the Klondike Highway to a gas station called Midway Lodge, about 10 miles from Minto. It is the first place where handlers and family can see their drivers and teams since the teams left Dawson two days earlier.

When Monson pulls into Midway Lodge in the early morning hours of the race's tenth day, he is 300 miles ahead of Ty Halvorson and John Ballard, the final two teams that are still on the Yukon River heading to Dawson. Between them are spread 34 more teams, of which only three apparently have a realistic shot at Monson's spot.

Although Monson stops and grabs what looks like a casual coffee and donut, his eyes keep glancing nervously down the trail. Somewhere back there in the trees and poor light are Riley and Swenson. They may be running without lights, creeping closer without being seen, or camping just around the corner, out of sight, hoping Monson believes they are further behind than they really are.

"My feet are really sore," he complains to a couple of bystanders. His nerves finally get the better of him and he pulls out after only 10 minutes. Riley appears just 20 minutes later and trots past without stopping. He passed Swenson sometime during the night, but she is just five minutes behind. She doesn't stop either.

Rick Atkinson is still within striking distance, but when he reaches Midway it is obvious that he doesn't really have a chance. While the front three are moving steadily forward, Atkinson's team is gradually losing speed. They look tired as they trot into Midway with their tails down, and flop gratefully onto the snow when he stops.

Bruce Lee, still at Stepping Stone and now too far behind to mount a threat at this late stage in the race, finds himself being pressured to maintain his top-five placing by a pack of teams, led by Kate Persons and John Schandelmeier, which are slowly but surely making up ground. Dennis Kogl, Ralph Tingey and Jim Wardlow are close behind.

But the pieces are still in play and anything can happen among the front three. Whatever traps nature doesn't set with snow or storm or encounters with wildlife (Vern Halter will be chased by a moose just out of Midway Lodge in 1990), can be set and sprung by a person.

Harry Sutherland found that out the hard way in 1986. Running down the side of the highway towards Minto he could see a road sign on the side of the road, telling him it was only two kilometres to the station. But he was tired and bored.

"You can only watch dogs run for so long." As is his habit on long, straight pieces of trail, he turned his back on the team and sat on his little seat, facing back down the trail.

"Suddenly the world went dark. Stars flew. Then I opened my eyes. I was lying face down in the snow and the team was heading on down the trail. I thought someone had hit me with a two-by-four. I lay there wondering, 'Who in hell would hit me here? Why?'"

Jeff King, Bruce Lee and Jim Wilson keeping close, 1989.

Then he looked directly above him and saw the road sign. It dawned on him that the trail didn't take a little loop to go around it as he assumed it would; it went directly under it. And it wasn't tall enough for him to get under without ducking behind the driving bow, even while seated.

Even with the finish line within sight, figuratively speaking, by this time the drivers are starting to get convinced that this trail is going to go on forever and there's no checkpoint at the other end, just more trail, a sort of eternal punishment in dog musher's hell. But even the road to hell has detours.

With their bodies and minds sapped by 10 days of driving and deprivation, it gets easier to become confused and get lost, even when you're not lost.

Sonny Lindner was out front by himself in 1984 when he stopped to camp. He was hoping to be able to time the next driver to follow. But, after six hours, nobody had turned up. Concerned that maybe he was on the wrong trail, he started back up the trail looking for markers. After a couple of hours he found Harry Sutherland.

"Is this the trail?" asked Lindner.

"I don't know," replied Sutherland. "I'm following your tracks."

Lindner smiles when he's reminded of that time. "I wasn't lost," he says. "I was misplaced. It was the right trail all the time. I just didn't think that anyone had let me get six hours ahead. You get a little confused in the middle of the night."

Ed Salter couldn't seem to locate anything in 1987, no trail markers, no tracks, nothing. After a while, he became convinced he was on the wrong trail.

"I finally stopped and said, 'Well, if I'm going to be lost, I'm going to be lost stopped.' It was the right trail but you're half fried, haven't slept, you can't see a marker even if you're looking right at one, and you don't know if you're on the right trail or not."

The race is no longer measured in distance. Now, it is easier for the driver to gauge performance by time. They know what time they left the last checkpoint and what schedule they're running to rest and feed the dogs, but it's impossible now to determine how fast the dogs are travelling.

"I don't know," Jeff King will answer in 1989 about how far it is from Maisy May to Dawson City. "I left there at 6:30 last night."

From Midway, the trail returns briefly to the Yukon River, then crosses a long hill strewn with loose "widow-maker" boulders (large rocks lying loose on the sides of hills which can be easily dislodged, crash down the hillside and kill someone) on a slope "so steep you need to take a run at it to get up," says Oettli. It then drops onto the Freegold mine road (an access road to several small mines in the hills south of Carmacks) for the final 20 miles into the checkpoint.

Monson's feet are still the first thing on his mind as he pulls into Carmacks.

"My feet are killing me. All I want to do is get out of these boots," he says, glancing at his watch. He has to stop here for the mandatory six-hour veterinary inspection before continuing. He can't afford to leave one second later than he is allowed to and he has to watch for the next two teams, to determine just how big a lead he has when he leaves. Even though the race takes almost two weeks to complete, there is not much room for error this close to the end.

The biggest margin of victory — 24 minutes — in the last three years was Bruce Johnson's triumph over Jeff King in 1986. In 1985, Joe Runyan reached the line just 20 minutes ahead of Rick Atkinson. In 1987, it was Monson himself who was nipped at the wire by Bill Cotter. The difference between the paycheques for first and second is $5,000. Monson can attach a dollar figure to each 60-second segment — $500 per minute. That's what his 10 minutes cost him last year.

Alone in the dog lot, Monson looks as though he is only concerned with one thing — feeding his dogs. Then his focus seems to come slightly unravelled and a startled nervousness flashes across his face as Riley rolls up a half hour later. It is supposed to be Swenson.

"I'm right where I wanted to be," says Riley. His persistent ability to catch Monson is obviously starting to have some effect on the younger driver.

Last year, Monson had been duped into dismissing Cotter as a threat, then didn't have the speed to overcome his lead at the end. That another master strategist can steal a second one away from Monson is looming as a definite possibility. Riley must be faster and stronger than everyone gave him credit for when this race started. But how much faster?

Swenson pulls up an hour later. Her team looks strong and confident, loping in across the line with their tails up. She parks her dogs then glances at Riley before walking over to Monson.

"He's chasing you big time." She indicates Riley with a nod of her head. Monson gives her a tight smile.

Later, looking across the yard at the two drivers, she laughs. "David's going to be driving with his neck backwards tonight, I think. He'll have a sore neck when he gets to Whitehorse." She makes no mention of herself being in the chase. She looks good. Her dogs look good.

The tight finishes that marked all three of the last races prompt former Yukon Quest International president Dick Underwood to observe, "the only thing I'm betting on is that a lead dog will be first across the line, but I won't bet which one."

(over) The view from above — locating a team by aircraft.

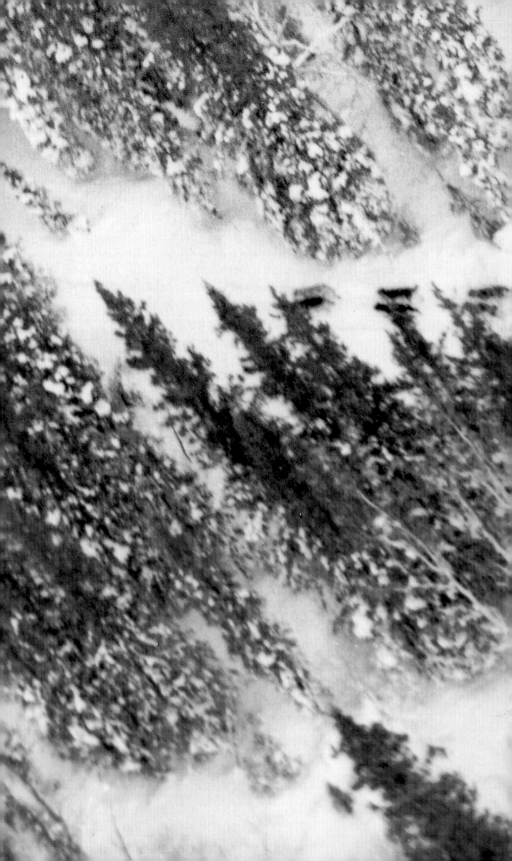

Stump country

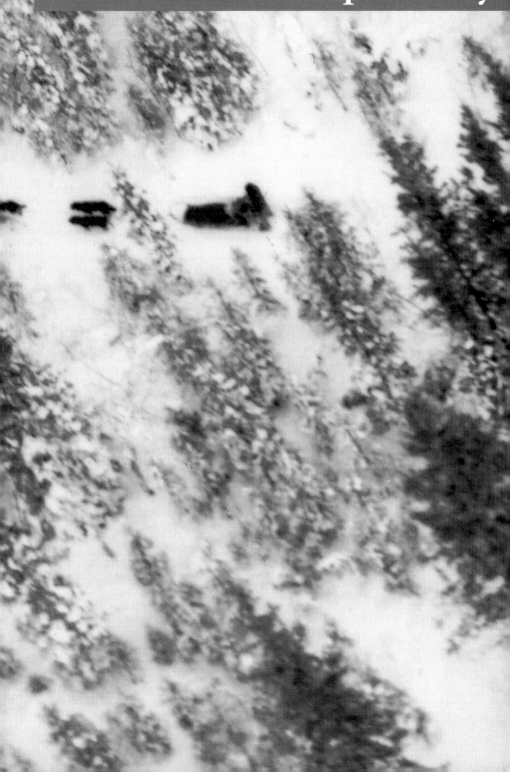

Stump country

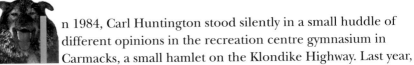n 1984, Carl Huntington stood silently in a small huddle of different opinions in the recreation centre gymnasium in Carmacks, a small hamlet on the Klondike Highway. Last year, Leo Oleson sat alone at a table in the checkpoint in Dawson City, rubbing the exhaustion from his eyes. Tonight, Jon Rudolph hunches over against the night's cold on the road outside Crabb's Corner in Central. They are all individuals poised on the brink of making a decision that may or may not affect the final outcome of the race; a decision that everyone will hate or a decision that only half will hate.

In every race, there must be one person who is the ultimate authority — who can mediate disputes, who can be the judge, jury and both lawyers when investigating protests, who can take abuse and can hand it out, who can enforce the rules or change their interpretation when needed, and who can apply common sense to situations that make no sense. When Carl Huntington took on the job in 1984, he stood up at the pre-race mushers meeting and faced the mushers. "I'm the race marshal," he said. "What I say goes. Any questions?" It was not an invitation to ask any.

Huntington's meeting with the race judges and race managers in the gymnasium of the Carmacks recreational centre demanded a resolution he knew would affect the final outcome of the race. The trail from Carmacks to Whitehorse ran alongside or right on the Klondike Highway for the first 40 miles or so. He had to sort out all the options: find an alternate route, run it as it stood or bypass the dangerous section. Everyone had a different idea, but it was on Huntington's shoulders that the final decision and ultimate responsibility lay.

"You can't run a dog team at night on or beside the highway with a tractor trailer coming down. The dogs will be blinded and turn right out into the middle of the road," he explained when announcing his decision.

He had spent several hours scouring the hills, seeking an alternate route that could be prepared quickly. There wasn't one. The teams would be loaded into trucks and driven past the dangerous section to Fox Lake, 50 miles from Carmacks and 75 miles from the finish line in Whitehorse.

Some drivers complained that the shortening of the final leg was a detrimental factor in their final positionings, while others lauded it for its safety aspect.

In 1987, another difficult decision had to be made. When an airplane pilot reported there were four teams on the wrong trail coming into Dawson, Leo Oleson just wanted to get away from the confusion of the checkpoint and sit by himself for a moment. He was tired and hungry and he knew what was coming. The four mushers had missed the marker at a turn-off on one of the ridges. They would blow into town on a plowed and broken pathway while behind them, the rest of the teams busted their way through the fresh windblown snow on the actual trail.

The protests made for a long sleepless night as Oleson and race judge Jon Rudolph pondered over what would be a suitable penalty. In the end,

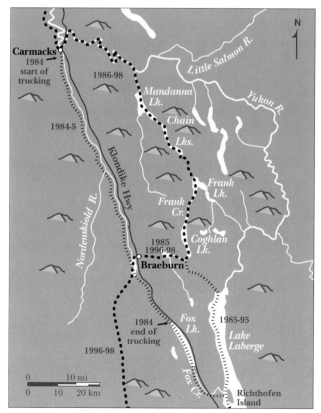

Carmacks to Lake Laberge

the four drivers were given a six-hour penalty, extending their mandatory stay in Dawson from 36 to 42 hours.

"Getting lost is part of the race," explained Rudolph, "but gaining a direct advantage by taking the wrong trail isn't allowed. There's a fine line there. Some people wanted them heavily punished. Some felt that, since it wasn't intentional, it should be light. We had to find a compromise, so we assessed them six hours. There were still a lot of bitter feelings, and no one was happy, so we sort of figured we must have made the right decision because everyone was mad at us."

"We didn't call it a penalty because it wasn't," says Oleson. "It was an attempt to put everybody back on an equal basis." One of the four penalized drivers, Bill Cotter, went on to win that race.

Tonight, Rudolph fills the role of 1988 race marshal. He stands on the road in Central and faces a hoard of angry mushers in the cold. Two teams had taken the wrong trail for a few miles, saying they knew it was the wrong one but that they couldn't find the right one. Other drivers suggest they opted for the road rather than breaking trail and gained a definite advantage because of it. As the protests continue, he makes two decisions. The first one irks the mushers.

"Look," he says to them. "Some of you guys also missed part of the trail out there. And it's too damn early in the race to be screwing around with this kind of stuff. Just get on the goddamn trail and keep racing."

The second one prompts phone calls from the organizers and the rules committee in Fairbanks.

"I made the decision to break a trail, to make sure there was a definite trail. Most of the infractions and major hassles occur because of trail conditions or markers. I was in that 1986 race when Bruce Johnson won it, and the trail conditions were the shits. We broke trail for 600 miles."

The order to have snowmachines re-break the trail all the way to Whitehorse raises a few eyebrows in Fairbanks. For the purists, it is contrary to the philosophy of the race. The mushers must be self-sufficient. If there isn't any trail, that is part of the wilderness experience and that's what they have to cope with.

"What the hell are you doing, Jon, sending snowmachines out to break trail?" demands the voice on the other end of the telephone. "That's not the intent of the race."

"Well," he replies, "if you put dog drivers in here as race officials, I guarantee you there's going to be a broken trail all the way to Whitehorse. If you don't like it, get a new race marshal."

"No. No. That's fine. Do whatever you're going to do."

So he does. The trail is broken for the rest of the way. In the end, Rudolph's insistence on sending out the snowmachines finds favour with the majority of the mushers and the majority of the organizers. He will be invited back as race marshal for the 1989 and 1990 races.

Not all the problems are so monumental or the resolutions so controversial. The marshal and the two race judges spend most of their time monitoring the teams on the trail, checking the tags to be sure the drivers aren't switching in fresh dogs and ensuring that the mandatory gear is in each sled at each checkpoint. They are the official backup for the veterinarians in enforcing dog-care rules and they watch to see if mushers receiving any kind of outside assistance are actually gaining an advantage because of it.

Penalties can range from disqualification to a time penalty, where a musher isn't permitted to leave a checkpoint for a specified period of time (as in 1987 in Dawson). One driver was penalized two hours in 1985 for outside assistance when he pulled dogs' chains out of his truck and used them. Another will be given the same handicap in 1989 for leaving Dawson before the end of his 36-hour layover. "If a trapper helps out a guy or gives him a place to stay, the trapper must do the same thing for every other musher," explained 1985 race judge Sam Johnston.

Officials are constantly bombarded with stories of violations, most of which are the products of vivid imaginations.

Vet Carl Monetti (l) talks with Bill Cotter (r), 1984.

"It's like a soap opera," says Rudolph. "Everyone's coming up, trying to dig up dirt, trying to get something going. The media's probably the worst for it, but the handlers are just as bad. The mushers aren't too bad, they're just out there racing.

"But you got the handler sitting there, they've got nothing to do, so they start making up stories, this guy's cheating or whatever. You sort of have to block all that out. If you start listening to it, you just get sidetracked. You've got to go with only formal complaints, a good eyewitness, or catch the guy yourself."

Just like the drivers, there's not much time to sleep for the race officials or the veterinarians. Not only do they have to keep track of the leaders, but they can't lose touch with the campers 300 miles behind, or any of the teams in between. And mushers don't exactly run on bankers' hours. They run when they feel like it, when their team will go or when the weather permits it. No matter what time of day or night, the officials and vets have to be ready.

A lot of their time is spent crammed into small aircraft flying back and forth between the checkpoints. In 1984, Huntington, Oleson, Roger Williams and Leroy Shank had to pile into a small Cessna in Dawson. Williams went up front beside pilot Les Bradley; Shank and Huntington crawled into the seats behind.

"The pilot looked at Oleson," remembers Williams, "and he just kind of pointed. Leo looked. 'You want me to lay down in the fuselage?' Bradley said. 'Yep.' So we all loaded up and Leo crawled back into the fuselage. All of a sudden the nose of the plane went up and the tail went 'thunk.' I look over at Les. 'Do you really know what the hell you're doing here?' He said, 'Don't worry. It'll straighten up just as soon as I get the prop going.' He fired it up, the nose came down and before I could think about it, we were in the air." It wasn't until 1985 that Oleson, in his first year as race marshal, was able to see the trail between Carmacks and Dawson from the air.

They ride in cars and trucks when they can (usually in the Circle District where so much of the trail is close to a road) or on snowmobiles, especially to reach the Yukon River checkpoints.

The snowmobiles put them on the same playing field as the drivers and they must cope with the same dangers. Williams and trailbreaker John Mitchell jumped on snowmobiles in Dawson City in 1986 and headed up the trail to see what damage had been done by a wind storm the previous night.

As Williams stepped off his machine to reset a marker about 20 miles from Dawson, the snowmobile cracked through the ice, then was slowly sucked into the black water. He looked over at Mitchell who had just stepped off his machine a few yards away and watched dumbfounded as the same thing happened to his snowmobile.

"We broke the first rule, we didn't tell anyone where we were going." The two built a fire and layered on clothes that Williams carried in a rucksack on his back. For almost 48 hours they tended the flames, kept warm and waited for a rescuer to happen by. Finally, a trapper did come by and he carried them to Dawson.

At any given moment during the race, and in any likely or unlikely location, the veterinarians can be found pinching the back of a dog's neck to test for dehydration, inspecting paws and leg joints for cracks or swelling, drawing blood or trying to coax a dog to urinate in a jar so they can screen it for drugs. The urine is collected in a small styrofoam cup hooked onto the end of a rod. They usually wait until after the dogs have been fed and watered before selecting an animal at random to be tested. There aren't any fire hydrants in the wilderness, so the dogs are led past trees, bushes, piles of snow, anything that may inspire them. When the animal gets the urge, the vet sticks the cup underneath and fills it. It's then sealed and shipped to a laboratory in Vancouver, British Columbia.

Steroids and blood-doping aren't their prime concerns. Drugs that can suppress symptoms of illness or mask injuries, such as common aspirin or

Vet Sue Cullen (l) and Tom Randall (r) taking a look, 1988.

anti-inflammatories, are their main targets. Finding traces of any banned drug results in automatic disqualification. So far, everyone has tested clean.

The vets wield the power to order the musher to drop a dog or to completely disqualify the team if, in their opinion, the dogs aren't healthy enough.

Lolly Medley, a veteran of the Iditarod, was forced to withdraw in 1986 after she got lost near King Solomon Dome and travelled an extra 50 miles in deep snow. The extra work burned out her team and caused serious foot problems. Upon arrival, the vets ruled that four of her dogs — one more than the drop limit that year — weren't capable of continuing.

Mike Maurer, a fisher from Salcha, Alaska, will be disqualified in 1990 after one of his dogs dies shortly after arriving in Carmacks. The injuries suffered by the dog will lead the vets to believe the animal was not given proper care on the trail. Maurer will protest the ruling, insisting that the autopsy gave the vets a false reading, but his disqualification will stand.

Usually, however, the musher already knows when a dog has been hurt or when a team has been burned and the musher will reach the decision to drop the animal, or to scratch entirely, before a vet even sees the dogs. Checking at each official checkpoint and turning up often at the unofficial ones is a safety feature to guarantee the dogs are getting the best of care.

Dennis Jackson will be the vet on call in Dawson City in 1989 when the Quest arrives. On his first Quest, he will quickly learn respect for the musher's relationship with the dogs. "One musher told me, 'It's like having 12 children.'"

"This is a race where the mushers have to take care of their dogs because there is a dog-drop limit and 1,000 miles is a long way to go," says four-time vet and one-time racer Karin Schmidt of Anchorage. The commitment of the veterinarians is so strong that they will fly from just about anywhere in the United States and Canada to work without pay for two weeks in the bush. There are usually 10 of them spaced out along the trail each year.

Jim Reiter has good reason to appreciate the extra effort put forward by the vets. When one of his dogs chewed off its foot after freezing it at Stepping Stone in 1987, Terry Quesnel, a vet from Vernon, British Columbia, flew in, landing on the snow-covered ice of the Pelly River, to perform a quick bit of surgery that saved the dog's life.

The dogs take all the pinching, poking of needles and peeing in jars in good humour. "The sled dogs I've seen back home are vicious," smiles New Jersey vet Jean Buist. "Here, the greatest danger I've had near a team is being licked to death."

The mandatory layover in Carmacks is a veterinary stop. It is the final opportunity to give the teams a proper checkup before they head off into the home stretch.

Dave Monson doesn't spend an idle moment in Carmacks. His stove blazes constantly as he feeds the team, then cooks up meals for further down the trail. Meals prepared in advance mean he can cut unnecessary time off any snack breaks, and he can leave the stove behind. He strips down the non-essential gear, reducing the weight of the sled substantially. There will be no stopping after this unless it is absolutely necessary, and with only 150 miles to go, sleep can wait until the finish line.

There is a sharp contrast between his intensity and the relaxed, confident Riley. Riley seems content. He is moving casually, but still managing to accomplish a fair amount of work. He had used subterfuge and sheer toughness to become an Iditarod champion a decade earlier and now seems to be using those same qualities.

"The dogs and I talked it over and tried to decide what we want the other mushers to do for us," he cracks. "Breaking trail seems to be what we hope they'll end up doing."

His history of mind games reminds everyone that they should be leery of anything he says. In 1984, he constantly mentioned to Jack Hayden that one of Jack's dogs looked sick, despite the fact that it was pulling well. Eventually, the conviction in Riley's voice convinced the less experienced driver that the dog was sick, although in fact it was perfectly healthy, and Hayden dropped it.

Monson keeps narrowing his concentration. He focuses on what he must do to win. "I was hoping that somebody else wouldn't have my mindset and say, like I was saying, 'I don't care what the lead is. I'm going to go for it anyway.'"

As the two leaders silently prepare for departure, Kathy Swenson is across the dog lot, apparently still in the race. She is doing all the right things, like lightening the load and cooking extra meals, but there is something missing. There's no air of anticipation, no tension.

Monson is obviously uptight. He can barely restrain himself. Riley seems casual, but his darting eyes and restless dogs betray that he too is struggling to keep his emotions under wraps. Swenson is methodical, stepping through a routine she knows well, but there is no competitive edge. Even her references to the race hint at capitulation.

"I don't have much reason to hurry now," she says. "I plan to turn on my radio to listen to the finish. Atkinson will have to sprout wings to catch up to me."

Atkinson, still in fourth, has slipped even farther back. He won't even arrive in Carmacks until shortly before Swenson is due to leave.

Monson slips off his boots and puts on his snow joggers (insulated running shoes). He rarely stops glancing at his watch; then, precisely on the second, he slips the snow hook and pushes off into the darkness.

Riley allows his departure time to slip past, taking his time to pack things the way he wants them before finally pushing off a half hour late.

Swenson leaves on time, 40 minutes later, just as Atkinson makes his appearance in the dog lot to start his six-hour layover.

The trail drops back onto the Yukon River for a short distance heading east, then turns south along Mandanna Creek, along the length of Mandanna Lake, then through a series of rolling hills before dropping into the Chain Lakes. Beyond that, it runs through a small group of hills, then onto Frank Lake and Coghlan Lake and, finally, along a series of small creeks that takes it to lower Lake Laberge, just 40 miles from Whitehorse.

In 1984, the trail bypassed all of the Chain Lakes area and ran along Fox Creek because of the trucking of the teams from Carmacks to Fox Lake. "A suicidal, really wild little piece of real estate," according to Lorrina Mitchell. It was a narrow path through a heavily wooded area that kept winding along trying to spear the drivers and dogs on dead trees that stuck out from the sides.

In 1985, after following the Klondike Highway for a while, the trail struck out cross country from Braeburn Lodge (famous for its huge cinnamon buns) to Coghlan Lake, then turned north. It was a clean, fast trail. Only Joe May had any real problems and that was because he lost his glasses. He mushed along, almost blind, until he noticed a sign on a tree. He kept peering at it, but was unable to read it, so he edged a little closer. It probably said something like "Danger. Steep Hill." But May never really had a chance to find out. His team and sled took off down the hill, with the driver virtually flapping in the breeze behind, hanging on for dear life. The dogs reached the bottom safely and continued trotting down the trail while May thanked heaven he couldn't see what had just happened. If he had been able to see, he probably would have tried to control it and ended up in a pile at the bottom of the hill.

It wasn't until 1986 that the present trail was put through. That year, the snowfall was so great that trailbreaker Tracy Harris could only manage to travel eight miles before turning around and breaking the same trail back the same eight miles through even deeper snow. The coarse snow crystals wore the hair off the dogs' legs up to their knees, bogged down the sleds, tripped up the drivers and turned what should have been a final sprint into an endurance test.

But the 1987 race to Fairbanks was undoubtedly the worst of the lot, giving this stretch a fearsome reputation. Not much snow fell in the months preceding the race. The stumps of cut trees stuck up through the meagre cover and felled trees, usually under the snow, lay on top of it. The trail twisted and turned back in on itself, much like what it had been like in the Enchanted Forest near Circle City in 1986.

Jon Gleason remembers his dogs missing a turn in the trail in 1987. He stopped the team and walked up to turn his leaders around, but just a few feet ahead of his team he saw the trail come back down and straighten out again. The turn he missed was just a very sharp loop. He led the dogs forward through the bush and skipped the loop completely.

Mitchell passed through the Chain Lakes at night that year. To help herself negotiate, she put fluorescent tape on her dog harnesses. "When the tape disappeared suddenly I slowed up, because I knew the team had rounded a sharp corner."

"I couldn't go five feet without barging into a tree," said Bill Cotter. "It was unbelievable. I got tipped over, banged into trees, thought I was going to get killed. I thought the sled was going to self-destruct and I'd just let all the dogs loose and walk home."

"If I closed my eyes to envision the worst trail I could," shuddered Ed Salter, "I'd never imagine anything as bad as that one was."

It was like a war zone. All along the trail, mushers were getting jammed between trees or they found themselves high-centred on stumps sticking three feet in the air.

The dogs seemed to form their own opinion of the trail. Don Donaldson, a security guard from Delta Junction, Alaska, finally pushed out onto a lake after missing a few turns in the bush. "My wheel dog, Dusty, looked at me like 'If you don't know how to drive this thing, come down here and I'll do it.'"

"There were places where prayers were more useful than a brake," said Mitchell. She remembers that the ice along the creeks was just as bad as the trees. She was crossing one patch of ice when she left the sled to assist the

Dog in a basket.

dogs. Suddenly, she heard a loud crash behind her and the dogs came to a dead halt. Turning, she found the sled had vanished.

Shell ice is formed when the water freezes high in the fall, then drops and refreezes at a lower level. On a river, the weight of the ice would collapse the upper crust onto the lower one. But on a creek, the top shell isn't that heavy and simply stays intact until added weight, like Mitchell's sled, causes it to cave in. Mitchell was fortunate. Her sled, although in a hole, was dry.

Kelly Wages and Larry Grout weren't so lucky. The water of Frank Creek was so crystal clear that the pebbles on the bottom could be counted through a small hole in the ice. It only seemed a couple of inches deep. As the drivers passed during the day a little more ice was broken loose around the edge and the hole got bigger.

By the time Wages came through in the evening dusk, the hole was substantially larger. His sled skidded sideways towards the hole, then caught on something and flipped upside down into the water with Wages under it.

"I panicked. I admit that," he said.

The water was about five feet deep and the stream had a fairly strong current. Wages unwrapped himself from the sled then threw himself back to the surface and out of the water. The dogs were tangled and confused but none had been dragged into the water.

"They strained to pull it forward but even when I pushed from behind, we couldn't pull the sled out. It was too heavy. Everything was soaked."

It was also cold, about minus 30, and everything he needed to survive was in the sled. He stripped naked, climbed back into the water and started unloading the sled. Some bags drifted away, only to get caught on the ice and a small log jam in the opening.

Larry Grout pulled up behind the hole. Not without hesitation, he also stripped down and jumped in to help. For five hours, the two wrestled with the current, the gear, the sled and the cold. When everything was out of the water, they both pawed through their gear in search of dry clothes. A plastic garbage bag had kept one pair of clothes dry.

Mud and water had penetrated everything else and was now starting to turn into ice. There didn't seem to be any point in starting a fire to dry out since all the wet gear was frozen solid anyway. Wages loaded lumps of clothes into his sled and both drivers headed off again. It was only 70 miles to the next checkpoint and getting wet just didn't seem like a real good reason to stop yet.

"Thoughts about quitting did cross my mind, but I figured nothing up ahead could be worse than what I went through back there." Wages and Grout eventually were forced out of the race at Stepping Stone by heavy snows.

The trail in 1988 is a vast improvement. It has been widened and the stumps and deadfall have been cleared out. There are even campsites set up: lean-tos with spruce bough beds, stumps to sit on and split firewood. Swenson can't believe her eyes.

"I'd go through these camps and...shoot...look at that! If I see one more of those, that's it, I'm stopping. Sure enough I come up on one. I knew nobody was right behind me so I stopped right in the middle of the trail." She stays for three hours.

Dave Monson decides this isn't the time or the place for a stop, despite the appeal of the campsites. He can feel the team as it methodically paces through the trees, and he can feel Gerald Riley breathing down his neck. He has eyes for only one thing: the trail ahead. Even his sore feet are forgotten for the moment.

"The perfect racing moment was between Carmacks and Coghlan Lake when the dogs were up on step. They were going. They were giving me everything I wanted. The trail was beautiful, the terrain was spectacular. It was a full moon, and I was pumped up, and the adrenaline was flowing. I wasn't going to let Gerry catch me. I wasn't going to make any mistakes. I wasn't going to lose the trail. I was pumping for eight or 10 hours until I got to Lake Laberge."

"Everything in that race is balance," says Frank Turner, "a balance between rest and stress. The only time the balance comes uncorked is right at the end, then you just let everything out. That's when you really start bearing down, physically and emotionally. You've got to be able to maintain, efficiently, the dogs in front of you and do it over extended periods of time when you're really tired. There's no more tomorrows. That's the thing that's hard to learn — that's exactly what we mean when we talk about driving dogs."

As Monson's team trots onto the ice of Lake Laberge, only 40 miles from the finish line, he starts to look back over his shoulder. Somewhere back there is Gerald Riley. How far back, Monson doesn't know. He only knows that every other time he had counted Riley out or thought he wouldn't ever catch up again, he'd turn around and find the old veteran right on his tail.

Monson knows he has run the best race he could possibly have run. But is it good enough? Above him, the face in the moon has a better view. It probably knows, but it isn't going to say a thing.

(over) Team crossing Lake Laberge with plane flying in the distance, 1987.

The absence of regret

The absence of regret

n 1984, when Lorrina Mitchell was within a mile or so of becoming the first woman to complete the Yukon Quest, she almost became its first fatality.

There was an open lead in the middle of the river and the trail crossed above it on a sidehill. At the top of the sidehill, her sled lost its grip and plunged down towards the water. Mitchell jumped off to try to control it, but her feet slipped and down she went towards the river. It could have swept her under the ice, leaving behind a mystery as to what had happened. But as she stepped from the sled, she had grabbed the gee rope (a rope used by the musher to help the dogs turn the sled) and when she slipped, she hung on desperately. Swinging down below the sled, she came up short of landing in the water.

The dogs had actually crossed the ice and had a grip in the snow. They strained hard against the tug line, gradually gaining the upper hand. With shouted encouragement from Mitchell, who was dangling helplessly against the icy slope, they pulled the heavy load past the point of danger. Their driver pulled herself up the gee rope, hand over hand, until she was no longer in danger of slipping back, then she just lay in the snow for a long minute catching her breath.

"That really got the adrenaline going. I was mad. I thought it would be really disgusting to drown within sight of Whitehorse after surviving all the other ridiculous stuff I'd been through."

Mary Sheilds is only four miles from Whitehorse when her team simply quits. They just stop running and lay down in the snow. Nothing she does is going to get them started again until they are good and ready to get going. She spends several hours on the ice, less than an hour's drive from the finish line, fuming in frustration, as other teams trot slowly past her. Even Frank Turner's dogs, who are mostly female and have been the object of amorous advances from the mostly male squad of Sheilds for most of the past few days, fail to raise more than an interested eyebrow as they go by.

There are lessons for everyone. Even with the finish line within sight, nothing on the trail is certain. The race doesn't end for each driver until the lead dog pokes its nose across the finish line.

For those who are driving for the prize money, there are few moments of certainty. Mushers contend with the environment, the emotional and physical state of themselves and their dogs, and their own strategy. They must also be aware of where their opponents are and what they are capable of, as well as be able to try to anticipate their thinking.

Physical toughness will keep a team in the race, but mental intensity is what will put them in front. In dog mushing, as in everything else, knowledge is power.

There are two basic strategies in long distance sled dog racing, but there are countless twists and variations to each one. The first game plan is when a group of mushers travels together as a pack, establishing themselves as the leaders. Usually, this group will be a mixture of drivers who have to struggle constantly to keep up, some who can keep up yet really don't have the dogs to win, and the true contenders.

The faster teams hold back, letting the struggling drivers and slower teams share in the emotional and physical burden of breaking trail. Then, when they believe the time is right, they pull out all the stops and sprint, leaving the others behind.

It is a conservative strategy, designed to give the faster teams control of the race by keeping themselves rested while staying in touch with the front

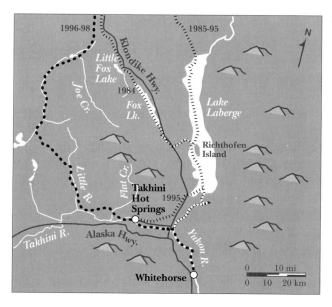

Lake Laberge to Whitehorse

runners. It reduces the chance that a sudden twist in the weather, like the snowstorm near Stepping Stone in 1987, or a change in the trail, such as the trucking of the teams at Carmacks in 1984, could give a slower team the chance to pull off an upset.

Joe Runyan was a couple of hours behind leader Sonny Lindner when he reached Carmacks in 1984. He still believed he had a chance at top spot, but the trucking ended it. Over 120 miles he figured he could catch Lindner and beat him, but over 75 miles, he knew he wouldn't have the opportunity.

"One thing I learned from that was that developments can change the race. If you're going to be racing, you've got to be right at the front."

The second basic strategy is one that requires endurance, speed and a lot of luck. It is a gamble from start to finish that often results in record fast times, but seldom pays off for the gambler.

The objective is to open a commanding lead early in the race, then try to hold it. If the trail is perfect and the team can endure the constant charge, it could work. Dogs that can force that kind of pace for the complete distance may be able to beat a team that is slightly slower over a distance, but has unbeatable speed in a closing sprint.

Nature must also play a part in this strategy. If a storm blows in behind the pacesetter and ahead of the rest of the drivers, the lead could increase while the drivers behind are delayed by having to bust their way through the snow and winds. There are too many "ifs" and "maybes" in this strategy to make it popular with the top drivers.

Both strategies have one thing in common — the timing of the break to establish a lead is crucial. Every advantage that can be used must be inserted into the driver's plan. There is a point in both strategies where cooperation is mutually advantageous, but near the end is another point where each driver must run strictly as an individual.

In 1984, all the teams initially travelled as a group, but the stronger teams gradually established themselves in a small front group that pulled a short distance ahead. Lorrina Mitchell, running in the second grouping of sleds, decided to push herself hard between Eagle and Dawson City. She moved along one night at a fairly fast clip, gradually opening a gap between her team and the others she had been travelling with.

Suddenly, she saw a fire on the ice ahead of her. Being in dire need of a rest, she took a moment to realize it was the lead group of teams camped just off the trail. She turned off her headlamp and drove along in the dark.

"I just motored past without stopping. I'm sure it got them real nervous, this team just appearing out of the night and blowing past."

Mitchell had vaulted into first place in one fell swoop. But it was short-lived. She stopped to sleep just past the camp and when she awoke, the leaders had packed up and gone past again. She didn't see them again until the end of the race.

Sonny Lindner says through his perpetual shy smile that he knew he would win when he looked at Joe Runyan's dogs in Dawson City. They were thinner than his and, in his mind, that was the edge he was seeking.

"You take two teams that can travel at the same speed, but one has to stop to feed more often than the other. That team can never make up the lost time."

He made his move shortly after leaving Dawson City, breaking away in the Black Hills. It was the right call at the right time. Runyan faded; Harry Sutherland and Bill Cotter kept pace, but they had been three hours behind heading out of Dawson and couldn't make up the ground.

Lindner claims he doesn't think about strategy either before or after the start, but there is never any doubt that he is in every race to win.

"I do the things that I enjoy. I like going fast. If that means I'm first at the finish line, that's great. When you're near the end and you know you're close, you give a little extra."

Because the race reverses direction each year, there are two ways for the drivers to approach the final stretch. In fact, the Yukon Quest is really two races in one.

From Fairbanks to Whitehorse (even-numbered years), the teams can start quickly, then they tend to slow as the distances between checkpoints gradually get longer. Physical endurance is a major factor in strategic planning once you move past the Circle District, because the teams tend to get spread out and mushers don't have the same opportunity to play head games with their competitors.

From Whitehorse to Fairbanks (odd-numbered years), the length of the early legs is draining on the teams. The race starts slowly, then picks up the pace as the checkpoints get closer together. The late race strategies are more emotional because the teams tend to group up in the latter stages and the drivers have more time to work on their opponents' psyche.

Timing is vital, no matter which direction you go. Waiting too long or making a break too early can be strategically fatal.

Joe Runyan tried to make his break early in 1984, pushing hard out of Eagle and going without a break to Dawson. He gambled that a 36-hour break would be enough for his team to recover totally. He was wrong.

"I found out that's not true. Thirty-six hours is not enough. Taking chances and breaking your rest-run schedule often gives results that aren't repairable. You can't make a mistake."

In 1985, he remembered his lesson and didn't panic as Rick Atkinson bolted out of Carmacks and rolled into Dawson City with a 12-hour lead.

"My strategy was don't pay attention to anyone else. Run the schedule you think makes sense. Establish what your boundaries are, what your dogs can do. The only thing that's relevant is your own dog team."

Runyan maintained his schedule. Run, rest. Run, rest. All he could do was hope that Atkinson's team couldn't keep up the torrid pace that the Scot had run to Dawson City. He realized his plan was working when he saw a headlamp bobbing along the river in front of him near Eagle. The only driver in front of him was a tired Atkinson, who had tried to bluff the gambler in Runyan, but didn't hold a winning hand of cards.

When he reached Circle Hot Springs, Runyan felt he was in control.

"Atkinson's dogs had lost a little zip and he was going to have a tough time bringing them back." The driver that concerned him most at this point, Sutherland, was a couple of hours behind, but, "Harry is the master of this end-of-the-race stuff. He's written the book on it."

At Chena Hot Springs, Runyan, who aided his dogs by running behind the sled most of the time, made his final move. It was time to depart from his rest-run schedule, time to pull out all the stops. The payoff was a record time to Fairbanks that will endure into the next decade. He will employ the same strategy to win the 1989 Iditarod.

In 1986, a snowstorm that buried the trail for 600 miles overshadowed any pre-race strategy that the drivers might have had.

Sonny Lindner had wanted to break away at Carmacks, but trail conditions were horrendous and anyone trying to shake pursuit that early would simply put his team under extra pressure. Cotter, Sutherland, Tim Osmar and Bruce Johnson shared some of the trailbreaking duties with Lindner all the way to Lake Laberge, through more than a foot of freshly fallen snow. When they crawled onto the ice and stopped to camp, Lindner's team, considered by all the drivers to be the strongest and fastest on the trail, was completely burned. He had carried the bulk of the work. The freshest was Johnson, who had lingered at the back and had only broken trail when everyone else refused to do so.

A short distance ahead they could see a broken trail, the first one since crossing Eagle Summit.

"We agreed that we were all going to water our dogs, then, after two hours, we were going to pull the pin and go for it. We were all going to race in," said Sutherland.

But Johnson didn't stay. He pulled out after only 20 minutes and headed down the lake. Then, down the trail the five had just exhausted themselves breaking, came a snowmachine towing a large toboggan. It was driven by a government employee who had been working in the bush and had simply followed what looked like a decent trail to the lake without realizing he was on the Quest trail.

"He's making a trail. He's coming down this thing that just took us four hours to go eight miles on. So here comes Jeff King and he goes by us. He did the eight miles in two hours. Even if that's slow, it's still twice as fast as we did it," Sutherland described.

"Osmar took off. Sonny decided to peel out. I took off. Cotter came behind me. We couldn't be more than five miles apart at that point. But we could never catch up again because we let Johnson go for an hour before we took off."

Johnson held the lead in what he later named "The Lake Laberge Charge." King kept closing but ran out of trail, finishing just 24 minutes behind Johnson.

"All we did was wear out our dogs," lamented Cotter, "especially out of Carmacks. We believed there was a broken trail, but there wasn't. If there had been a trail, it would have been a different winner that year. That time it was a disadvantage to be at the front that close to the finish line."

But all gave due credit to Johnson. While a faster trail may have produced a different winner, his team was the best in the conditions in which they raced and his strategy was the one that worked.

Ironically, Johnson's winning effort was the slowest of the three races he ran. His previous two finishes had been almost two full days faster. His winning race was the longest of the Quests, taking more than two weeks to complete, and is still considered one of the toughest races ever run.

Cotter kept re-running the first three Quests through his head, trying to determine ways to cut time and where the optimum point was to make a break. He thought he had it all figured out, but all that planning almost got wasted when he was penalized six hours in Dawson for taking the wrong trail.

"It was demoralizing. I knew how much I had lost by in previous years."

But by Eagle, he had caught up to the leaders again. There he took the time to reconsider his strategy. He vetoed trying to make a break on the Yukon River before reaching Circle City.

"Other people who tried this strategy always did it too early."

He decided to wait until he was in the Circle District, but he also knew he would have to have a distinct advantage before he reached Angel Creek.

The 1987 race was possibly the most strategically demanding of all of the Yukon Quests. There were four teams — Cotter, Monson, Swenson and King — all relatively equal in strength. They were each looking for any weakness that might provide insight into the others' plans or physical conditions, seeing how the dogs held their weight in the cold, looking for signs of tender feet by counting the booties that each team used, trying to interpret the run-rest schedules, to see if they could estimate how long and how far a team would run once it left a campsite, guessing at the fast leader, hidden in the team dogs, which could be pulled out and put up front at the crucial moment (a strong, rested pace leader can add a mile an hour to a team's speed).

"Sometimes they'll pack their sleds, tie it all down and pretend they're ready to leave," says Cotter. "Then they'll find some reason to delay, hoping that someone else will panic, cut their rest time short and head out too fast. It's serious, but at the same time it's fun."

The weather played a major role in Cotter's strategy, although it was not meant to be a factor. It was cold, too cold.

"I was so cold, I couldn't warm up. I could only build a fire and cook for my dogs." He decided that he would only feed his dogs at checkpoints where there was pre-heated water for the team and prepared food for himself.

The cold also aggravated a back injury he had suffered the previous month and he developed a limp. The pain was draining his energy, and when he pulled off the Yukon River into Circle City, emotionally it was the lowest point for him in the race. He was sore, cold, tired and disoriented.

"I know that after the race some people said I faked it. I may have played it up later on, but at that time, I didn't know what I was going to do next. I was so cold I didn't know if I could go on."

But when Jeff King loaded his sled, Cotter was right behind, limping all the way to Circle Hot Springs. He looked so worn, it seemed like just a matter of time before he would pull out of the race altogether. His back was obviously causing him a lot of discomfort. Monson, King and Swenson had to make a quick evaluation and they decided he wasn't a factor any more. Behind his painful facade, Cotter smiled to himself.

The back was sore all right, but it didn't hurt as much as it had in Circle nor was it as bad as he made it look at the Hot Springs. Two warm checkpoints had taken the chill out of his bones and while he was still tired, his adrenaline had started to flow. He went on to Central and stopped for one last big feed.

As he sat in the corner of the restaurant, King, Swenson and Monson arrived. They only had eyes for each other, spending a long time manoeuvring into sleeping positions to keep track of the other two.

"So I said, 'This is it. This is my chance to go. I win the race right now or I don't.'"

He strolled out, apparently to feed his dogs. As the three other lead mushers dozed fitfully and monitored each others' activities, Cotter kept on going, climbing onto Eagle Summit on a rare storm-free night. It took about four hours before the other three mushers realized that no one had seen Cotter for a while.

"When I got to the top and looked down that long valley and didn't see another team, I knew I had it," Cotter said. When he reached Angel Creek, he had a three-hour edge on Monson and King.

"I figured I could just cruise into the finish line." So he ran leisurely towards Fairbanks, oblivious to the fact that Monson was making one last charge.

A few miles from Fairbanks an aircraft circled over Cotter, then headed further down the river.

"I knew it would circle again over the next team, so I watched. When I saw it circle again just a mile or so behind me I thought, 'Oh shit, I'd better get serious.'"

He reached the line 10 minutes ahead of Monson. As he threw his arms in the air and passed under the banner, the pain in his back vanished for the moment and he was more awake than he had been in days.

Jeff King will run a textbook race in 1989. He'll travel most of the way with the established front pack of Vern Halter, Bruce Lee, Kate Persons, Sonny Lindner and rookie Jim Wilson (a commercial fisher in his first long distance race).

At Angel Creek, King will be the third driver to start out on the home stretch to Fairbanks, behind Wilson and Halter. Knowing he has run a perfect race so far, King will let it all out. "I started the dogs into overdrive, and they bolted by, and the other teams weren't able to catch me."

Wilson, who will finish third, was flabbergasted at the speed King's dogs had so close to the end. "He left me in the dust. His dogs went by like their tails were on fire."

Vern Halter will watch King vanish down the trail ahead of him in 1989, but he knows he is only a dog or two and a year's experience from having the same kind of finish. The team that Vern Halter will lead to the start line in 1990 is possibly the single strongest squad of dogs to have ever run the Yukon Quest. The power of the team will be demonstrated when he waits an extra five hours in Dawson City for the second musher, Kate Persons, to leave ahead of him so he won't have to break trail. Giving up his five-hour lead so easily is a mistake, the other drivers will say, but by the time he reaches Midway, only Jeff King will be close enough to be a threat.

"They were almost connected," King will say of the team that plays catch-us-if-you-can with him over the last leg from Carmacks, and which he will not be able to catch. "They had a spirit about them, the whole team, that was almost supernatural." Halter and his dogs will be the first team to complete the Fairbanks-to-Whitehorse race in less than 12 days.

"Winning," says Dave Monson, "is the absence of regret." In 1987, he had two things to regret. Not having reached the finish line 10 minutes earlier was one of them. He had underestimated Cotter. The award-winning acting performance had duped him completely.

"In Central, we sat around like a couple of weasels watching each other in a woodpile while the fox stole the golden egg."

The second regret came a little later in the race, when he allowed his anxiety to overrule his caution. In his hurry to make up lost ground, he didn't notice an area of weak ice that had broken when Swenson went over it just ahead of him. Dogs, sled and driver all plunged through into Birch Creek. Working the team out of the hole and drying off by rolling in the snow, he pushed on until he ran into Swenson.

"I said, 'Kathy, I just fell in the river there and I'm soaked.' My gloves were like seal flippers. Kathy monkeyed around, tried to chip the ice off the gloves and zippers. We stopped for over an hour which, at that point in the race, is ridiculous, but my decision was to take the best care of my dogs and myself."

Then he missed the turn into Angel Creek and spent some time backtracking to find it again.

Monson remembers the 10 minutes he has had to regret for the past year. But as he balances on the runners of his sled in 1988, looking back at the north end of Lake Laberge, he knows he has made no mistakes he will regret.

"I just stood backwards and concentrated on that one spot in the woods where the trail ended. I watched for 15 minutes, a half hour, an hour, an hour and a half. Finally, I couldn't see that spot any more and, after two hours, I knew that Gerry or no one else had entered the lake. That's when I knew I was way ahead. It would take something superhuman to catch me at that point. The race ended."

Riley is almost nine hours behind by this time. While Monson has enjoyed the feel of a fast, effortless sprint for the past 100 miles, Riley's young dogs have finally run out of steam. They have been catching up to Monson for 11 days and they just can't do it another time.

Crossing Lake Laberge, made famous in "The Cremation of Sam McGee."

Now, resting at an unofficial checkpoint on Coghlan Lake, in a cabin belonging to Tracy Harris, he is in danger of being caught by Swenson. But she is unaware of his problems and doesn't realize that second place is within her grasp. At one point she comes within a few hundred yards of him, but her team has also hit the wall (run out of steam).

"I was bummed out because I had a chance to catch Riley and I blew it. My dogs were gaining on him until we lost the trail. We went around in circles for about 30 minutes before we found it again." But the extra stress drains her team. They stroll the rest of the way to Whitehorse.

As the drivers approach the north end of the lake, the last few miles become the hardest part of the trail for them.

The ice that forms over Lake Laberge has a natural beauty to it. It seems to be the perfect surface for the long, narrow lake walled on each side by high cliffs. When the sun rises or sets in winter, it turns the ice a light, glowing pink.

The First Nations people thought it was so awesome that when they described it to Michael Lebarge, a surveyor with the Western Union Telegraph Expedition in 1866, it was in such terms that he envisioned a lake of beauty beyond belief. Although he never saw the body of water that was to later bear his name (spelled slightly differently), he described it constantly and in great detail for the rest of his life.

The sun's light gradually creeps down the hills on the west side and touches upon the rocky merge of the lake (where Robert Service chose to cremate Sam McGee in one of his most famous poems) and on Richthofen Island, where a group of cabins used to provide service and shelter for the riverboats that plied the Yukon River from Whitehorse to Nome. Some of those riverboats, having been caught in the sudden windstorms the lake is notorious for, now lie wrecked on the shore.

But the history and the poetic setting aren't enough to give the tired driver more than a momentary thrill. The bruises and aches of abused muscles can no longer be overpowered by a rush of adrenaline. Once the emotional race is over, there is nothing left except to complete the physical part. Time starts to feel like an anchor. The hours spent alone on the lake ice are the longest ones the drivers will ever endure. It's only 40 miles to the finish line, but the dogs are moving unbearably slowly. At times it seems like they're not moving at all. Every second becomes a minute; every minute, an hour.

"I must have fallen asleep 20 times on the lake," Vern Halter will say in 1990.

Dave Monson, a wounded warrior waiting to do battle with an opponent who never showed, feels lonely and sore as he drives the length of the pink ice into the rising sun.

(Over) It's over. I'm done!

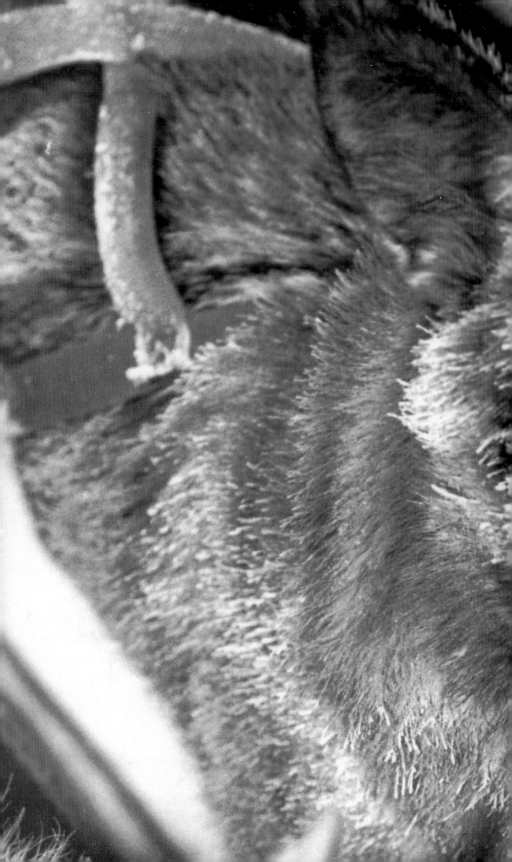

Sleeping dogs

Sleeping dogs

The finish line is the last half-inch of space that the mushers must travel in the Yukon Quest. But that final half-inch is what has kept the drivers on the trail. Without it, everything that came before, the 1,000 miles of trials and tribulations, is incomplete.

For almost two weeks the drivers have lived an intense life patterned exclusively around their racing timetables, their dogs' needs, and the environment and geography. They and their dogs have run, rested and eaten in eight-hour shifts, three shifts a day, all aimed at one ultimate goal — to pass under and beyond the finish line banner. Then suddenly, in the space of that one second it takes to complete the race, it's technically over.

Pressure becomes relief. Solitude changes to crowds. Wilderness trail turns into city streets.

Whitehorse.

Nobody's exactly sure where its name comes from. The term "white horse" was commonly used in the late 19th century to describe the waves or white caps in the river. Whatever the origin, the area was known as White Horse by 1887. (In the early 1900s, the two words became one.)

Whitehorse is the exception to the historical background of the Yukon Quest. It is the only area that had no gold discovery of its own to bring in the first residents. It served as a sort of checkpoint on the trail to the Klondike goldfields.

While the city of over 21,000 is known primarily as the hub of transportation in the territory, for the dog drivers this year, it is the end of the trail.

Their first clue that the end is nigh is an old abandoned garbage dump on a high bluff about three miles out of town. People often drive out to it, then clamber down to river level to watch the teams go by. Soon, the drivers see a power line stretched across the river. Get around the next bend and there are cabins in the distance on the far bank of the river. Another corner and they can see the shacks in the old shipyards.

There is one more little handmade trap to dodge. The trail passes under a footbridge, leading from the shore to a mid-river island, where one of the support cables under the bridge hangs low enough to decapitate the unwary musher. The cable is wrapped in reflective aluminum foil and, after dark, a car is parked with its headlights shining on it. So far, everyone has ducked under it.

Then the mushers follow a boat launch road that leads up from the river ice to the railway. The sleds travel alongside the tracks for a hundred yards or so to the parking lot beside the White Pass and Yukon Railway's two-storey log train station.

The finish line itself is somewhat unimpressive — a small motorhome parked to one side, two powerpoles with the banner stretched between them, some wooden road barricades to hold back the spectators, and three or four sets of portable bleachers so those in the back can see over those at the front.

Sonny Lindner, the first Yukon Quest champion, 1984.

Inside the motorhome can be found volunteers like Peter Garside and Doug Baird, non-mushers who take holidays or leave-without-pay from work to satisfy their own fascination with dog mushing. They have been race officials for sled dog races in the Yukon since the early 1970s. Along with finish line organizer Dolores Smith and Quest archivist and soon-to-be-mother Edna Knight, they sleep, eat and wait patiently in shifts, 24 hours a day, watching the river for approaching teams. They move into the vehicle a day or so before the first musher arrives and won't leave the area unstaffed until the last one is safely across the line. It can be minutes, hours or even days between teams.

Because of the uncertainty of predicting the exact times of arrival, crowds at the finish line tend to be small. A few minutes after each musher crosses the finish line, the crowd size almost doubles as news of a new arrival is spread. Those who wait at the line between arrivals are dedicated musher supporters.

When a musher does roll in, the crowds see some unusual things.

Sonny Lindner was the first musher to ever complete the Yukon Quest. When confronted by the media, he shifted uncomfortably from foot to

Joe Runyan, Yukon Quest champion, 1985.

foot, gave shy one-word answers to the questions, then walked past the 166-ounce Texas Mickey of rye whiskey that awaited him as the victor and went shopping instead.

"One good reason for not winning," he will confide a few years later, "is that you don't have to talk to the press or give a speech at the banquet."

In 1986, Joe May finished his 12-year racing career, which included a win in the 1980 Iditarod, with a camp fire in the finishing chute. Gently, solemnly, a small tear freezing on his eyelash, he officially confirmed his retirement by placing his snowshoes on top of the fire and watching them be consumed by the flames. He is one of the few who retired and didn't come back — yet.

Ron Aldrich is probably the only musher ever to be greeted in the finish area by a woman standing in the snow wearing a yellow polka-dot bikini. It was minus 20 degrees when Aldrich finished in 1984 and his wife wore a warm overcoat that she opened to flash her garb at him at the appropriate moment. A lot of the bystanders never knew who she was or what she wore, if anything. All they could see were her bare legs under a long coat.

Bruce Johnson,
Yukon Quest
champion, 1986.

Lorrina Mitchell was the first woman to ride to the finish line in that first Quest in 1984. Only a few spectators were on hand to greet her, but the one she remembers best was sitting across the river from the finish line.

"It was a cat and, you know, the dogs didn't even look at it. They couldn't care less. They could see the finish line across the river. This cat was sitting on the riverbank just terrified, staring at us, but we went right on by."

When Frank Turner and Wilson Sam trundled into Whitehorse in 1984, the big money was gone, but there was still a little cash to be had. They had travelled together for 600 miles. Now, 100 yards short of the finish line, they stopped, drew a line in the snow and sipped on a beer supplied by a bystander. The next one across the line would be 14th, which would earn $100 more than 15th, the last position that earned a cash prize.

The two lined up abreast. The bystander counted down to zero and the race was on — it was Turner by a nose.

William Kleedehn, finishing in 1990, will have found answers to the two questions he started with — he has a long way to go to be able to compete with the Alaskan mushers and his artificial leg isn't a handicap. In fact, it's almost an advantage. He only has to worry about frostbite on one foot instead of two.

Bill Cotter winning the 1987 Quest.

Jeninne Cathers will make her mark in history by finishing the 1989 Quest as its youngest-ever competitor. And she'll be back in 1990 for another shot at it. She aspires to be the first woman to win.

Now, in 1988, there are perhaps three or four hundred people waiting to greet Monson as he races in to claim the championship prize and belt buckle (a custom scrimshaw piece of mastodon ivory).

"When I realized the finish line was there and I was going to cross it, I didn't even have time to really emotionally prepare myself for the fact that I was going to win the Yukon Quest," he said. "I'd gone from absolute solitude to total pandemonium." A set of headphones slapped on his head connected him with his wife, Susan Butcher, in Anchorage preparing to defend her Iditarod title.

"I hear in my ear...Susan is talking to me. She's not even there and it's like, 'What kind of a dream am I having?'"

Gerald Riley, who plods across the finish line about nine hours behind Dave Monson, finishes what may well have been his last realistic shot at the winner's circle. He'll be back for another effort in 1989, but the big high-tech kennels, like those of Monson, Runyan, Swenson and King, will keep getting stronger and faster and those from the old school of dog mushing will realize their day is done.

Dave Monson, Yukon Quest champion, 1988.

Kathy Swenson, who in 1987 had been the first woman to finish in the top 10, trails in a couple of hours later to take third place.

Between the championship contender and the one who will light up the red lantern — the traditional prize for the final finisher of a dog sled race — comes the rest of the pack.

Rick Atkinson. Bruce Lee, who finally gets a last minute burst of power from his dogs to hang onto a top-five finish.

Kate Persons, who many believe will actually become the first woman to win the Quest. She will be back in 1989 and 1990; both times, like Kathy Swenson, coming close.

John Schandelmeier. Dennis Kogl. Ralph Tingey.

Jim Wardlow. Vern Halter. Frank Turner.

Mark Elliott. Lorrina Mitchell. Frank Ganley.

Mary Sheilds, whose uncooperative dogs are now rested, perky and happy, have finally got up off the ice and brought her the rest of the way to Whitehorse.

Ron Rosser. Mark Stamm. Ned Cathers trots in a few hours ahead of Lena Charley. He's tired, but he had fun. "I'm only going through life once and I have no intention of not enjoying myself." The outdoor adventure guide will return in 1989 and 1990.

Lena Charley pulls up after 15 days on the trail. The quiet, durable grandmother was 20th in 1986 and she's 20th again this year.

Dave Dalton. Jim Strong. Jim Reiter. Jeff Fisher. Tom Randall.

James Poage. Marc Poage.

The red lantern finally goes to Ty Halvorson. He out-delays John Ballard to wander casually across the line over a week after Monson finishes.

He joins the ranks of other notable slow-pokes such as Shirley Liss in 1984. She actually had to finish in Carmacks because the ice on the Yukon River was too rotten to travel on when she reached it. Jim Bridges in 1985. Michael Schwandt in 1986 and Allen Dennis in 1987. Peter Butteri in 1989 and Esa Ekdahl in 1990 will also collect their own red lantern.

Behind them, left behind in checkpoints along the way, are Jon Gleason, David Sawatzky and his constipated dog, Don Donaldson, Clifton Cadzow, Bob Bright and his futuristic sled, Adolphus Capot-Blanc, Jeff King and François Varigas. All have scratched for this year, but most will return in 1989 and 1990.

In all, 30 of the 47 mushers who pulled out of the starting chute in Fairbanks two weeks ago will reach Whitehorse. And when they arrive, each one wants to do something different.

In 1985, Jon Gleason just wanted to go dancing. As a past president of the Alaska Trappers Association he wanted to arrive in time for the annual Trapper's Fling Ball. He rolled into Fairbanks at six in the evening, and the ball was scheduled to start at eight. After a shower and a meal, Mary Gleason wanted to get her husband home.

"No," he argued, "We've got to go to the fling."

He sleepwalked into the ball, yawned at a few friends, then turned around and headed to bed without dancing a single step.

It will be in the 40-foot chute beyond the finish line, in 1990, that Will Forsberg will finally catch his wife, Linda. She will be ahead of him all the way from Fairbanks, leaving taunting notes at each checkpoint to goad him on his way along the trail. By the time he arrives, she will have had a shower and a sleep before coming back out to greet him.

This year, Jeff Fisher, a carpenter from Cantwell, Alaska, is sitting in the checkpoint when last-place musher Halvorson rolls in. Tired and dirty after three weeks on the trail, he is helping to staff the checkpoint at the finish line because his handlers are travelling with Halvorson's handlers. Neither group of handlers had arrived in Whitehorse by the time Fisher did, so all he could do was sit and wait.

Jeff King, finally a Yukon Quest champion, 1989.

Fisher is a Quest rookie, running his first long distance race after getting hooked on mushing when he did a friend a favour six years ago and took his small dog team out for a little exercise.

"It's a personal challenge, kind of an ego thing," he says, looking wistfully back down the trail. "It builds confidence in a person. If I can mush a dog team for 1,000 miles, I can do anything."

Then his eyes, weary and haggard a moment before, brighten as he looks beyond the finish line, up the river past where the teams stop, and the Quest blood starts to boil in him again. There is a broken trail, made by a snowmachine, wending its way along the edge of the ice, under the bridge that spans the river and around the corner to...

"Is there another town I can run to...? I might as well hitch 'em up."

It is later, as Dave Monson rides to his hotel, that it gradually seeps in that he is the first and, so far, only finisher, of the 1988 Quest — which means he is probably the winner. But there is little peace for him in the first few hours; no time for him to think about what it means or to appreciate it.

Even sitting in the bathtub, trying to scrub two weeks of grime and sweat off his body, he is talking to a reporter perched on the lid of the toilet next to him. He dozes off in the middle of another media interview in his room.

It will be three days before the final banquet. There are teams who will still be on the trail. For those who finish, there is plenty of activity between times spent catching up on long overdue sleep.

The drivers have had plenty of time to look over their opponents' teams during the past two weeks and now is the time to talk trading and selling dogs. The mushers' marketplace is open all year round — it's not unusual to find a musher in midsummer or mid-race wrangling with another musher over a dog or two — but the post-race period is the most frenzied. It is similar to athletes from professional sports franchises being swapped when the season wraps up, as teams try to improve for next year.

It takes a while for the dogs and drivers to settle into a normal routine. Like jet-lag or the adjustment a shift-worker has to make, the pattern of run-eat-sleep doesn't just vanish in the one second it takes to complete the race, or even with one good night's sleep.

Even something as simple as breathing is an adjustment that has to be made. The warm, more humid air inside a room or building is in sharp contrast to the cold, dry, brittle air they've been inhaling. The driver's sinuses and nostrils, now adapted to a steady diet of outdoor air, react with the indoor air and become constantly plugged, making breathing difficult. A large room that others feel is chilly, will be tiny and stiflingly hot to the musher.

There's nobody to tell the dogs it's over. They've passed under banners, stopped in crowds and been poked, prodded and needled by veterinarians a few times over the past two weeks. To them, this is just another temporary stop, albeit a little more populated than some. The first difference they notice is when they're loaded into their dog boxes and trucked away from the city, to be kenneled on rural lots for the next few days. When they arrive, they curl up motionless on beds of fresh hay for a few hours.

When their internal clock tells them it's time to get up and go, they awake, but there's no one there to take them and no place to go — just a bowl of water, some food and maybe a handler sitting nearby, keeping a careful eye on them. The sled isn't behind them, the tug line and harnesses are gone. There's nothing to pull and no way to pull it if there was.

Confused, they eat and drink, and wait, then lie down and curl up again. Two or three times they repeat that. Eventually, they stop waking up and drift into a deep dream-filled sleep. Even then it doesn't end. They pant, their legs twitch and their sides heave. Their imaginations literally run wild.

For the first few days, the handler will take the dogs for a jog to loosen them up and take the ache out of their legs. They will welcome the easy jaunt. It tells them that the hard stuff is over for a while. They may get a week or two of easy exercise, then it's back to the racing circuit. The big-money middle distance races are scheduled to be run during the next month. They will greet the reappearance of the sled and harnesses with grins and wagging tails. This is what they were born to. Running is their life.

The drivers also keep waking up, ready to run.

Vern Halter, Yukon Quest champion, 1990.

Whitehorse, the finish line

Frank Turner wakes up with a start in the middle of the night: reaching for his boots, wired up with nerves and perspiring heavily, wondering which way his team is facing, who is passing and uncertain of exactly where he is on the trail. And why is the sky so strange. Then he realizes he's in the cabin and the sky is his loft ceiling. There is no sled passing, no trail, and the boots in his hand are his bedroom slippers.

Jim Reiter opens his eyes at night and shifts uncomfortably under the covers on his bed. His feet feel strange — instead of being bare, they should be sheathed in mukluks or bunny boots. The blanket feels weird — a parka or sleeping bag would feel more natural. And there's the frustrating feeling of thinking you should be doing something, but you're not sure exactly what.

Jon Rudolph finds that day and night have no meaning.

"It takes me about two weeks to get back into a normal routine, going to bed at night and getting up in the morning. You've been awake all the time. You slept when you could and if you could."

Strange things happen in the twilight zone. Rudolph arrived at the finish line just before two in the morning in 1986 and his wife drove him home. On the way he noticed the road to his house had drifted over with snow and thought to himself, "I should plow the road."

The next thing he remembers is waking up five or six hours later in the cab of his grader. But instead of plowing the road, he was 12 miles away, heading down the highway into Whitehorse.

"What the hell am I doing here?" he asked himself. "Taking a grader downtown?" He turned around, returned home and plowed off his driveway before returning to bed.

"I was able to run the kind of race I wanted to at the end. It paid off for me. I was really happy," Dave Monson says in his victory speech at the mushers' banquet. "To me, the Yukon Quest is a spirit of adventure, of travel through some of the prettiest country in the northern latitudes… certainly, in its own respect, the prettiest in the world.

"It's about camaraderie and companionship, competition, loneliness, hardship and pain, the will to persevere and succeed.

"It's all these things rolled into one.

"It's the musher and dogs in companionship against the elements, and the teamwork between the two, that helps you overcome the obstacles and make your goal."

At the banquet, he basks in the public's adulation and hero worship for the newly-crowned champion.

But later, in his bed that night, it is a good feeling being alone. In the solitude, he savours his accomplishment. He is proud of his dogs. He is at peace within himself.

The dogs

by Erin Briemon

The little dogs had the hardest of times getting over the long, long trail. The trail is a very rough trail to get over.

When your little dog finishes the QUEST what do you do to it? Do you thank it? I think it is hard on the dogs and you don't know what it would be like to be the dogs. I think that all your dogs need a lot of credit for pulling you and your things over the finish line.

I know that the first person over the finish line gets a trophy and 20,000 dollars, but think of your dogs. Don't forget to thank your dogs. They did most of the work.

Erin Briemon was an 11-year-old resident
of Whitehorse when she wrote this piece in 1990.
She liked to watch the Yukon Quest, especially the dogs,
either in Whitehorse or on Lake Laberge.

(over) Frank Turner, Yukon Quest champion in 1995.

Whitehorse, the finish line

Races of future past

Races of future past

NOVEMBER 22, 1993. There was no sunset. Instead, the day had just started to fade into dusk under a high overcast sky. Bruce Johnson, winner of the 1986 Yukon Quest and runner-up in the 1993 race, hitched up a couple of his regular dogs and six young up-and-comers. This was just going to be a short training run, a chance for some of his younger, future team members to get some work behind experienced leaders. Pulling his ice hook, he jumped on the sled runners and rode out of the yard amidst the howls of the other dogs, dismayed at being left behind.

The team ran true for several miles, faultlessly following the marked and packed trail skirting the shoreline of Little Atlin Lake. Then, as they made the turn at the southernmost end of the lake, something happened. Exactly what occurred will never really be understood.

It is assumed that Johnson lost control of the team, possibly even lost control of himself. He continued to ride the runners, but made no apparent efforts to influence the course of events that followed. His experienced leaders appeared to panic, making a sharp right turn off the trail, then travelling straight towards the centre of the lake.

Winter had been a little late in arriving. The temperatures had been warmer than normal, slowing down the freezing process. The ice around the shoreline was firm, but the centre was treacherous. Pressure ridges were just starting to build, a sure sign that the ice was just forming, too thin to bear any stress. A knowledgeable northern traveller like Johnson, had he been in control, would normally be nowhere near the centre of any lake at this time of year. Had his leaders not been panicked, they would have sensed the danger and changed direction.

The tracks showed the team getting onto the weak ice, which sagged, bled water and threatened to collapse under them. They almost made it.

For over half a mile, the ice bent but didn't break. Then, just a couple of hundred yards from solid ice, it suddenly folded and buckled underneath them, opening up a lead over a hundred yards long. Johnson, the sled and his dogs vanished from sight.

Johnson, a veteran of 20 years of northern travel and sled dog racing, was always aware that competing in a race, even one as isolated and arduous as the Yukon Quest, was as safe as a musher could be. There were constantly other competitors, officials or aircraft monitoring him during the race. But during training, he also knew of the greater chance for disaster, when he was alone and the only people waiting for him to come in were his family.

His body was cremated and, in the spring of 1994, his ashes were privately buried in an undisclosed location somewhere in the Little Atlin Lake area by his wife Jeaneil and daughters Elizabeth, Zea and Bronwyn.

When the 1994 Yukon Quest started on February 11 in Fairbanks, the starting flag was dropped for team number one to leave the chute. But no roar came from the crowd. No dogs lunged forward. No snow hook was pulled. Instead, there were two minutes of silence as mushers and spectators alike looked forlornly at the empty trail ahead, remembering the intense, quiet-spoken competitor who had mastered the head games, perfected the strategies and babied his dogs.

Then the next team pulled up to the start line, the flag dropped again and the race was on under a high, overcast sky.

Bruce Johnson, 1986.

1991

Warm weather can affect a race in many ways. It can slow it down by softening up the trail and making it punchy or by making it too hot for the dogs to race, forcing teams to rest during the day and travel only at night. It also creates perfect conditions for dog viruses to emerge and spread.

The "Healy Virus," which drains the energy from the dogs and causes them to come down with vomiting, coughing and bloody diarrhoea, erupted during the first 48 hours of the 1991 Quest. Before colder weather finally started to dampen its effect midway through the race, eight teams withdrew due to sick dogs and 35 other animals suffering from the virus were dropped.

Switzerland's Ruedi Indermuhle had been forced to use his healthy dogs to assist his sick dogs through the final series of hills heading into Carmacks. Leaving his sled at the bottom of each hill, he would hitch a sick dog in harness behind a healthy dog, then lead them up the hill. Once on top, he would let the sick dog rest and would go back down to pull another one up. Once all the sick dogs were at the top, he would hitch the healthy animals to the sled and pull it to the top of the hill.

"I did this four or five times and then I was so tired," he said, "I was thinking I'd never arrive in Carmacks."

Once in Carmacks, Indermuhle scratched from the race. But his ordeal wasn't over yet. The dogs were still sick and he spent the next several hours using a syringe to force water through the clenched jaws of the dogs who had started refusing food and water. Eventually, his team started to come back. In the end, with rest and colder temperatures, all the dogs recovered.

THERE'S NOT MUCH FLAMMABLE MATERIAL ON THE TRAIL DURING THE QUEST. Dry wood. Clothing. Gas in the cooking stoves. The mushers themselves.

While lighting his stove one night on the Yukon River between Circle City and Eagle during the 1991 Quest, Peter Butteri managed to set his head on fire, singeing off half his beard, one eyebrow and most of his hair on one side of his head.

"I did something that, when I did it, I didn't think it was very stupid. But it was definitely stupid."

He doused the flames by burying his head in the snow, the position he was in when the veterinarians happened upon the scene. The mild burn was treated with canine tit-salve, which they rubbed all over his face.

"The dogs all thought it (the burning hair) was great. They all started howling and jumping around."

THE 1991 YUKON QUEST BROUGHT A NEW DIMENSION TO THE TRADITIONAL strategies employed in a long distance race.

The field featured two former winners, Sonny Lindner and defending champion Vern Halter. John Schandelmeier, Jim Wilson, François Varigas, Linda Forsberg and Bruce Lee (who never ran a race he didn't think he could win), were also pushing at the front of the pack.

"This is different than other Quests," said Lee. "There are more people who want to win. People always dream of winning, but there are six or seven out there who want to win this year. It's the toughest field I've ever seen."

A surprise among the leaders was Charlie Boulding.

Charlie Boulding looked like he always did. His trapline dogs were a motley crew. His sled was old and loaded with black and white plastic bags. He claimed his gear was worn because he couldn't afford new equipment.

"Maybe that's why our gear doesn't look as good as the others," he drawled. "But on the other hand, there's an awful lot of pretty gear behind us. People used to say, 'Charlie Boulding's leaving,' and everybody would go, 'Oh yeah? So what?'" It was his own private joke.

The truth was that, while Boulding was low tech with his equipment, his team was high tech. He had been methodically building a new team, using young dogs bred from his trapline dogs and mixing them in with shrewd purchases of animals from other powerful racing kennels. His laid-back mannerism and the apparently random manner in which he acquired his dogs prevented the other mushers from realizing what he was doing in the off-season.

Charlie Boulding, Yukon Quest champion, 1991 and 1993.

He had a 20-minute lead over Bruce Lee and two hours over John Schandelmeier when they reached Circle City. No one else was even close.

Bruce Lee now recognized the intense competitor underneath the gray pigtails and ragged parka.

"He ran the same schedule I did and he did it well. I realized then (near Eagle) that he was going to be something to deal with."

The three teams travelled close together across Eagle Summit to the final mandatory checkpoint at Angel Creek. Then, dumping all unnecessary gear, they started the final sprint through the night to Fairbanks.

"I'm just gonna go as fast as I can," said Boulding, and he did. The teams flew through the night at a frantic pace.

Headlamp bobbing and every muscle in his body simply screaming with agony as he pushed for the finish, Lee chased Boulding all the way to the finish line. But, in the early morning mists on the Chena River near downtown Fairbanks, Lee came up short, finishing only five minutes behind. He was still more than 15 hours faster than the previous record time for the Whitehorse-to-Fairbanks race. Schandelmeier rolled in 46 minutes later to claim the show position.

DANIEL BOURASSA COULDN'T BELIEVE IT WHEN HIS SLED STOPPED MOVING BUT the dogs kept running on Coghlan Lake. His tow line had broken, leaving him with only two wheel dogs in harness while the rest of the team cavorted on ahead. The Quebec musher and his two dogs battled with the heavy sled through the snow and hills of the trail, running towards Carmacks for three and a half hours.

Eventually, cresting a ridge, they came upon their team members, tangled up around a tree, waiting for the food to catch up. Bourassa fed the team, repaired the line and continued on down the trail.

THE "HURRY UP AND WAIT" GAME AT THE CHECKPOINTS, PLAYED BY HANDLERS, checkpoint officials and veterinarians while waiting for the teams to arrive, usually consists of playing cards (cribbage, which is a northern obsession), talking, sleeping, drinking coffee, heading out to the nearest bar for a beer, reading or staring vacantly at the wall.

One handler decided to bring his hobby along with him for the endless hours he would be spending in checkpoints along the way. He would find a table, set up a lamp and bracket and proceed to tie flies for fly fishing. The children hanging around the checkpoints found this fascinating, as did the adults. They spent hours watching and asking questions. This year the Quest may not only have inspired junior dog mushers, but it may also have produced a future fly fisher.

1992

The veterinary program in 1992 featured the beginning of research specifically designed to determine the differences between the pet dog and the working dog. During the race, in addition to the day-to-day care and monitoring, blood tests and EKGs were regularly administered by two specialists from Ohio State University.

"If we take an EKG from a sled dog," said Dr. Ken Hinchcliff, "we find there are a number of changes which, if you didn't know it was from a sled dog, you would say are abnormal. They are changes you see in sick pet dogs, but are normal for working sled dogs. In the same way you would expect to see larger hearts in marathon runners or other world class athletes, you see them in sled dogs. It is a result of all the training."

The blood tests were being done to determine why sled dogs have fewer "free radicals" in their blood. Normally, using more oxygen causes more free radicals, which damage muscle tissue and are responsible for sore muscles following extensive exercising.

"The more free radicals you make, the more damage it does, but that doesn't happen in these dogs. What we want to know is why."

The program also had its controversy. Head vet Jeannie Olson was relieved of her responsibilities by the rules committee because she was using acupuncture to treat dogs with minor leg problems.

EKG machine in use on the trail.

Races of future past

There is no restriction to the use of acupuncture on the Quest, but Olson was the only vet doing it. Whether it was effective or not apparently was never questioned by the race rules committee. The decision was made because equal access to dog care is a fundamental part of the rules and "she is only one person and she could not be everywhere 24 hours a day."

Olson apparently offered to make the treatment available to all the mushers in Dawson City only, thus meeting the equal access requirement, but the offer was declined.

"I said I could no longer serve my oath, which says you perform to the best of your ability based on your knowledge. So I took my needles and went home."

Just as holistic medicine is a controversial topic in dealing with human health, it is also a heated debate in the canine world. One of the arguments against acupuncture in dogs is that it might be used to mask pain. But several mushers, including Frank Turner, feel it has its place in the racing dog health field.

"It doesn't enhance the performance. It doesn't make the dog go past its performance levels...but it definitely makes the dog more comfortable." Turner uses acupuncture on his lower back as a means of pain management.

The theory behind acupuncture is that the insertion of needles into specific points on the body helps to balance the circulation of energy, which helps the body to heal itself. However, needles are not always necessary. Finger pressure can also be used and Olson has taught several of the competitors how to apply those acupressure techniques.

While the use of acupuncture and acupressure by veterinarians is frowned upon by the mushing establishment, it is actually in use on the trail by the mushers themselves.

JENINNE CATHERS BECAME A POSTER GIRL IN 1992, BUT THE MAIN BENEFICIARIES of her efforts never got to see it.

Her primary goal in running the race for the fourth time was to raise money for the Canadian National Institute for the Blind (CNIB). She collected pledges from donors who contributed according to how far she got. All proceeds from the sale of the poster bearing her image went directly to the CNIB. When she finished the Quest in 15th place, she had raised almost $15,000.

IN WHAT HE CALLED "THE TOUGHEST RACE I HAVE RUN," JOHN SCHANDELMEIER held off a late charge by Sonny Lindner and finally won the Yukon Quest in 1992. It came down to whose dogs were faster over the final 50 miles of trail and who could stay awake.

"I was dreaming about Sonny's lead dogs coming up and hitting me in the back of the legs while I was asleep on the sled," Schandelmeier's grin broke out under his ice-encrusted moustache as he hugged his mother at the finish line, "but I felt confident I was going to outrun him. My dogs were faster. I asked them to do it and they did it."

The two had camped together on Coghlan Lake early that morning to feed their dogs, having finally left defending champion Charlie Boulding behind in Carmacks the night before. The three teams had juggled top spot between them ever since Eagle Summit, running on a trail that varied from soft snow, in which the dogs bogged down, to a hard crystalline track that was like sandpaper. The temperature, which had been unseasonably warm in the early goings, leaving long open leads in the Yukon River between Circle City and Eagle, had plummeted and the second half of the race had been run under bitterly cold conditions.

Schandelmeier, Lindner and Boulding had been "in a league all their own," according to Frank Turner, and until Linda Forsberg made a late run at Charlie Boulding, finally finishing only seven minutes behind him in fourth place, nobody else had really been close.

ONCE THE FIRST TEAMS WERE IN, THE WEATHER STARTED TO WARM UP AGAIN. BY the time New Hampshire's George Cook arrived four days behind Schandelmeier, the trail into Whitehorse had literally melted away. The red lantern carrier actually completed the race at a relocated finish line on the Yukon River 20 miles short of Whitehorse. It was the first time since Shirley Lish had been declared a finisher at Carmacks in 1984, also because of rotting river ice, that a musher didn't have to complete the entire distance.

One other driver, Doug Hutchinson of Fairbanks, almost made it to Whitehorse just ahead of Cook, but "lost it" and actually turned around to return to Carmacks. It took him 18 hours to return to the checkpoint, where he scratched from the race. It would have taken him less time to complete the run to the finish line, even if it had still been in Whitehorse.

"Anytime you see a musher who wants to turn back on the trail, you know his mental state has really been affected," said Cook.

1993

Jimmy Hendrick didn't have to wait until the finish line to find out if he was in the money; he knew it before he reached Carmacks. Trundling down the trail to Coghlan Lake, he noticed a wallet lying on the ice and scooped it up as he passed by. Opening it he discovered it was full of cash.

"I thought, 'here is my lucky day.' I figured I could take a trip wherever I wanted." He dug further, finding keys and identification that told him the wallet belonged to Dave Dalton, who he knew was just ahead of him.

As the teams reached the Yukon River just outside of Carmacks, Hendrick passed Dalton.

"Lose something?" he asked casually, with the wallet in plain view stuck under his arm. It turned out that the cash was Dalton's gambling money for Diamond Tooth Gerties in Dawson City. He got it back from Hendrick, but lost it anyway.

AS THE TEAMS RACED ALONG THE YUKON QUEST TRAIL, THEY WERE MORE THAN A little surprised to encounter two skiers pulling pulks (sleds) full of equipment. The two were Bob Baker of Fairbanks and Tim Kelley of Anchorage, 10-year veterans of long distance cross country ski racing in Alaska who had skied the Iditarod Trail in 1990, taking 23 days to complete the 1,000-mile distance.

The Quest represented a unique challenge for them since there were only five locations where they could pick up provisions, compared to the 17 re-supply drops they had had on the Iditarod three years earlier.

By the time they reached Dawson City, 10 days after starting, Kelley was fighting a nagging lung infection and Baker's feet were a mass of bleeding

Bob Baker and Tim Kelley skiing the Yukon Quest trail while pulling pulks, 1993.

blisters. But they were thriving on being fringe participants in an event that had a sense of timelessness to it.

"Here you go days without seeing a snowmachine or a plane. That doesn't happen in Alaska. The only people you see here are mushers. The equipment is different, but essentially, it's the same as it was 100 years ago.

"We have the best view of anyone. We're right out there with them. We have a front row seat and get to meet a lot of mushers. Everyone has a fantasy of what the Yukon or Alaska should be. My vision has come true on this trip."

IT WAS NO SURPRISE THAT HUMANS AND MOOSE SHOULD FINALLY CONFRONT EACH other somewhere along the Quest trail. After 10 years without any problems, heavy snowfalls in the early winter of 1992-93 forced the moose out of their usual haunts in the forest onto machine-made trails, where walking was easier and food more accessible. The trains running to Fairbanks had been colliding with the frightened, hungry ungulates at a record pace all winter long.

Jimmy Hendrick had encountered a moose on dog trails while training near Fairbanks. It hadn't charged his team, but had stomped another team who was running with him. Hendrick acted as an ambulance for one dog who was hurt in the encounter.

Race marshal Ed Salter had encountered a moose while snowmobiling and Iditarod champion Susan Butcher had two dogs injured in a confrontation while training near Fairbanks. Both of these incidents occurred just prior to the start of the Quest.

Charlie Boulding rolled into Angel Creek in a pretty anxious mood. He had spent a half hour "dancing with a cow moose" just outside of the checkpoint. The animal refused to relinquish the trail when Boulding attempted to scare it off. It charged the musher, who dragged his team out of harm's way. Then he broke a new trail around that section of trail, avoiding the angry animal.

Bruce Johnson came along about four hours later and encountered the same moose in the same spot. This time, it ran off as the team approached.

Up until now, it had been "man" meeting moose. Now it was to be Mann meeting moose.

When Jeff Mann arrived, the moose was in a belligerent mood again and charged the team, storming into the middle of the dogs.

"I couldn't believe it. I thought for sure this was the end. After my ordeal on Eagle Summit, I thought I was going to see my dog team killed right in front of me."

Miraculously, none of the dogs were injured by the kicking hooves of the moose. It travelled right through the middle of the team, then crashed into Mann with its front legs, knocking him off the trail. The musher rose like a phoenix out of the snow and the moose retreated momentarily. Then it charged again.

Mann grabbed his axe, swung it over his head and brought the blunt end of the axe head down between the moose's eyes. The moose dropped to its knees. Mann hit it again and it rolled over, dead.

Quest rules require that when a musher kills any wildlife, they must butcher it and deliver it to fish and game department officials. When Mann arrived at Angel Creek, he reported the attack, fed his dogs, then returned on a snowmobile to butcher the carcass.

VETERINARIAN KEN HINCHCLIFF WAS BACK FOR HIS FINAL YEAR OF STUDYING THE physiology of sled dogs. This time he was trying to determine why some dogs finished the race and others didn't.

"The obvious reason for some is they are lame. But there may be a reason why some are more susceptible to lameness than others."

Dogs are dropped by mushers for various reasons — sore muscles, stiffness, virus, injury, dehydration, or pregnancy. Their mental state is important. Some will just stop pulling for no physical reason but simply because they're not happy anymore or just don't want to go any farther. Often, some young dogs are dropped intentionally by the musher who only wanted to run them for half the race anyway, just to give them some experience.

Last year's stress test results had surprised the vet.

"The most surprising thing we found is how minimally stressed they are by competing in a race like this. It was not outside the normal range of a household pet."

Hinchcliff didn't expect any surprise results from this year's testing.

"I don't expect we'll find any earth-shattering reason. But I won't be surprised to find that dropped dogs, even if they are lame, have something in common in their blood."

RIGHT FROM THE START IT WAS CHARLIE BOULDING'S RACE. HE LED THE WAY into Carmacks. In Dawson City, he strolled into the checkpoint just minutes after Quest officials had arrived to set up. They hadn't expected him for another four hours.

His competition initially appeared to be coming from Jeff Mann, so the wily Boulding started playing head games with the younger driver early in the race. When Mann had passed him just before Sulphur, at the foot of the climb over King Solomon Dome, Boulding held back until Mann camped with David Sawatzky. Then he left the marked trail and sneaked around the sleeping duo before coming back onto the trail. It was another hour before Mann and Sawatzky realized what had happened and gave chase.

Then Mann started to make mistakes. Already three hours behind Boulding at Circle City, he was penalized a further 90 minutes for accepting outside help in the checkpoint at Eagle. His headlamp had packed it in, so he borrowed another one from a reporter.

According to the rules, mushers must be self-sufficient for the entire race. They can provide assistance to each other, but, with the single exception of the 36-hour stop in Dawson City, they can't accept any assistance from outside the race (unless that same assistance is offered by the individual to each and every musher). The reporter had only one headlamp and she couldn't offer it to anyone else after it was gone.

Trying to make up extra time, Mann pushed his team and paid the price. His team quit climbing three-quarters of the way up Eagle Summit and laid down.

"Spending a night and a day on a mountain, you learn a lot about humility and humour."

Four teams passed Mann as his dogs sat on the hillside. No one was going to prevent Boulding from becoming the first musher to win the Quest twice, but second place was still up for grabs.

A heavy fog blanketed the Chena River on that final morning. It prevented spotters from reporting what was happening up the trail. No one was surprised to see Boulding roll in, but the second team to arrive caught everyone off guard.

Bruce Johnson and his dogs chugged out of the mist, crossed the line and ground to a halt. Looking over at a startled group of officials which included Will Forsberg, Johnson smiled.

"Sorry. I ain't your wife."

The Canadian musher had been riding in fifth place for most of the race and never really appeared to be a threat. Even as late as Angel Creek, it had appeared that Linda Forsberg and David Sawatzky were the only real contenders for the runner-up spot.

But Johnson, the 1986 winner who had not really been having any fun until he finished the climb over Eagle Summit, decided to liven things up.

"This is the most boring race I've ever been in," he had said the day before. "It's weird. There's nothing happening. It's just a day-to-day grind. I think it's gotta get more exciting. It's got to or I'm gonna die of boredom." At that point, he cut his rest stop short and headed out two hours ahead of his planned departure time.

From Angel Creek, he just let the dogs have their head and hung on, holding off David Sawatzky by three minutes at the finish line, followed 40 minutes later by Forsberg.

THE CLOSEST FINISH CAME FARTHER BACK IN THE PACK. ED HOPKINS WAS following behind Larry Grout in the snow chute with only 100 yards to go, when Grout's leaders suddenly decided they wanted to visit someone in the crowd. The team veered right and started over the top of the snowbank. Hopkins' leaders started to follow, but the musher leaped off the runners, ran ahead and turned them back towards the finish line. Grout did the same and side-by-side they sprinted (as well as anyone can sprint after two weeks on the trail, sort of a slow-motion shuffle on shaky legs) up the chute, the two mushers dragging their teams behind them. Hopkins beat the Alaskan by a stride for 19th place.

JEFF MANN'S PROBLEMS DIDN'T END WHEN HE FINALLY CROSSED THE FINISH LINE and for Frank Turner, the weeks following the race were possibly the worst time he could have imagined ever having on the Quest.

Both mushers had dogs test positive for Ibuprofen, an anti-inflammatory drug used to mask pain. They were fined by the organization, forfeiting half of their winnings (Turner, $1,700 and Mann, $3,250).

Turner accepted the penalty administered. The drug had been given to his dogs accidentally during the 36-hour layover in Dawson City.

Mann appealed his fine, denying the use of the drugs. The original ruling was upheld when re-testing showed that the dogs had indeed been given the drug. Mann still maintains he did not administer the drugs to his dogs and hasn't entered the Quest since.

1994

The past came back to haunt Bruce Cosgrove of North Pole, Alaska, before he even left the start line in Fairbanks. The Quest sends a list of competitors, veterinarians, officials and handlers to both American and Canadian immigration officers for pre-approval in order to reduce the paperwork in Dawson City and Eagle when the teams cross the border. Entrants can be deemed inadmissible if they have a criminal record for indictable offences, but exceptions can be made if it is deemed to be in the interests of the country.

Only once has anyone been refused clearance to enter the country by either side. Cosgrove was denied entry to Canada in 1994. When apprised of the situation, the Quest organization started negotiating with Canadian Immigration to reverse their decision and, at the same time, allow Cosgrove to start the race. The decision to deny entry was not reversed, even after his team left the start chute.

"With an event that is this important to the community," said Canada immigration manager Piers Drew in Whitehorse, "we make every effort to make decisions as favourably as possible. At the same time, the Immigration Act can't be declared null and void because the race is going on."

As the organization tried to figure out how to inform Cosgrove of the decision, he took the pressure off everyone by scratching at Central because of sick dogs.

THE MEMORY OF BRUCE JOHNSON WAS ON EVERYONE'S MIND DURING THE 1994 race, but it was foremost in Peter Butteri's mind when the Yukon River ice started to crack under his team just outside of Eagle.

"I was scared. I was as scared as I've ever been on a dog team. I thought about Bruce for a second, and then..." his front six dogs went through the ice. Then the sled dropped. Totally helpless, Butteri just clung to the sled wondering if he should let go or hang on.

Underneath the first layer of ice, there was a second one, but it also was starting to crack. Butteri grabbed his lead dogs and dragged the team to thicker ice near the bank of the river.

"I'm afraid of rivers to begin with. That's why I have trouble with them. I don't like to train on them."

THERE IS A SCULPTURE IN EAGLE, ALASKA — A SMALL SILVER GLOBE IMPALED ON a pedestal in a small park. It commemorates the arrival of Norwegian arctic explorer Roald Amundsen in Eagle in 1905. At that time, the isolated community was the northernmost communications link on the continent. Amundsen had just finished discovering the Northwest Passage (the navigable water link between the Atlantic and Pacific oceans across the north end of North America) and came to this place to broadcast that fact to the world.

Eighty-nine years later, his granddaughter, Suzan Amundsen, drives her Yukon Quest team off the Yukon River and into Eagle. It takes a special kind of person to explore unknown corners of the world under the most brutal of environmental conditions. If Amundsen was anything like his granddaughter, it's no wonder he left his mark on history.

Suzan Amundsen started this race by wearing to the banquet "the" dress, a strapless sequined number designed to make it perfectly clear that she was all woman, even if she was just a rookie.

By the time the single mother of two girls reached Eagle, she was unrecognizable. Swathed in layers of parka, fur mitts, snowpants and boots, she hadn't washed in five days. Her hair hadn't been combed. It hung like dreadlocks "with rats in it." Her eyes were puffy from fatigue. Her face was raw and peeling where the frostbite had gotten at it. The only thing left over from the banquet, where every male eye in the place followed her every move, was the red polish on her fingernails.

A few days earlier, while she was at 101 Lodge, waiting to go over Eagle Summit, a man approached her, looking her over closely, obviously uncertain to whom he was going to talk. Finally, in an incredulous voice, he asked, "Are you the woman who wore the dress to the banquet?"

She laughed. "Talk about deterioration."

Suzan Amundsen.

In a year where the minus 50-degree temperatures and stiff north winds knocked several more experienced mushers out of the race with frostbite and viruses, Amundsen was still having fun learning how to run the Quest. Even when her handler quit in Central, informing her that, in addition to driving the dogs, Amundsen would also have to figure out how to get her truck to Dawson City and Whitehorse, she simply waxed philosophical.

"It's a drag being a handler for someone at the back. I realize that, but I never intended to be at the front."

By Eagle she still hadn't figured out how to get the truck from Fairbanks, but her drive to finish was stronger than her concern over the lack of a handler down the trail.

"I just want to finish. I didn't cut my finger off (referring to David Sawatzky, who almost severed a finger in the first day of the race, forcing him to scratch). My dogs didn't balk going over the summit.

"I'm going to be a heck of a dog driver by the time I'm done this race."

Taping chemical warmer packets onto her feet, sticking some under her parka and into her mitts, Amundsen headed back out into the cold to pack her sled. On the way out of Eagle, she turned down Amundsen Street and passed by the small sculpture which she acknowledged with a brief nod of her head.

"MAYBE I'LL FIND MY BRAINS IN HERE," MUTTERED BARRY EMMETT AS HE rummaged through his sled in Circle City, looking for his mandatory gear. The Fairbanks musher was, of course, questioning his sanity just as any musher should.

The comment came at the tail end of a day where he had temporarily blinded himself by rubbing his eyes when he had foot cream for the dogs on his hands. The dogs hadn't been cooperating. He had arrived in Circle hours after everyone else had left and there wasn't any food in the checkpoint for him.

"The first half of my day was the worst. I was going to shoot the dogs, shoot myself and scratch. It was terrible. This race can be the ultimate downer at times."

Later, his dogs fed and a couple of hours of sleep under his belt, he headed out again.

Approaching Eagle a few days later, he was "taken hostage by a wolf" near Trout Creek. At first, the predator stalked him from behind, then it sprinted up ahead of the team and parked itself in the middle of the trail. The team stopped and for a moment Emmett, dogs and wolf just stared at each other under the northern lights. Then Emmett threw a piece of ice at the animal and it scampered away into the cold dark, not coming back.

His arctic survival skills were tested to the maximum in this race. For most of it, he had to cope with temperatures near minus 50 degrees. Then, in the last two days, he encountered fierce head winds that buried the trail with drifting snow and knocked over the trail markers. For much of that time he broke trail for his team and led the dogs through the deep snow. It was a time when Emmett discovered the depth of the energy reserves that nature instills in all of us, to be drawn upon when there's nothing else left.

"When you're exhausted and feel like you can't move, you find you have a little more because you know you have to spend an hour taking care of the dogs."

The Fairbanks musher was a collector of red lanterns from races he had entered. Already, he had five or six hanging on his wall at home.

"People pay attention to who's one, two, three and who's last. The middle ones are also-rans."

He crossed the line with all 13 of his dogs in harness, with their tails high and grins on their faces after almost 18 days on the trail.

"They're good dogs, a little brain-dead at times, but so was I when I signed up."

WHEN LARRY "COWBOY" SMITH ARRIVED IN CIRCLE CITY, HE WAS TOLD HE HAD recorded the fastest time ever between Circle and Central. He shrugged.

"There's a difference between what looks like what went on out there and what really went on out there."

That observation came early in the race, but it summed up perfectly the 1994 Yukon Quest. It was a race in which the winner was virtually ignored until the final checkpoint. And where a slight, painfully shy woman made a decision about who wasn't going to win, thus determining who would.

The pace was frantic, even with the cold temperatures and swirling winds. Dawson City's Cor Guimond led the way over Eagle Summit with John Barron and Smith nipping at his heels. Then Linda Forsberg led the charge to Circle City, followed by John Schandelmeier, Jim Wilson and Kathy Swenson.

Swenson was the first into Eagle, then she and Forsberg led the way out of the Yukon River ice fog into Dawson City with Schandelmeier and Guimond close behind. It was the first time a woman had led the race into Dawson City to claim the four ounces of gold for being the first to arrive.

Swenson led the way up the dike towards the checkpoint, then her team veered left. Forsberg, right behind, sank her snow hook, waited for Swenson to regroup, then followed her into the checkpoint. She hadn't realized that there were four ounces of gold waiting for the first team to finish. Had she passed Swenson, the gold would have been hers.

"Don't forget," admonished Will Forsberg when Linda was preparing to leave 36 hours later. "First one into Whitehorse gets $20,000. Second one gets $16,000."

"I know that," she snapped back. Her team continued to roll, leading the way into Carmacks.

Jim Wilson had arrived just behind Forsberg in Carmacks and was surprised to find, not Guimond, Swenson or Schandelmeier riding behind him, but Lavon Barve just six minutes back. Wilson had been studying all the other teams, looking for the weaknesses and strengths of each, but until Carmacks he hadn't had an opportunity to view the dogs trotting in behind him. They looked a lot stronger than he would have liked.

The pre-race advice given to Barve, from Wasilla, Alaska, was to hang back, take care of his dogs and start racing in Carmacks. Riding along in 14th place for most of the early going, the veteran of 12 Iditarods (finishing as high as third in 1990) realized near Dawson City that he may be hanging back a little too far. Every stretch of the race had been run in record time and the leaders had been gradually pulling away. He started to slowly inch up in the standings, moving to seventh out of Dawson and, finally, third into Carmacks.

Lavon Barve, Yukon Quest champion, 1994.

There was a unique quality to the team driven by Linda Forsberg. Hers was the only team that Barve didn't believe he could beat. Hers was the team that Guimond, now back in seventh place, believed would win the race.

Forsberg is unlike any other musher who runs at the front of the pack. She is competitive, but won't push her dogs just to win. Her strengths are the power and speed of her team, a result of the meticulous care she lavishes on the dogs. This was not the first time she had brought a team that was capable of winning the race, but it was the first time she was really in a position to do it.

Her dogs fed and resting, Forsberg sat in the checkpoint with husband Will. Their hands interlocked, they talked quietly between themselves. Finally, one line emerged from the intimate conversation, overheard by only one other person in the room.

"I don't want to win this race. I don't think I could get up in front of all those people."

From her husband, "O.K."

When Forsberg reached Coghlan Lake, she was still alone in front with no one in sight on the trail behind her. She stopped and made camp.

Eventually, Barve passed her, then Wilson came by 15 minutes later. Still, for five hours, she sat and waited before finally pulling the hook again. This decision satisfied her need to give the dogs the best care possible and the shyness that made her so reluctant for public acclaim. But it probably cost her the opportunity to become the first woman to win the Yukon Quest.

When Barve motored across the finish line in Whitehorse — two hours ahead of Wilson, who had finally hit the wall and was walking slowly down the river — he had knocked 18 hours off the previous record time.

"I said I just wanted to have fun. I guess that was fun."

Wilson dragged himself and his dogs in for second place, arriving just five minutes ahead of Forsberg.

"I got a little lucky today [being able to finish ahead of Forsberg]," said Wilson. "There were some tired dogs out there. We were kinda barely moving."

Peter Butteri tried to steal fourth place from Schandelmeier and Swenson that night. He switched off his headlamp and passed a cabin where the two teams were parked. But they were listening to the radio and the announcer gave away the trick since there was a reporter standing right there. Schandelmeier did catch Butteri, but Swenson ran out of steam and hung on for sixth.

1995

In 1980, 15 years earlier, Larry "Cowboy" Smith changed long distance sled dog racing forever. He had entered the Iditarod — at that time the only long distance race in the world — and said it could be completed in 10 days. Then he set out to do exactly that. Prior to his arrival, the Iditarod was a glorified camping trip for 800 miles, then an all-out sprint for the final 200. The winner usually finished in just over 15 days.

Smith started out racing and applied relentless pressure from beginning to end in every race. He never achieved the 10-day standard, nor did he ever win the Iditarod (his highest finish was third, in 1983), but his intensity spurred other teams to strive for the same goal. The 10-day time limit was reached, then breached. The "Cowboy," who hasn't raced the Iditarod since 1983, is still a legend in the villages along the Iditarod Trail.

It had been a long time since Smith had the type of team that he could drive relentlessly and the last time it had happened, in 1983, he had been 12 years younger. His 1995 Quest team had all the appearances of those glory days and the way Smith drove them, it looked like he had shed years off his age. But Smith also had a history and, in the end, it was history, along with the eternally patient, persistent Frank Turner, who won the day.

The start line in Whitehorse, 1995.

Smith rolled in and out of each checkpoint the same way — quickly, quietly and efficiently. Trotting along in his wake were Cor Guimond, Jay Cadzow, Turner and pre-race favourite Jim Wilson. Always the first to arrive and usually the first to go, there was no doubt about who was setting the pace.

"You separate the faster teams from the slower teams to here," said Cadzow, keeping an eye on the activities at the Carmacks checkpoint. "Everyone that gets here is going to keep an eye on everyone else. From here, it's a mind game. If Smith goes 40 miles before resting, I'll go 40. If he goes 50, I'll go 50. Never trust him."

There was Smith the legend ("He's tough. He's as tough as they come," admired Guimond), intense, private, always pushing for that little extra edge that could put him over the top. And there was the Smith that nobody knew except those drivers who spent time with him on the trail (a great sense of humour, a sense of fair play, the entertainer — "It depends on which side you see of him," said Turner).

As hard as he pushed, with speed records falling between every checkpoint, Smith just couldn't shake his four pursuers. Then, just as it looked like he had gained the edge he needed, history interfered.

Smith was 200 yards from the peak of Eagle Summit on the steepest portion of the ascent. He finally had the time buffer he needed. Once over the top, with the lead he had finally manufactured in the approach to the final hurdle, "Cowboy" could have walked to Fairbanks and still won the Quest, but his dogs decided they had had enough and lay down, just 200 yards from winning the Quest.

In his Iditarod years, Smith hadn't found a team that could match his stamina; they faded in the final stretch every time. In 1995, on Eagle Summit, he discovered that this team, possibly the best one he had ever driven, just couldn't do it either. Smith anchored the sled, fed the dogs and settled down to rest. He would complete the event, but for him the still-elusive dream of victory was over.

Once over the top, it was the speed of Turner that took control.

"If there's a proper way to do this race, Turner did it right," said Wilson. "We came in pretty good to Angel Creek; we were moving what I thought was pretty fast, but he was flying. Frank was sort of holding back all this whole race. I only really saw him in Dawson City and I didn't see him again until he caught me coming into Angel Creek. That's when I knew he had a real good team."

Turner had known since Eagle that he had the fastest team on the trail. "I don't think there's a team right now that can catch me if I get a lead, not after what I've seen over the past few days," he said in Central. That speed had enabled him to stop and rest his team more often while still keeping in touch with the front pack. His biggest worry had been not letting Smith get too much of a jump on him over Eagle Summit. He found it impossible to hide the emotions that threatened to overwhelm him at the end.

The previous two years had provided trials for Turner, almost forcing the musher, who was considered "too nice" to be a serious contender, to develop a mental toughness to go along with his physical prowess.

His fine, in 1993, for drug use involving his dogs had been a personal challenge for the Quest veteran, who had developed a reputation for quality dog care. The death of his friend Bruce Johnson that same year, then his being forced to scratch in 1994 due to sickness (Turner was ill, not his dogs), had both been devastating experiences.

"I sort of owed it to the dogs and to a lot of people to make sure we didn't underachieve on this one," he choked out the words. "Winning has never been a motivation for me. It's never been a personal goal.

"I had a lot of time to think about what winning means on a personal level and on a competitive level. Often during this race, I have felt very close to Bruce. I think the way I ran this race is really closely associated with him. This would have been Bruce's type of race."

Jay Cadzow was also delighted that Turner, the only musher to have entered all of the Yukon Quests, had won.

"We're all tired, but the toughest team won. That's good for the race, because now Frank has to come back and defend his title."

BUCK, FRANK TURNER'S LEAD DOG, NEVER LET FAME TURN HIS HEAD. WHEN Buck and Turner appeared on CTV's Canada AM show the morning after their win, while Turner fielded the questions, it was Buck who provided the program's most memorable moment.

In front of a television audience of millions across Canada, Buck first of all tried to find comfort by burying his head under a pillow on the couch. Failing that, he promptly started to clean himself, as a dog will, by licking his testicles.

WHILE WOMEN AS MUSHERS HAVE THEIR PLACE AMONG THE ELITE ATHLETES OF the long distance dog driving world, there were no female race marshals prior to 1995.

Lorrina Mitchell of Whitehorse, a three-time veteran of the Quest and, in 1984, the first woman to finish the event, was race marshal for the 1995 Yukon Quest.

The appointment was initially greeted with skepticism and apprehension, a nervousness which seemed to boil over when Mitchell was confronted by her first major crisis.

The snow cover on the trail between Whitehorse and Carmacks was thin, exposing large stumps and deadfall (fallen trees lying across the trail). Teams travelling fast through the woods, especially at night, faced a very strong possibility of injuring themselves badly.

Bush trails are never flat.

Mitchell ordered all the teams to drop two dogs before starting in Whitehorse, then granted them the right to put the teams back in harness in Carmacks. Having fewer dogs would slow the teams down, she said, creating safer conditions.

The mushers revolted temporarily. ("I didn't train my dogs to run 800 miles. I trained them to run 1,000," grumbled one musher.) When Mitchell refused to be cowed by the uproar, they grudgingly obeyed. Mitchell proceeded to make arrangements for the teams to be able to make extensive sled repairs in Carmacks, then put first aid workers and veterinarians on alert. She also decided not to accept any scratches from mushers who had just arrived.

"We'll let them rest first. Then, if they still want to scratch, we'll let them," she said.

"It was the right decision," said Frank Turner when he arrived in Carmacks. "It was simply brutal out there. The more dogs we would have had, the more dogs we would have hurt."

There were no further challenges to Mitchell's authority. She was invited back for the 1996 race, but declined because of personal commitments.

Mitchell also became known for another idiosyncrasy. She has an intense dislike for small aircraft and refused to fly over the trail or to the Eagle checkpoint. Instead, she assigned those jobs to her race judges and, when the teams left Dawson City, she drove almost 1,000 highway miles to rejoin the race at Central.

HIGH FASHION MET THE BUNNY BOOT IN 1995.
With the Quest facing financial hardship, internationally known Vancouver fashion designer Catherine Regehr (whose dresses hang in Neiman Marcus, Holt Renfrew, Saks and on the bodies of various singers, Hollywood actresses and politicians on the world stage) offered her assistance.

She volunteered to show her fall line of outfits at a professionally produced fashion show staged as a fundraiser for the Quest. For Regehr, a veteran of shows in all of the fashion capitals of the world, the Whitehorse show ranked as one of the most nerve-wracking she had ever put on.

She was born and raised in Whitehorse and still owned property near Atlin Lake, about 100 miles south of Whitehorse. The north, she claimed, was her inspiration and this is where she came when she needed a time and place to get creative. The Quest, she said, symbolized all that she believed the north to be and that was why she made the offer to assist in fundraising for the event.

The show also unveiled a hitherto unknown side of quest veteran Jeninne Cathers. Celebrating her 24th birthday on stage as one of the models, she strutted the high fashion garments in high heels, then traded in the fancy footwear for bunny boots.

"The first thing I wanted to be was a can-can dancer. If I didn't have a dog team, I would probably have been a dancer, but I don't think that not having a dog team will ever happen."

THEY CALLED DIETER ZIRNGIBL THE "MUNICH COWBOY." THIS MEANT THAT for much of the race, there was a cowboy at either end of the standings.

Mushing was just another challenge for the bulky German. He had already played professional football, been a sea captain for 30 years, captured the German national power-lifting championship three times and wrestled professionally.

"That's one of my big problems. I just keep fulfilling my dreams. I was a professional wrestler when I was 19, not because I needed the dollars, but because I wanted to get into that kind of circus."

Despite the fact that one of Tim Mowry's dogs used his sled as a fire hydrant on the Takhini River, Zirngibl was captivated by the north and the whole idea of the Yukon Quest.

"I always think, when I pass along the trail, about the old mail carriers who did it, the gold diggers who did it. After the Klondike, there wasn't so much gold, so they went to Alaska and I think about how they weren't as well equipped as we are."

For someone who is used to testing his capabilities, Zirngibl encountered conditions unlike anything his years at sea could have prepared him for. Travelling with Alaskan Kurt Smith from the Fortymile River to Eagle, Zirngibl drove his team above the treeline on American Summit into a blizzard. The snow swirled so thickly that neither driver could see his team in front of him. The howling wind made communication impossible.

Standing nose-to-nose, the two shouted at each other, trying to figure out the safest way to battle the storm. First they tried leading their teams by hand. That worked for a while but the sleds, without their drivers, kept falling over into the soft snow. Even Zirngibl, the powerlifting champion, had never encountered a harder nor more vital lift than putting the sleds upright again.

Then they worked together, one taking the lead dog, the other handling the sled. Slowly, they led the team through the whiteout. After awhile, they would secure that team, then crawl back on their hands and knees to locate and bring forward the second team.

Five times they repeated this procedure before they dropped down out of the winds. The experience generated a bond between the two drivers and they drove together for four days, the flamboyant German and the unassuming Alaskan, until they reached Central. There Smith scratched with sick dogs while Zirngibl travelled over Eagle Summit and down the Chena River to etch his name in Yukon Quest lore.

THE 1995 QUEST WAS GOING TO BE THE BEGINNING OF THE END FOR BOB Holder, and he came awfully close to finishing before he even began.

Holder, a veteran of several Quests, Iditarods and numerous other shorter races over the previous several years, was on his way to Whitehorse when his truck left the road near Haines Junction. While the accident didn't damage dogs, musher or truck, it did prevent him from being present at the mushers' meeting the morning of the day prior to the race start. Technically, missing the meeting means automatic disqualification.

However, race marshal Lorrina Mitchell waived the rules, saying that Holder's absence was due to circumstances beyond his control.

When the Alaskan musher left the start line on his way to Fairbanks, it was the beginning of a three-race odyssey that he had decided to complete before finally retiring from the sport.

Holder did start and finish the Quest, the Iditarod and the Hope Race (across the Bering Strait from Alaska to Russia), the only person to have completed all three races in the same year.

1996

Every person has their limit of endurance. Most people will never reach that level; a few will exceed it. And when they do, they become a danger, not only to themselves, but to everyone and everything around them.

Most of the mushers on the Quest have tottered on the edge of going over their limit. They hallucinate. They fall asleep while travelling along the trail. They lose control momentarily. It is the result of sleep and food deprivation, which weakens the physical body and befuddles the intellectual capacity. Most of the time, they can pull themselves back by taking an extra couple of hours of sleep or eating a meal while stopping to feed the dogs.

Every once in a while someone hits the wall, going completely over the edge. When that happens, they become incapable of caring for themselves or their teams.

Dieter Dolif, a 56-year old doctor from Munich, Germany, stopped just outside of Eagle. He camped for a day and a half, for no apparent reason, since the checkpoint was only a couple of hours ahead of him. He started to get hypothermic. Still totally disoriented, he headed off down another trail in the wrong direction. Searchers sent out from Eagle by concerned race officials located him, got him turned around, then led him to Eagle where he scratched.

Bill Stewart was just 40 miles from the finish line, almost to Takhini Hot Springs. The team was working like a piston engine, smooth and flawless. The charge was on. He was riding the heels of the two lead teams, not making any ground at this point, but not losing any either.

Then he lost it.

Frank Turner suddenly appeared to Stewart to turn a corner ahead of Stewart (the real Turner was several hours behind) riding a small sled, pulled by a small team.

"This is my own private training trail," said the illusionary Turner. "Besides that, you're going the wrong way."

Stewart turned the team around and headed back up the trail for four hours. He encountered a real life Mark May.

"Hey. You're going the wrong way buddy," shouted May. So Stewart obediently turned the team around again and started heading back towards Whitehorse. Then he came across Larry "Cowboy" Smith (who wasn't even in the 1996 race, but still back at his home in Dawson City).

"There's a hotel over there," said the fictional Smith. "Go get a room." Stewart stopped his team and walked into the centre of a small meadow. Unable to locate his hotel, he lay down in the snow and fell asleep. It was minus 25 degrees. Stewart hadn't eaten for over 24 hours. He hadn't slept in almost two days. Since losing the ability to make rational decisions, it had been close to 10 hours since his dogs had last eaten, been watered or had a rest stop.

The real life Mark May came up the trail. Spotting the stationary team, he stopped and went looking for Stewart. He found him, then led him back to the sled.

"He suggested we get some sleep and reorganize ourselves. He wasn't sure where we were geographically and I was psychologically lost. It had the potential of being really bad out there for myself and my dogs had Mark not arrived. From that perspective, I owe him a big debt."

The Stewart incident brought to light the fact that, while veterinarians and race officials are constantly monitoring the condition of the dogs on the trail, there is very little attention paid to the condition of the musher.

It is, according to Frank Turner, a health and safety issue that needs to be addressed. "There are some real issues there that might be worthwhile discussing. The results of Bill's experience could have been far more serious."

Stewart did finish the race, in third place. He retired from long distance and competitive dog mushing. Several of his dogs suffered damage as a result of the long period of time that they ran without any food or water and they never raced again, something that Stewart regrets to this day.

SCOTLAND'S ALISTAIR TAYLOR WAS FERRYING SCIENTISTS AROUND THE ANTARCTIC in 1994 when he heard about the Yukon Quest. One of his trips took him near a construction project which had been contracted out to Pelly Construction, a Yukon company. A few of the workers told Taylor about the race and suggested he might be interested. He was.

"They were quite a bunch of characters, those guys, telling tall stories about the Yukon. They were always going on about the Yukon Quest, so I'm hoping one of those guys will buy me a beer when I get to Whitehorse."

TECHNOLOGY ARRIVED IN 1996, WHEN THE QUEST HAD VETERINARIANS INSERT microchips into all the dogs prior to the race.

Under the rules, it is illegal to substitute for dogs that are hurt or sick and have to be dropped. The only means of keeping track of which dogs were originally in the team had been to mark their forehead with a dab of paint. This wasn't a popular method since it was neither pleasing to the eye nor good for the dogs when they licked their fur.

Until microchips came along, however, there wasn't any other reliable method of monitoring the dogs. Using a needle, the microchips are inserted under the skin just between the dogs' shoulder blades. Each microchip has its own code number which is picked up by a monitor passed over the animal at each checkpoint.

The microchips can be left in the dogs since they do no harm and can be used again in following years. Other races that use the same technology can use the same chip. The code number is distinctive to that animal alone.

The communications systems used by the Quest to maintain radio contact with isolated dog drops and unofficial stops along the trail also went high tech in 1996.

Mobile Satellite (MSAT) radios were used for the first time and proved to be a resounding success. About the size of a briefcase and as heavy as a suitcase twice its size, the units are essentially telephones that use specific satellites to connect with the regular telephone system. Unlike ham radios, they aren't restricted by environmental conditions. As long as the receiving-sending dish can be pointed into the southern sky, the phone will work.

The technology was subjected to the Quest's greatest challenge, the communications "black hole" that surrounded the Scroggie Creek dog drop. Although various forms of equipment had been hauled into the dog drop over the years, nothing seemed to be able to reach the outside world.

The MSAT delivered to the camp went into operation the first day and continued to grind out information until the battery unit died. The aircraft that was bringing in the generator to recharge the batteries was prevented from landing by low clouds.

ON THE SURFACE, THE BELT BUCKLE LOOKED LIKE A GREAT IDEA. APPRAISED AT A value of $60,000 U.S., it was made from gold, silver and turquoise and studded with 186 diamonds. It weighed 13 ounces and it cost the Yukon Quest absolutely nothing. The buckle was a donation from Dieter Zirngibl's business partner, Alex Durek of Munich, Germany. It was to be awarded to the winner of the 1996 Yukon Quest.

But there was a catch that the donor never anticipated. The winner of the Quest would have to pay tax on the buckle — almost as much tax as the $25,000 purse. "I couldn't afford to win even if I did win," joked John Schandelmeier at the start banquet. "I need that money to take care of my team."

Durek came up with the perfect solution. He had his lawyers draw up a document which guaranteed he would loan the buckle to the winner of the

1996 Quest indefinitely, until the winner either sent it back to Durek or died, in which case it would be returned to Durek.

THE FINISH BANQUET, WHICH WAS PLANNED FOR A FRIDAY NIGHT, WAS postponed, midway through the race, for 48 hours. "We thought it might be a good idea to have some mushers at the banquet," said one of the race organizers. The banquet schedule had been based upon results from previous races. Had the teams encountered the fast conditions of the past few years they might have finished the race in under 11 days. But heavy snowfalls and water, where there should have been ice, had bogged the race down early. It would take over 12 days for the first team to finish.

"In the winter we call it overflow," muttered Paddy Santucci, while sitting in one of the small cabins at 101 Lodge, in the shadow of Eagle Summit. "In the spring, we call it water. This, the first patch of overflow just past Angel Creek, was water."

Dieter Zirngibl spent almost an hour up to his chest in the frigid water, fishing out his dogs, sled and equipment, while shouting warnings at the teams coming behind him. Dieter Dolif, a doctor from Germany, tried to go

Jon Rudolph (l), Susan Whiton (r) and drying booties and gear, Eagle, 1987.

around the hole, but his team tangled. As he tried to creep along the edge to help the dogs, his feet slipped and he plunged into the hole.

"I took a bath at minus 40 degrees."

Haines musher Dan Turner helped drag one sled out of the water, then had to rescue two dogs who were tangled up in the frigid water and in danger of drowning.

Beyond the deep hole the trail was covered by almost six inches of snow, which effectively disguised other, less deep, overflows. If dogs' feet get wet, they get sore, and the teams travel more slowly. At 101 Lodge, finally past the overflow area, mushers and vet worked relentlessly, applying foot ointment and checking for any more serious problems.

"All this fresh snow," muttered Jeninne Cathers, "it could be worse. We could have a big storm blowing."

When Frank Turner reached the top of Rosebud Summit, he found himself at the tail end of a convoy of sleds, backed up behind Peter Butteri and John Schandelmeier, who were out front trying to slug a trail through the snow.

The snow and overflow never stopped coming. Outside of Eagle, it was snowing so hard that Suzan Amundsen couldn't see. "I needed wipers on my goggles."

John Schandelmeier, Yukon Quest champion, 1992 and 1996.

While Bill Stewart and rookie Rick Mackey stuck close for most of the race, they had basically conceded that the 1996 Quest was John Schandelmeier's to win or lose.

Even as early as Eagle, Mackey dismissed his chances of winning. He pointed out that he had dropped four dogs already and was down to 10 while Schandelmeier was still running with his full complement of 14.

"John will have to go the wrong way to lose the race," he muttered. Putting himself into the underdog role is part of the head game that Mackey plays with his competitors. But there weren't many in Eagle, or anywhere else along the trail, who would question his observation that year.

Schandelmeier held the lead and broke trail most of the way, a gamble, since that strategy had backfired on most other teams who had tried it. It wasn't his idea, he insisted, it was because nobody else wanted to do the job. He publicly fretted about what the extra effort might be ultimately costing him and his dogs.

"You know, if you want help breaking trail...slow down. Wait for us," said Stewart at one point. Schandelmeier just grinned and pulled the snow hook.

"He has broken every inch of this trail," said Mark May. "We have to buy him a dozen roses. The whole thing stinks, but the only way he can get away from it is to let one of us lead."

Schandelmeier never really did let anyone take the lead from him. He simply observed in Carmacks, when the top four teams arrived within minutes of each other, that the apparent closeness of the race was an "illusion" of the true picture of who was actually in control of the race.

They were still only minutes apart on Coghlan Lake, but when Schandelmeier rolled off the Yukon River and into the finish chute on the Whitehorse waterfront, there was no one else in sight.

RACE JUDGE JOE MAY JUST SHOOK HIS HEAD IN DISBELIEF WHEN OLD CROW musher Stanley Njootli reached the finish line to claim the red lantern four days later.

"That's the healthiest looking team I've ever seen arrive in the red lantern position," he said. "I'm really impressed with what Stan has done and with what he's learned about dog care since he started this race. I was quite worried about the dogs after his team came over Eagle Summit, they looked so bad. But everyone looks bad after Eagle Summit. When I went out to talk to him, I watched him with the dogs and decided to just let it go and see how they did.

"Ever since then, they've just looked better and better."

Races of future past

1997

Just in case anyone got lost on the trail that year, all they had to do was find Mike King to figure out where they were. King was so thrilled with finishing the Quest in 1996 that he had his finishing time tattooed on his left shoulder, directly above the full colour tattoo of the trail map which covers most of the top part of his back.

IN 1997, THE MEDIA, IN ADDITION TO REPORTING THE RACE, BECAME PART OF the story.

It started with the arrival of the "Red Army," a group of 30 German television and print media journalists who were brought to the race by the event's first European sponsor, Fulda Reifen, Goodyear Tire's European tire manufacturer and distributor.

The journalists didn't do anything to attract attention to themselves. But Whitehorse, in the middle of winter, is a pretty sleepy town until the pre-race activities of the Quest start to wake up the population in early February. To roll over and find 30 red parka-clad journalists (thus the name Red Army) running around in your front yard comes as a bit of a shock.

The shock was even greater for the village of Carmacks and for Dawson City, both of which have winter populations of under 1,000. By the time the Red Army reached Eagle, it had been pared down to seven (the others had to return to Germany because their newspapers or magazines couldn't afford to have them away for two weeks).

In addition to the German journalists, two French television crews also arrived. (They made headlines later when three of their journalists were deposited by a helicopter on the wrong trail, then had to spend a very cold night out in the bush.) A reporter from *Paris Match* came, a TV crew from Japan turned up, and Canada's own CBC sent out a camera as well. Add these extra 45 people to the usual crew of journalists who cover the event, and the Quest organization was suddenly faced with an unprecedented media presence and a logistical dilemma.

In addition to finding itself in unexpected competition for accommodations and facilities along the trail, the organization also discovered they had gotten complacent in dealing with the media. In previous years, journalists had been experienced and knew how to conduct themselves around the dogs. (For instance, don't make contact with the dogs unless told you can do so by the musher. When a team is travelling up the trail, you can be close but not too close, otherwise the dogs will get distracted. Don't disturb them while they're resting.)

The new journalists weren't familiar with the rules and, on occasion, made mistakes. In Pelly Crossing, some of the German journalists wandered around through the dogs during dog rest time. Mushers complained about the intrusion and expressed concern that an inexperienced person could potentially step on one of the dogs, causing injury. The journalists were warned and it didn't occur again.

John Schandelmeier left the Dawson City checkpoint late at night and trotted down onto the Yukon River. Suddenly, he and the team were blinded by a spotlight from the CBC television camera. "Turn that damn thing off," raged Schandelmeier as he untangled his confused dogs.

However, the journalists also added dimensions of media coverage to the race that hadn't existed before. Few journalists have ever seen Eagle Summit. Most of the stories written are from descriptions given by the mushers. No documentaries in previous years had included scenes from the Eagle Summit area. In 1997, a tent was set up at the summit specifically for the media. Only a few television crews actually used it, but they produced some of the most extraordinary video footage ever taken of the Yukon Quest.

Frank Turner noticed them right away.

"It was icy and we were struggling up the hill and I was breathing so hard. I just couldn't get enough air and I was gasping and choking. And I get to the top and there's this big, grey, furry thing — the microphone — stuck almost in my face, recording every wheeze I made. And the TV camera is there and everything. I'd never seen anything like that up on Eagle."

They also assisted the Quest organization. When a communications tower went off the air between Eagle and Dawson City, the Red Army provided their helicopter to Quest organizers, allowing them to fly over the trail to check the location of the teams and to lift a technician up to the tower for repairs.

BY THE TIME THE DOG DOCTORS REACHED DAWSON CITY, THEY NEEDED A people doctor. A flu bug rampaged through the ranks of the veterinarians in the early stages of the race. Combined with the lack of sleep they normally have to endure, the vets were physically and emotionally burned out when they finally rolled into Dawson. Although Dawson has always been a place for them to rest up before facing the second half of the race, it was never needed more than it was in 1997.

Several vets were bedridden for their entire stay in Dawson, putting an extra load on the healthier vets. One of them was finally sent home because he hadn't been able to assist in any way since Carmacks and didn't seem to be recovering. He was only the first in a slow trickle of vets leaving the race because they were too ill to continue.

Races of future past

It was an unfortunate postscript for a veterinary program that had established a new standard for pre-race care and was breaking new ground with portable ECGs so the dogs' hearts could be monitored along the trail. Head veterinarian Wendy Royle had started a series of kennel visits three months prior to the race so the mushers could have the benefit of a Quest vet in the training stage. The purpose of the visits was to enable her to monitor all of the Quest entries and possibly identify any problems that might occur before the dogs ever reached the start line. The program was voluntary, but all the mushers took part.

When the dogs went through their mandatory pre-race physicals, the attending vets were impressed.

"These dogs are in the best shape I've ever seen before a Quest," said Whitehorse vet Jim Kenyon.

The tests conducted along the way enabled the vets to monitor the recovery rate of the dogs when they were resting and possibly pick up any heart irregularities that might not have shown up before the race.

A manual, compiled by Royle, was published by the Quest. It contained articles on dog care written by veterinarians. It was the first manual of its sort to deal exclusively with the care of racing dogs.

Vet Wendy Royle (l) and "Cowboy" Smith (r) examining a dog.

"That manual is like a bible to me," said Frank Turner. "I keep it on the kitchen table and we read it almost every night. We discuss what it says and how it might apply to my dogs."

Other racing organizations, including the Iditarod, were also provided with copies upon request.

While the flu was devastating the ranks of the veterinary core, Arizona vet Al Hallman, who took over the head vet duties when Royle couldn't continue past Dawson City, was impressed with the performance of the decreasing crew.

"I've said it before and I'll say it again. This, in my mind, is absolutely the best veterinary sled dog care in the world."

THE "THOUSAND-MILE STARE," THAT VACANT, GLAZED LOOK THAT THE MUSHERS start to wear in the later stages of the race, isn't just the result of a lack of sleep or proper nutrition. It is due, in part, to the truth behind the mushing joke, "the view never changes unless you're lead dog."

In an average Quest race, the drivers spend close to 200 hours behind their sleds. There's not a lot that one can do standing on sled runners for that long. Some admire the scenery. Others sing or whistle to themselves. Some fret about where they are, where everyone else is and how far it is to the next checkpoint. For the most part, however, they watch the back ends of their dogs as they trot or walk down the trail ahead of them.

Rookie Dave O'Farrell watches the gait of his dogs. "After you've been out for so long, you know what each dog is supposed to look like and how each dog moves. When it's not moving the way it should be moving, then you know something is wrong."

John Schandelmeier makes note of every little detail. "I spend a lot of time trying to find something going wrong and trying to catch it before it occurs eight or 12 hours down the trail." He looks for and questions the things that ordinary people wouldn't even think about: "When did that dog pee last?" or "What colour is the urine?"

It's the endless hours of watching the back end of their dogs that gives the drivers that empty stare, but it's that constant observation that is the groundwork of good dog care. While the vets at the checkpoint may detect that an animal has problems, it's often the performance of the dog on the trail, and not its condition at the checkpoint, that can identify a potential danger.

Jim Hendrick229 decided to bring all his old canine buddies in 1997. After six years of racing with them, he had grown sentimental about the team members.

By Pelly Crossing, he recognized that his dogs were too old for this game and that it was probably time to start building a new team.

"I don't think we're sunk, but we're definitely leaking bad." He glanced over at his team, now rested and starting to stand up. "I guess owners of a football team must feel the same way when they've had a guy playing the defensive end for 10 years and they've got to look at him and say, 'Guess what? You lost your job.' You care about him, but you've gotta think about the future of the club."

Then, standing up, he headed out toward the dogs who are anxious to get going. "We're ready to go home, to scratch, but we ain't gonna."

CHRIS WILLINGHAM TRAVELS FROM HOUSTON, TEXAS, TO SPEND A MIDWINTER holiday in Dawson City every year. Her presence is the result of one comment made to her during a discussion about dog mushing several years earlier. "You don't know anything unless you know about the Yukon Quest." She is one of a surprisingly large number of people who travel from around the world to help in one way or another with the Quest.

In 1997, Jamie Main, a former Royal Marine from Perth, Scotland, was spending his midwinter holiday working in the Quest office in Whitehorse. He had found his way north after stumbling across the Quest web page on Internet.

Willingham is one of the first people the mushers want to see when they reach Dawson City, even though she's not even an official part of the organization or checkpoint. Willingham is a masseuse and she has volunteered massage services to all the mushers, veterinarians and officials.

"The mushers are really sore. They've worked really hard. A lot of them come in really banged up. It's like any athlete who puts forth tremendous effort. They have a build-up of lactic acid and I can help flush some of that out.

"They need to be relaxed by a full body massage. I bring them down, then get them ready to go, mentally and physically."

NEAR TROUT CREEK, JUST PAST EAGLE, RICK MACKEY CAUGHT UP TO THE front three teams, John Schandelmeier, Frank Turner and Mark May. They were together in a cabin, warming up and cooking themselves some food. Their dogs, already fed, were dozing in the snow.

Rather than stopping at the cabin, Mackey decided to sneak past them, then camp a short ways down the trail. Turning off his headlamp, he used the moonlight to guide his team as they slid by silently. Then they stopped and he changed their booties and started feeding them. (He had warm food in a cooler in his sled for the dogs, so he didn't have to start his stove.) Chuckling with delight as he sat back with a cigarette, Mackey tried to imagine the faces of the three when they found him parked ahead of them. They were probably sitting in the cabin thinking that he was taking a longer break in Eagle.

Inside the cabin, his three opponents weren't even entertaining the possibility of Mackey still being in Eagle.

"Why is he out there camping in the cold?" asked Schandelmeier. The other two just shrugged and settled back for a couple of hours of warm napping, chuckling to themselves that Mackey figured he had pulled a fast one on them.

It was that kind of race. The four teams had separated themselves early from the pack, then spent most of their time watching each other and trying to play little games to give themselves an edge, all the while claiming that they just ran their own race and didn't pay attention to what the other drivers were doing.

"Rick tries to create an environment in which he is the underdog," explained Turner. "'Everybody else is against me' is a motivational tool for him. But at that point in the race, the reality was that we weren't racing against Rick Mackey. What he did or didn't do never altered our plan."

Schandelmeier insisted that he never lets anyone else affect his system. "It doesn't matter where the other guy is. If I have a four-hour rest scheduled, then I'm going to take a four-hour rest. The whole race could pass me by and I wouldn't budge. Those dogs need a certain amount of rest and they're going to get it."

Mackey seemed to think he was having an effect. "I got a good break there," he gloated later in Central. "As far as I knew, they didn't know I was there."

In the end, it really wasn't the game playing and strategies that decided the 1997 winner. It was Rick Mackey's sleeping patterns, combined with some alleged outside interference, and a mix-up in the screwdrivers that Frank Turner had with him in Angel Creek.

Four days earlier, approaching King Solomon Dome, the four lead teams stopped at a cabin for a rest. After a short nap, Schandelmeier, Turner and May woke up, then quietly trotted away. Mackay continued to snore as Keizo Funatsu of Japan loped by with his dogs. For four and a half hours after the other teams left, Mackay slept.

Then along came Jerry Louden. He stopped and woke up the sleeping driver. Louden wasn't particularly concerned. He was just curious. Why would one of the favourites be asleep here at Granville (Sulphur) when everyone else was on their way to Dawson?

"How come you're still here?" he asked Mackey. "What did you do? Give up?"

Mackey hadn't given up, but he did have to catch up.

"I thought I had blown it when I didn't wake up at Granville. It was a costly nap in that I had to work awful hard to get back that four hours. But it worked well."

In Dawson City, Mackey fumed over his four and a half hour deficit. Then it seemed to dawn on him that there was a history of teams coming from several hours behind in Dawson to win. He rolled out of Dawson, determined to get himself back in the race, then win it. When he camped at Trout Creek, the first part of his mission had been accomplished.

Until Angel Creek, it had been, for all four lead drivers, one of the most enjoyable Yukon Quests they had ever run.

"I had a good time on the race," smiled Schandelmeier. "It was a good group to travel with. It was interesting because everyone was travelling the same speed. There was no dominating team. It was a matter of who had the best run between Angel Creek and Fairbanks."

At Angel Creek, with only minutes separating the top four teams, the need to sleep started to show up as Mackey's potential Achilles heel. He settled his team down, then crawled into a cabin to sleep. This is where the story takes a nasty twist away from the camaraderie of the friendly Quest.

Mackey's family was sitting outside the cabin in Angel Creek, getting worried. He had been awakened by a checkpoint official (it is a service

Rick Mackey, Yukon Quest champion, 1997.

available to all the drivers, so it is not a rules violation) close to the end of his eight-hour mandatory stop, but he had simply rolled over and gone back to sleep.

According to Frank Turner, the Mackey family stopped the official and ordered him to return to the cabin and not leave until Rick was up and active. The official complied. "Getting outside assistance is against the rules. If you can't get yourself up, then you shouldn't get up. So I really wasn't very happy about that." Turner didn't bother to file a formal protest.

It came down to four teams virtually lining up for a final sprint to the finish. The 1997 Quest would be decided by sheer speed and trail knowledge. According to Mackey, the race wouldn't necessarily be won by the fastest team, but by the driver who made the fewest mistakes on the last day.

"There's a lot of trails down between Angel Creek and Fairbanks, where the rest of them could take the wrong one pretty easy."

When the time came to go, Mackey, Schandelmeier and May left on schedule, but there was no sign of Turner for almost 45 minutes.

Near the end of his rest Turner decided to change his runners. He was using soft Teflon runners, but the trail conditions ahead were more suited to a hard plastic runner. It's a job that usually takes about five minutes.

When Turner pulled out his screwdriver, it turned out to be the wrong size. Worst yet, it also turned out to be the wrong place to have the wrong size. He was using a Robertson style of screwdriver, which is made in Canada and isn't generally available in the United States. There were no replacement screwdrivers to be had.

It took him almost an hour to complete the change, but it was an hour he really couldn't afford at this late stage. It probably cost him the race.

Mackey pulled away steadily, opening a substantial gap between himself and Schandelmeier and May. He already had almost an hour on Turner due to the screwdriver problem. It was a deficit that none of them would be able to overcome.

As his dogs pulled him across the finish line, Mackey broke into a huge grin. "I can't believe it."

Schandelmeier and May were pretty much considered to be the second and third place teams, but Turner wasn't finished yet. In a stunning display of speed, he overtook and passed both teams, to claim second place.

"People on the river were telling me that my dogs were looking really good, they could see the way we were moving. I knew that Schandelmeier and May's teams were tired. It was just a question of whether I had enough time to catch them. I couldn't judge exactly how far in front of me the other teams were, so I just kept the dogs moving."

Races of future past

COLD WARS

Politics plays a role in almost every organization and the Yukon Quest is no exception. Despite the lofty goals of the Quest in fostering international cooperation between Alaska and the Yukon, the world's longest undefended border has on occasion resembled an iron curtain.

The first shot in the cold war came in 1992, when the Alaskan board of directors informed the Yukon board that they were seriously considering cutting the Canadian portion of the race and holding an all-Alaskan event.

The reasons, they claimed, were because of the reliance of the event upon Alaska's greater ability to raise funds (the population of Fairbanks alone was twice that of the entire Yukon — a difference that had been recognized in the early years of the organization and that earlier Alaskan boards had accepted as being a circumstance that couldn't be controlled) and communications problems. (While the boards of directors were supposed to meet together several times each year, the distances involved made it difficult. As a result, the two boards rarely met more than once a year.)

Having an all-Alaskan event, they said, would be much easier to manage, thus the Yukon had to go. It was alleged by several Alaskans who were opposed to the suggested change, that, behind the scenes were some of the larger Alaskan sponsors who had no presence in Canada and felt that running half the race in a foreign country wasn't worth their involvement.

Cooperation on the route.

Canadian board president David Knight was able to cope with the crisis diplomatically with his Alaskan counterpart, Greg Ashback. The Canadian financial commitment to shared expenses was increased and an agreement to establish the groundwork for a joint board of directors to oversee the entire event was reached. It also became apparent that popular support didn't exist in Alaska for anyone to start tampering with the historical route of the Yukon Quest.

It seemed the issue had been addressed and groundwork for a solution put into place but, like any volunteer organization, leadership changes and political will were altered by the next group of people.

The second shot was fired in 1994 when Alaska president Tom Nixon announced that the 1995 Yukon Quest would run from Fairbanks to Dawson City and return for, allegedly, the same reasons outlined in 1992. The real reason was that the organization was awash in red ink. The economic downturn in Alaska had resulted in sponsorship dollars being tight and the Quest organization was feeling the pinch. The board of directors went looking for a scapegoat, saying that an all-Alaska race was financially feasible but that running across the border to Canada was too expensive.

The Canadian board didn't even blink. Totally ignoring the Alaskan announcement, they continued to plan for the 1995 race, announcing a start date for entries to be accepted (George Aplustill, an Alaskan, was the first one to sign up on July 1 for the Whitehorse-to-Fairbanks Quest), naming a race marshal and hiring a race veterinarian.

"The trail will be in from Whitehorse to Eagle," stated Yukon race manager Tom Randall. "If there's no trail from Eagle to Fairbanks, I guess the race will only be 500 miles long this year."

In Alaska, the issue imploded on the board of directors. The membership demanded their resignation. The board responded by declaring that a vote of the full membership would decide the issue in August, 1994. President Nixon, however, stepped down before the vote was taken. An anonymous caller in the middle of the night had phoned Nixon to voice his displeasure by threatening to shoot him if the Yukon Quest was changed.

"It must be something in the name 'Nixon' and presidential positions," commented Yukon board past-president Elsie Wain when informed of the resignation.

Following a heated debate, in the same room in the Fairbanks library where Leroy Shank and Roger Williams had held the first meeting to found the race in 1983, the Alaskan membership voted 98 percent against the proposed change. A new president, Scott McManus, was elected and the Alaskan organization started to work its way out of the financial morass. By the end of the 1995 race, the Quest was back in the black.

In addition, the formal structure for a single board of directors to oversee the race was finally worked out and agreed upon. But before it could be put into effect, the leadership changed and the joint board concept was set aside once again.

In 1997, the Alaskan board tried once more. Again, the Yukon was to be cut out of the Quest. This time, it wasn't because it couldn't hold up its end of the race financially. It was because the Yukon board had negotiated a major sponsorship with a European tire manufacturer. While the Canadian board was financially stable and agreed to handle half the shared expenses of the event, the Alaskan board members were angry because they were once again deep in debt. The Canadian board refused to pay the Alaskan bills because the sponsor had provided the funds to assist in the 1998 race, not to pay outstanding accounts from the 1997 race.

The Yukon board had also contracted with a professional fundraiser to work with both boards to find sponsorships in Canada, the United States and Europe. The Alaskan board apparently felt that a professional fundraiser poised a threat to their traditional relationship with sponsors.

The Yukon board considered its options, then decided to head over to Fairbanks and deal with the Alaskans nose-to-nose. When they arrived in Fairbanks, the issue had already been resolved by the Alaskan membership.

"We were told they were holding a press conference when we arrived," said Yukon board president Tom Randall. "When we walked through the door, they were announcing their resignation en masse. The entire board! We were absolutely floored."

A new Alaskan board was elected, headed by former president Bob Eley. The political will to resolve the dispute was once again in place and this time the two boards were determined to deal with it before future leadership changes could derail the process again.

On November 2, 1997, the two boards of directors signed an agreement that constitutionally bound them to a joint board of directors, whose role was to handle all major sponsorships on behalf of the race, to work with the professional fundraiser to develop relationships with local and international sponsorships, and to oversee the fundamental philosophy and operations of the race.

ROUTE CHANGES

While temperatures and snow conditions can change the trail from hour-to-hour during a race, in 1994 the race organization started to change the trail on a year-to-year basis.

In previous years, mushers had started dropping dogs at Biederman's Cabin, approximately midway between Circle City and Eagle, and McCabe Creek, 50 miles north of Carmacks. At the time, the rules dictated that dropping a dog at any location other than a checkpoint was subject to an eight-hour time penalty. The mushers opted to take the penalty rather than carry a sick or injured dog over the trail to the next checkpoint.

For the 1994 Quest, Biederman's and McCabe were named official dog drops. Another official dog drop was added for the 1995 Quest, the Dog Drop Inn, at Scroggie Creek, on the Stewart River, approximately 100 miles south of Dawson City. Braeburn, about 90 miles north of Whitehorse, was added in 1997. Previously the only official dog drop that wasn't a checkpoint had been 101 Lodge, just below Eagle Summit.

In 1995, the organization decided to re-route the southernmost 50 miles. Previously, the teams had started in Whitehorse, then travelled down the Yukon River to Lake Laberge. Now they would follow the Yukon River until they reached the Takhini River. Turning west up the Takhini for a few miles, they would climb off the ice and onto a road that would take them to Takhini Hot Springs. Then the teams would travel a trail that paralleled the

Bill Stewart crossing the road near Takhini Hot Springs, 1995.

Klondike Highway for approximately 10 miles before crossing the highway and dropping onto the southern end of Lake Laberge.

Another change that year was the rerouting of the trail from the Ridge Road to its new route along the Bonanza Creek Road on the northern side of King Solomon Dome, just south of Dawson City.

"That was a good move for trailbreakers and mushers," said Canadian Ranger Sergeant John Mitchell, who coordinates the trailbreaking crew from Dawson City. "You could break a trail in there and it would be five feet deep in snow two hours later. It was tough enough setting a trail, but it was just brutal if you had to run dogs in that stuff."

It was a phone call in mid-August, 1995, from Teddy Charlie, a resident of Pelly Crossing, that initiated the first of the major changes for the Quest trail that would characterize the 1996 and 1997 races.

"You guys ever consider making Pelly a checkpoint?" he asked.

"Actually, Teddy, we have for a number of years, but we could just never really identify a trail that would get us there," replied a Quest organizer.

"Oh," he replied. "Well, I think I've got an idea for you. Can I come over?"

Unrolling his maps, Charlie described a new route for the Quest that would bring the teams to Pelly Crossing, then down the Pelly River to Stepping Stone to rejoin the original route.

"It would be great, Teddy, but there's no trail there and we don't have the budget or people power to cut one."

"Oh, that's no problem. We've already started cutting it. It's a little more work than we expected, but we'll have it ready by Christmas."

The checkpoint was officially added to the Yukon Quest in November, 1995.

The second change for the 1996 race was slightly more controversial. The organization decided to eliminate Lake Laberge from the race by bringing the teams home along the old Dawson-Whitehorse Overland Trail (the original winter stage route between the two communities, in use until the mid-1950s).

"The mushers do not like Lake Laberge," said organizers, "because it is a lot of ice running, over 60 miles from the north end of the lake to Whitehorse. The dogs get bored and the mushers get bored." The new trail was a fairly well used snowmobile trail and fit the Quest's mandate to commemorate transportation history.

Once the teams left Carmacks, they would follow the original Quest trail until they reached Coghlan Lake. From there, there was a trail that took them out to Braeburn. From that point they could travel along the old road bed until approximately 20 miles from the Takhini River, when the road virtually disappeared, turning into a bush trail.

It was the bush trail portion that sparked the controversy. On the maps, the entire distance from Braeburn to the Takhini River was a public thoroughfare. In fact, it is still legally considered to be a territorial highway. However, the bush trail didn't follow precisely the surveyed route of the former highway and it also happened to be the access for one of the more successful traplines in the Yukon.

The trapper, Jurg Hofer, didn't like the idea of the teams coming down what he considered to be his private trail. Backed by the Yukon Trappers Association, Hofer claimed the Quest would destroy his livelihood. The mushers, many of them trappers themselves, claimed it would actually enhance his trapping. In 13 years of running the race along trap lines in Alaska and the Yukon, no other trappers had ever complained that the Quest affected their profession.

Having made the decision to travel down what they considered a public trail, the Quest also made preparations to ensure that the teams would be safe. The Canadian Rangers would escort the teams through the approximately 10 miles of trail that Hofer was using and would identify the location of traps alongside the trail. (Trapping on the trail is illegal, so the traps would have been located alongside or just off the main trail. It is illegal for anyone but the trapper to touch the traps, therefore the Quest

What goes up...

couldn't close the traps.) With the lead teams preparing to leave Carmacks, the Yukon government stepped in and paid Hofer to spring his traps.

For the 1997 race, Hofer voluntarily sprung his traps for the Quest and the organization, in cooperation with the TransCanada Trail and TransCanada Snowmobile Trail committees (which had been involved with the Quest in making the decision to travel the stage road in 1996) agreed to assist him in relocating his trap line before the 1998 race.

The trail change for 1997 was at the northern end, where the Alaskans added a loop in the trail to carry the teams from the Chena River up a flood channel (an artificial river bed constructed to handle flood waters during the spring melt) to the community of North Pole, then back down to the Chena River. An official dog drop was also added at North Pole.

In total, the changes added just over 100 miles to the race. There had been some question as to whether or not the Quest Trail had been an honest 1,000 miles in previous years.

"It was a 1,000 mile race," maintained organizers. "It still is a 1,000 mile race. It's just a little longer 1,000 miles."

Dreaming about being in the Yukon Quest.

WORLD NEWS

Sledog racing is spelled with one "d" in Europe. Not only is the spelling different, so is the way the Europeans approach the sport of dog driving. The checkpoints and the start and finish areas are like a carnival: bright, colourful and noisy. Military bands greet or send off the teams. Dining is gourmet food and fine wines. Accommodation is four-star hotels. Thousands of people flock to see the dogs, from crowds of 10,000 at small regional sprint meets to teeming masses in excess of 50,000 per day lining the route of the Alpirod.

"In Alaska we're not used to seeing a lot of people. It's wilderness and forests of trees," says Joe Runyan, winner of the 1988 Alpirod. "In Europe, there are forests of people and the trees are rare. It's really very confusing for the dogs every once in a while." Runyan is the only musher to have won all three of the world's long distance sled dog races — the 1985 Yukon Quest, the 1988 Alpirod and the 1989 Iditarod.

To actually drive dogs in Europe is expensive. Teams must be flown over from Alaska at great cost. Teams based in Europe are owned by those who can afford them. With the exception of the Alpirod, there are no cash prizes for the drivers, and professionals are unheard of. Despite the lack of cash prizes, the Alaskans like going to Europe. Success there can mean large endorsement contracts with outdoor equipment manufacturers, a trend which is just starting to reap rewards — although limited — for the Americans in their own country.

In Europe, dog driving is a sport only for the wealthy: buying and maintaining a team is an expensive pastime. It is no wonder, then, that it was only a small, select group that kept the sport alive until the last decade. Not many of European aristocracy and society wanted to be seen in the company of a bunch of dogs — but times change, as do the views of what is socially acceptable and what isn't.

Now it's a rapidly growing activity. New sledog racing clubs are being formed almost every six months. The number of regional races has grown from two or three per country in the mid-1970s to eight or 10 by the early 1980s.

There are national championships and European championships that attract up to 300 teams from Germany, France, Switzerland, Austria and northern Italy.

The Alpirod, a four-country 1,000-mile event, was the brainchild of Armen Khatchikian, an Italian who got hooked on sledog racing when he won a national "What is your desire?" contest in his home country. His desire was to run the Iditarod, and that's what he did with the $50,000 in prize money.

When he returned home, he set about organizing a major European long distance race and, in 1988, his dream came true.

Joe Runyan beat 25 other teams to the finish line in the 10-day event, including four-time Iditarod champion Rick Swenson and the first woman to ever win the Iditarod, Libby Riddles.

In 1989, it was Kathy Swenson's turn to step into the Alpirod winner's circle. With Libby Riddles and Susan Butcher winning the Iditarod, only the Yukon Quest (of the three major long distance races in the world) still waits for a female champion.

The Alpirod has struggled since its beginning. The only long distance race in Europe, it battled through years of no snow and no money. In 1994, it reduced the distance from 700 miles to fewer than 500 in an effort to cut costs and eliminate areas where snow was too unreliable. Yet even that didn't help.

In December, 1994, just a month before the 1995 race was due to start, the Alpirod called it quits. They announced that the race wouldn't be run for one year to allow organizers to restructure the event and make it more viable. In late 1997, there were rumours in the mushing world that the Alpirod might be revived in 1999.

The Alaskans are still the cream of the world's mushing family, but the Europeans are starting to make major progress towards that domination. Some Europeans, like Switzerland's Martin Buser and France's Tony

What a tongue!

Andreonne, originally got started in mushing while in Alaska and have acquired most of their experience and training in North America.

Around the world, interest in dog mushing has been high enough over the years that it was actually a recognized demonstration sport in the 1932 Lake Placid Winter Olympics. Canada's Emile St. Godard won the gold, edging out American driving legend Leonhard Seppala.

In 1988, the Alberta International Sled Dog Classic was held as a demonstration for the International Olympic Committee just two weeks before the Olympic Games in Calgary, Alberta. Over 170 teams from nine countries took part in the three-day event, held in the hopes of earning Olympic support to reinstate the sport as an official event.

Wherever there are winter wonderlands, there are sled dog clubs. Canada, a country covered by snow over 90 percent of its area for almost 50 percent of each year, has clubs from the mountains of the north, to the plains of the central provinces, through the lakes of Ontario and onto the rocky shores of the Maritimes.

The northeastern United States — Maine, New York, Vermont, New Hampshire and New England — have a history of using dog sleds going back to the early 19th century and an organized racing circuit since 1922. Across the north central states, middle distance races, like Minnesota's John Beargrease 400, are popular. And in the far west, dog drivers can be found racing in northern California, Arizona, Oregon, Washington and Utah.

If there are sand dunes instead of snowdrifts, mushers run dogs pulling sleds on rubber tires.

Terry Quesnel was a vet for the 1987 Yukon Quest and one of the organizers behind the 1988 races for the Olympic community before the Calgary Olympics. "It's an elegant sport," he says, "with lots of romance and history to it."

Even when they're not being used in a sport, dog teams are invaluable. They have been used extensively in both arctic and Antarctic exploration. At one time, in Nome, Alaska, they were even used to pull a railway train when no engine could be imported.

Somewhere in the world, at any given moment, a driver is hitching up a team. They may "hike" their dogs with a southern drawl, the clipped perfection of the Queen's English, a rolling Scottish brogue, the structured formality of German, the romantic flow of French, the emotion of Italian or the casual tones of the Alaskan driver.

Individually, they are as different from one another as thousands of individual people can be. But when they step on those runners, something happens that transcends all the cultural, political and personal boundaries. They all seek the same fantasy: adventure, glory and wealth.

END OF AN ERA

The mail is still carried by dog sled in the north, although it is now a purely ceremonial function. Cachets of mail are carried as mandatory gear by mushers in the Yukon Quest. The limited edition envelopes are stamped and the stamps cancelled in both Fairbanks and Whitehorse each year. Then they are sold as collectibles by the organization. There is a complete collection of envelopes dating back to the inaugural race in 1984.

There are other races, such as the Iditarod, that also deliver mail cachets, but the Quest is the only race designed specifically to retrace the original mail routes.

The 1996 Yukon Quest was dedicated to Charlie Biederman, the last of the Alaskans who delivered the U.S. mail by dog sled in the 1930s and 1940s. Biederman had hoped to be at the start line of the race, but he died in late 1995, just after the Smithsonian had honoured him in their new National Postal Museum in Washington, D.C. The hickory sled he used to deliver the mail is on display at the museum.

The last of the Canadian dog sled mail carriers died the next year. Ed Whitehouse of Whitehorse had delivered the Royal Canadian Mail upriver from Dawson City by dog sled in the winter of 1928-29.

Limited edition envelope from 1984.

THE TRAIL

less travelled. Sitting in the Eldorado bar in 1995, Yukon Quest head vet Wendy Royle spent a long minute staring out the window into the Dawson night. Around her and her cup of coffee (she was due to go on night shift at the "doggy hotel" across the Yukon River), the cigarette smoking, beer-swilling denizens of the dark bar talked dawgs and dawg mushin'. They partied on, speculating on strategies, where the teams were, how fast they were moving and who was the toughest one of all. They remained drunkenly unaware of the anguish and frustration seething under Royle's apparently complacent exterior.

"I love this race," she started, suddenly, without taking her eyes off the window, "but I have to wonder if we're going about doing this all wrong. It's times like this that I wonder whether or not we're running some of these dogs to death." Just a couple of hours earlier, she had lifted a dead dog from the sled of Jay Cadzow — the second one she had to deal with in the past two days. John Peep had lost a dog just after leaving McCabe Creek. (Peep was so upset he immediately withdrew from the race. Cadzow wrestled with the issue for most of his 36-hour mandatory stop in Dawson City, then decided to continue.)

Cadzow's dog had died when it stumbled, running down a hill, and the sled rode up on the animal before the musher could stop it. Peep's dog hadn't shown any warning symptoms at all; it had simply collapsed and died in the harness. (The death was eventually attributed to "sled dog myopathy," the sudden death of a sled dog for no apparent reason. It is a little understood condition that many now believe is the result of a genetic predisposition.)

Despite all the studies, despite the superior training and conditioning, despite the care provided by the mushers and vets, despite programs designed to weed out the weaker animals, dogs still died on the trail.

Statistically, the odds of a dog dying on the trail are less than that of a pet dog dying in front of the fireplace. Less than one third of one percent of dogs involved in long distance mushing will die while training or competing. Royle's words were indicative of the impact that a dog's death will have on the individuals whose job it is to care for the animals.

Her anguish came from having to cope with death. The frustration came from not knowing, whether, as good as the dog care was, it couldn't be better.

There were some groups out there who were trying to improve dog care. There was common purpose, but no joint ventures. The International Sled Dog Veterinary Medical Association (ISDVA) was trying to establish uniform veterinary standards in all the races, but they were also not involved with every race — the Quest being one they haven't worked on. Mushing with PRIDE, founded in the early 1990s by Will Forsberg, was an organization for the mushers that provided practical guidelines on improved raising, handling and running of dogs.

Royle started out on a one-person crusade to see if she could resolve her personal reservations about "going about doing this all wrong."

She drew on the collective knowledge of groups like ISDVA and PRIDE, plus input from numerous other professionals from across North America, to compile the comprehensive manual on dog care, from the practical to the purely scientific, that was published by the Yukon Quest just before the 1997 race and she continued to research for the second edition.

Knowing that prevention is better than treatment, she had initiated the system of pre-race kennel checks, so the race vets would actually be monitoring the dogs for several months before the event started. During the race itself, in addition to the regular functions of the vets, she also introduced the program of on-going EKGs and ECGs and blood tests to seek out any irregularities that might escape a routine vet check.

After setting new, higher standards in quality dog care programs and knowledge, Wendy Royle finally called it quits following the 1997 Yukon Quest. She was emotionally exhausted by her passionate pursuit of the perfect program and disheartened by the fact that, after two years of working with veterinarians and organizations, it was still a one-person crusade.

Tom Randall, president of the Canadian board for the 1998 race, stopped driving dogs altogether several years ago. He was a veteran of two Yukon Quests.

"I haven't told many people this story. I've always told them that because I had snapped my Achilles tendon and couldn't walk without pain, I stopped driving dogs. But this is the real reason for it."

His last race had been in northern Alberta. He was close enough to the lead to possibly mount a challenge. He had a scheduled two-hour rest stop coming up, but if he didn't take it, he could have a shot at catching the leaders. So he kept on running.

A few miles down the trail, the team dropped onto a river. After a while, Randall noticed his lead dogs were starting to wander a bit, weaving back and forth across the icy surface. He stopped to take a look. The leaders had hit the wall. They couldn't go any further. He had pushed them too hard for too long. Randall parked the team and waited on the river for five hours before the dogs would continue.

"What in hell am I doing?" he asked himself, and stopped racing dogs at that moment.

"I let speed and position get in the way of dog care. I was lucky I didn't hurt any of those dogs. I decided there and then, it wasn't worth it. If I could make that mistake once, I could make it again."

These are the kinds of issues that plague the mushing world, the issues of conscience.

Over the past half-decade, the dog mushing business has started to attend to the business of making the dog, and not just winning, the focus of the sport.

"I came to the Quest because it's a dog care race," said Rick Mackey, when, in 1996, he switched from the Iditarod (which he had won in 1983) to the Quest.

It is that perception of the Quest that makes it stand alone in the sport of dog mushing. One Alaska-Yukon Trail Association article of incorporation, on which the race was founded in 1983, states that the race was "to commemorate the historic dependence of man on his sled dogs for mutual survival in the arctic environment and to perpetuate mankind's concern for his canine companion's continued health, welfare and development."

The Yukon Quest traditional veterinary program and the vets who must make it work are possibly the best in the world today. It is a testing ground for new and, sometimes, unusual concepts for improving dog care.

But the time is coming for making some very difficult decisions.

Trevor Braun and companion.

There is a great deal of pressure to change the Yukon Quest, to turn it into a stage race. A stage race is a series of short runs of 50 to 100 miles between checkpoints. The Iditarod, for instance, has 27 checkpoints over a 1,200 mile route. The teams run from one checkpoint to another in only a few hours. The musher need only carry enough food and gear to last until the next checkpoint and there is no requirement to camp in the outdoors since, every night, the mushers can sleep at a checkpoint or, in some races, in a hotel room. Some stage races are set up so a team will race only a specified distance each day, then stop and rest overnight, before repeating the process the next day. The idea is to keep the sleds lighter so the dogs can run faster.

"That," said former Quest driver David Sawatzky in 1996, "is what mushers want now. They don't want a true endurance event any more because they can make more money running easier races. Stage races are the future of dog mushing.

The major criticism is that a stage race doesn't permit mushers to test their ability to care for themselves or their dogs. It can be perceived to be simply a test of how well a musher can hang onto the back of a sled that is moving fast. The dog care can be inconsistent. Mushers don't have to care for their teams in the checkpoint; they can hand that responsibility over to a handler. With shorter distances and the ability to drop more dogs, it is easier to push a dog to its limit and drop it, than it is to care for the dog.

To survive financially in the 1980s, the Iditarod was forced to compromise and change to a stage race, shifting away from the principles it was founded upon. The result was a race where speed was everything and dog care took a back seat. It was the voices of animal rights activists in the early 1990s that forced the organization to review its priorities.

It was partly that shift away from the endurance and dog care aspects of the Iditarod that prompted Leroy Shank and Roger Williams to found the new race that eventually became the Yukon Quest.

While the Quest is still perceived as the "dog care" race, that aspect of the event has started to be overshadowed by the need for speed.

At one time, the rules read that a team could start with a maximum of 12 dogs and could drop only three along the way. It took exemplary dog care to accomplish that, but most of the competitors managed to do it. Then some of the mushers wanted to go faster and be able to drop more dogs. So, the organization bent a little and the limit was raised to 14 dogs, with the musher finishing with no less than six dogs in harness.

In the years following that change the number of dogs dropped at checkpoints increased, as did the incidence of dog deaths on the Yukon Quest trails.

The purse for winning the race went from $15,000 in 1984 to $30,000 in 1997. The Veterinarians' Award for the best dog care was $1,000 in 1984. It is still $1,000 in 1998. The award for dog care should be no less than the prize for being the first musher across the finish line. That accomplishment is no less worthy of reward than are the exploits of the fastest team, and recognition for their efforts should be no less.

In the five principles outlined in the articles of incorporation, there is no reference to the Yukon Quest being a "race." It is "an epic event," an "experience," a "recognition" and an "opportunity."

It would be unrealistic for the Quest to deny that competitive teams aren't necessary. Without them, there'd be no race. They must be compensated accordingly and usually are among the best in terms of dog care.

Future purses should be directed equally towards those whose actions exemplify the fundamental philosophy of dog care. This way, the Quest won't be recognized solely by the speed of its champion, but by the quality of its field from back to front, on and off the trail.

How can the Quest go about accomplishing this? The musher who pushed his dogs too hard, Tom Randall, is hoping to spearhead a move towards setting up an association of established middle and long distance races around North America. The idea is to set up a points series where each musher would score a certain number of points in each race, based upon placement and dog care, with the individual collecting the most points being declared the world champion.

The higher the finish position, the more points an individual would receive for that part of the event. Dog care would receive equal weight in the scoring, with the race veterinarians and officials being the sole judges of that aspect. There would be no first or second in dog care. Every musher could potentially score exactly the same amount. The dog care points, when combined with the placement, could radically change the final results of a race. A team finishing back in the standings, if it scored higher in the dog care, could actually end up winning the race.

The scheme is grandiose, maybe too big to ever be completely successful. But to take those fundamentals and apply them to one race is more than possible. Every great accomplishment begins with some kind of vision or dream. Dreams precede reality. They nourish it. Perhaps they even create it. The Yukon Quest started in 1984 because two people had a dream.

In an era where political and sponsor agendas will pressure the Quest to conform and compromise, perhaps it's Tom Randall's dream of a sport that gives its caregivers equal respect or Wendy Royle's dream of a perfect veterinary program, that will help the Yukon Quest to retain its integrity and take leadership in determining the future of driving dogs.

(over) Doug Harris and checkpoint official, 1996.

Races of future past

Rules and Statistics

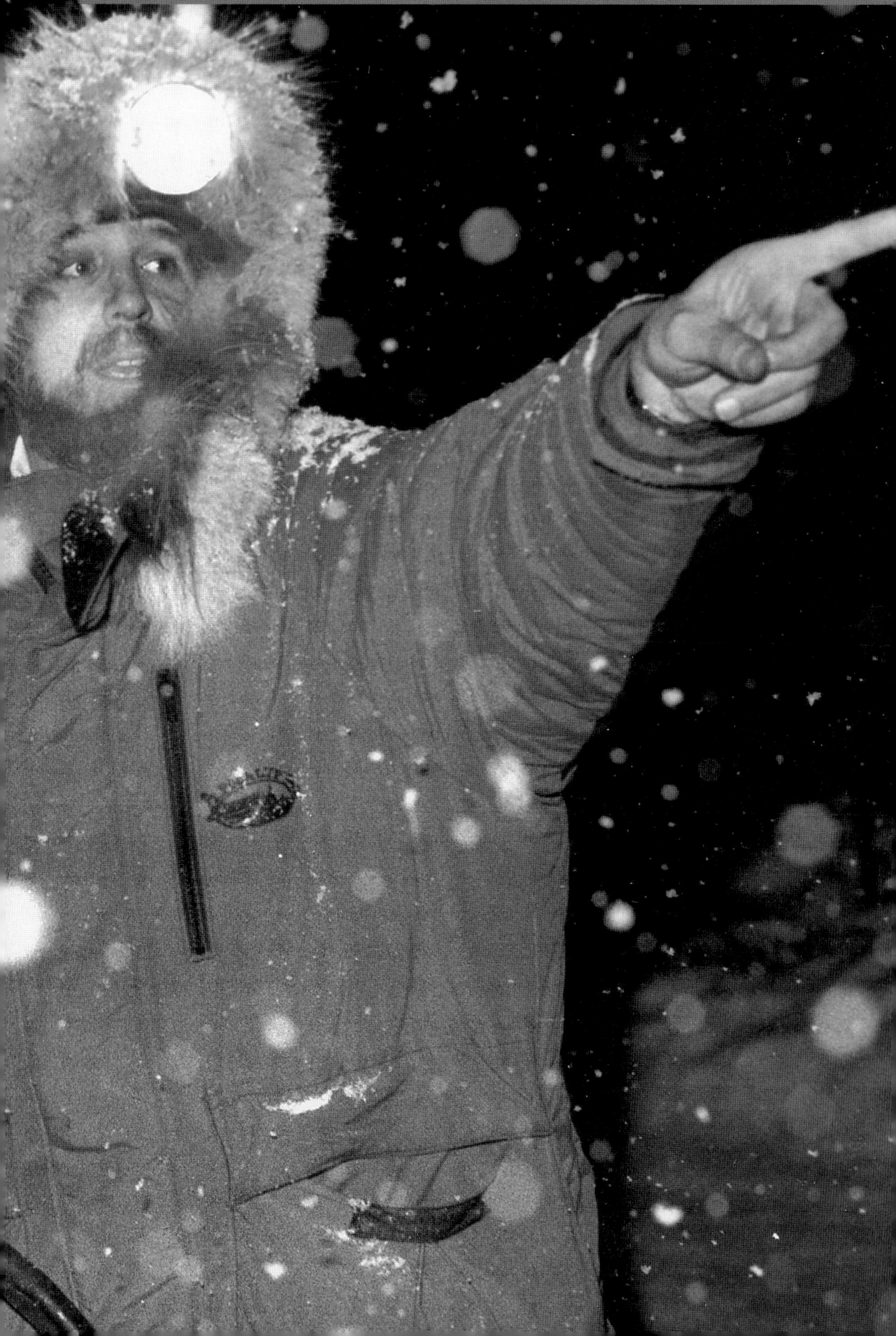

Official 1998 race rules

Box 5555
Whitehorse, Yukon
Canada Y1A 4Z2
867-668-4711

Box 75015
Fairbanks, Alaska
USA 99707
907-452-7954

15TH ANNUAL YUKON QUEST INTERNATIONAL SLED DOG RACE™

As adopted by Yukon Quest International, June 7, 1997

English is the official language of the Yukon Quest International Sled Dog Race™

■ GENERAL RACE PROCEDURES

1. RACE START

The official starting date for the 1998 race will be Sunday, February 8,1998 at 1:00 p.m. local time. The official starting place will be Whitehorse, Yukon, unless otherwise designated by Yukon Quest International™ (hereinafter referred to as YQI) . The race will be held as scheduled, regardless of weather conditions. Each year the starting date and time will be determined by YQI. For safety reasons, changes to this rule may be made by the race marshal with approval from the YQI Rules Committee.

2. ENTRY FEE, DATES, LIMITS

1998 Yukon Quest Sled Dog Race™ entry opens July 1, 1997. Receipt of the entry fee and completed forms will constitute the driver's intent to enter the race, and further acknowledges that the driver understands and agrees to comply with each and every rule as stated. YQI reserves the right to reject any entry. Entries are determined on a first-come, first-served basis. Entries close at midnight local time December 31,1997. Certified postmarked entries by this date will be accepted.

The maximum number of teams for the race is fifty (50). Once the maximum of fifty is reached, a waiting list will be established, again on a first-come, first-served basis. To qualify for the waiting list, the official entry form must be completed, and a $25 non-refundable fee paid. If a driver withdraws from the list of fifty, the name at the top of the waiting list will be moved up to the entry list, upon receipt of the rest of the required fees. The entry fee will be the fee applicable on the date the wait-list deposit is posted with YQI. The slot will be held open for no more than seven (7) days after notification. Entry fees including food drop, membership, and race entry are as follows

- July/August: $800
- September/October: $1,000
- November/December: $1,200

(All dollar amounts are in U.S. currency)

Conditions of entry

All drivers entered in the race must be members in good standing of YQI.

Kennel entries must name a driver to enter. Drivers may be changed or entries transferred for a fee of $100. Transfers are not allowed after 50 teams have entered nor after December 31,1997.

Drivers must be a minimum of eighteen (18) years of age by the start of the race.

Drivers must have a demonstrated ability to complete a long distance sled dog race. Rookie drivers must submit written proof to verify their completion of a YQI approved race of at least 200 miles in 1996, 1997, or January 1998. Completing at least 400 miles of the Yukon Quest™ or the Iditarod in 1996 or 1997 will be accepted.

All applicants will have their applications to enter the Yukon Quest™ reviewed by the YQI Rules Committee.

YQI will honour censures from the Iditarod Trail Sled Dog Race. Censures from other sled dog racing organizations may be honoured. Unpaid fines to YQI are equal to a censure.

No one convicted of animal abuse or neglect may enter the Yukon Quest™.

Each driver shall sign any and all documents or promotional material requested by YQI prior to or at the drivers' meeting. Failure to comply will result in disqualification.

Definition of rookie

Any first time entrant or any previous entrant of the Yukon Quest™ who has not reached Dawson City, Yukon, from either direction.

Substitution of drivers

Substitution of drivers for medical reasons will be permitted up to the start of the pre-race drivers' meeting, upon approval of the YQI Rules Committee and payment of a $100 fee.

Withdrawal before race

An entrant withdrawing for any reason on or before midnight December 31, 1997 will be refunded all but $50 of the entry fee. An entrant withdrawing after midnight December 31, 1997 will forfeit the entire entry fee unless the entrant can provide a certified medical reason for the withdrawal, in which case, the entrant may recover all but $200 of their entry fee.

3. COURSE AND CHECKPOINTS

The course covers approximately 1,000 miles/ 1,600 kilometres of mostly arctic wilderness, much of it on and along the Yukon River. The trail will be broken and marked prior to the race, but due to weather conditions there will be no guarantee of broken trail during the race. Checkpoints are as follows

1. Whitehorse
2. Carmacks
3. Pelly Crossing
4. Dawson City
5. Eagle
6. Circle City
7. Central
8. Angel Creek
9. Fairbanks

4. FOOD/EQUIPMENT SHIPMENT

All food and equipment shipped to checkpoints for the race must be in cloth burlap bags or woven poly-bags, permanently marked with the driver's name. Gross weight not to exceed 60 pounds/27.2 kilograms. Straw is mandatory at every checkpoint and must be shipped as a wrapped bale. Bags must be turned in to YQI prior to food shipment deadline or delivered to the checkpoints prior to the start of the race. No food or equipment will be delivered to checkpoints after the start of the race with the exception of Dawson City.

If a driver obtains dog food between checkpoints, that driver may be penalized or disqualified.

5. PROMOTIONAL MATERIAL AND VETERINARY RECORD BOOK

YQI may require a small amount of promotional freight as part of the mandatory load. Promotional material and veterinary record book must be turned in to a race official at the completion of the race, or when scratching.

6. SHIPPING DROPPED DOGS

Drivers will pay for all transportation expenses incurred by or relevant to the return of their dropped dogs. YQI will supervise the transportation of dogs from "fly-in only" checkpoints and dog drops. Transportation for dogs dropped at other checkpoints or dog drops (along the road system) may be arranged for by the driver, or will be provided by YQI at the driver's expense.

7. RACE OFFICIALS (RACE MARSHAL AND RACE JUDGES) AND RACE VETERINARIANS

The intent of the rules will guide the race marshal and race judges in their decisions. The race marshal is in charge of all aspects of the race from the pre-race drivers' meeting to the awards presentation. Race judges will act as deputies of the race marshal. The race marshal may waive or reduce monetary or time penalties for unforeseen calamities that may befall a driver.

Race veterinarians are present throughout the race to monitor the health and welfare of all dogs, advise drivers in caring for their dogs' medical needs, and provide veterinary treatment for dropped dogs, if necessary.

Race veterinarians in conjunction with the race marshal or a race judge shall have final authority to remove a dog from the race for medical reasons.

8. VET CHECK

All dogs will undergo a thorough physical examination before the race starts. Any dog which cannot qualify for a certificate of good health will not run in the race. All examinations must be done within ten (10) days prior to the start of the race. All dogs entered in the race shall have had parvo, and distemper vaccinations within the last 12 months. Rabies vaccinations must be current. Certificates and invoices will be required to prove vaccination status. All dogs must be examined by a qualified YQI-approved, licensed veterinarian of the driver's choice at the driver's expense, or by a licensed veterinarian sponsored by YQI at an official vet check. YQI will not provide this service after the official vet check. The race marshal and head veterinarian have authority to disqualify unfit teams examined outside of the official vet check up to the start of the race.

Rookie entrants must have their dogs examined at a YQI official vet check. Rookies that cannot participate in the official vet check cannot start the race.

The official YQI health certificate must be presented at the pre-race drivers' meeting. Failure to comply will result in disqualification. The time and place of the vet check will be announced by YQI.

9. DRIVERS' MEETING AND DRAWING

It will be mandatory for all rookies to attend a meeting at 10:00 a.m. local time the day of the start banquet. All entrants are required to attend the drivers' meeting at 1:00 p.m. on the day of the start banquet. Failure to answer all roll calls in person will result in a $500 fine. A handlers' meeting will be held at the beginning of the drivers' meeting. The location of these meetings will be announced by YQI. Each driver must draw their starting position in person at the banquet.

10. PRIZE MONEY (U.S. CURRENCY)

1. $30,000
2. $24,000
3. $18,000
4. $12,000
5. $8,000
6. $6,000
7. $5,000
8. $4,200
9. $3,700
10. $3,300
11. $2,900
12. $2,500
13. $2,100
14. $1,800
15. $1,500

In the event that more or less than $125,000 is raised for prize money, the awards will be paid on a percentage basis of prize money available in relation to $125,000.

11. SLED

Only one (1) sled per driver will be used throughout the race. Each driver has a choice of sled, subject to the condition that some kind of sled or toboggan equipped with a brake must be drawn. The sled or toboggan must be capable of safely negotiating a 1,000-mile trail, and of hauling any injured or fatigued dogs and the required food, materials, and equipment. In the event of repairs, there must not be significant alteration of size or reduction in weight. Help with sled repairs, that is available to all drivers, may be allowed with prior approval of the race marshal and/or race judge. On prior approval of the race marshal, a destroyed sled may be replaced by a comparable size and weight sled, with a time penalty of eight (8) hours at the next mandatory stop (Angel Creek, Dawson City or Carmacks).

12. AWARDS PRESENTATION

The awards presentation ceremony at Fairbanks or Whitehorse will be held approximately three (3) days after the first team crosses the finish line. All drivers who have crossed the finish line up to two (2) hours before the ceremony will be present. The winner will have a representative of his/her dog team present for recognition. An official finish is a prerequisite for receiving awards. Drivers will only receive $500 of their prize money at the finish banquet. The rest will be disbursed to the driver after negative drug test results have been confirmed, or within 30 days, whichever is shorter. Those who do not attend the awards presentation ceremony may be fined up to five hundred dollars ($500). A recognition party will be held for those drivers unable to finish the race in time for the awards presentation ceremony.

13. CLAIMS

Each driver agrees to hold YQI, the race sponsor(s), and other contributors (that is, sponsors and contributors of the race corporations, as distinguished from the sponsors of individual drivers) harmless from any claim or demand based on any alleged action or inaction by the driver, his/her dogs, agents, or others acting on his/her behalf. The driver also agrees to release YQI, race sponsor(s), their agents, employees and volunteers from any claim or demand resulting from injury to the driver, his/her dogs, or his/her property. Further, YQI has the unqualified and unrestricted authority to permit the race sponsor(s) to photograph and otherwise collect information for advertising, public relations, or other publicity purposes.

14. DRIVER'S REPORT/PROTEST FORM

This sled dog race will not survive if the competition is not conducted fairly and the dogs are not well cared for and humanely treated. It is the duty of every driver to report all violations of these rules to the race marshal or race judges. The forms for reporting violations or protests are available from the race officials and at checkpoints.

15. CENSURE AND/OR FINE

In reference to action taken by the YQI Rules Committee, race marshal or race judges during the race, the board of YQI may censure and/or fine a driver for cause, including prohibition from entering a future race or races. The driver so involved may request in writing an informal hearing by a written review board within thirty (30) days of the date of censure and/or fine. In the event that the driver so involved may by clear and convincing evidence show that the action taken should be reversed, the driver so involved understands and agrees that the maximum financial recovery shall be limited to the prize money for the finishing position that the driver so involved could realistically have attained but for the action taken. The driver so involved further agrees that this remedy shall be the sole and exclusive remedy. In no event shall the driver so involved be entitled to incidental or consequential damages as they are outside the sole and exclusive remedy above provided.

16. FAILURE TO COMPLY

All decisions by the race marshal and/or the race judges shall be final. Failure of a driver to comply with the published rules of General Race Procedures and Trail Procedures will result in disqualification or a monetary or time penalty. In the event a fine is imposed, application to enter a future race will not be accepted until full payment is received by YQI. Disqualified drivers will forfeit all placements and monetary values.

■ TRAIL PROCEDURES

1. COMMON START/LATE START

Teams will leave the starting line at two-minute intervals. Any driver who cannot leave the starting line in the order drawn will be started after the scheduled departure time of the final team. Any team that cannot leave the starting line within sixty (60) minutes of the last team's departure may be disqualified. The starting time differential will be compensated for during each team's mandatory thirty-six (36) hour layover in Dawson City. For elapsed time purposes, therefore, the race will be a common start event. Before the start of the race, YQI will give to each driver their total layover time in Dawson, which will not be changed in the event of a late start.

2. MANDATORY GEAR

Each driver must have in his/her possession at all times the following items:
- Proper cold weather sleeping bag.
- Hand axe with an overall length of at least twenty-two (22) inches/56 centimetres.
- One pair of snowshoes with bindings, with an area of at least two hundred and fifty (250) square inches/1,612 square centimetres each.
- Veterinary records (loss will incur a one (1) hour time penalty to be taken at the last mandatory stop or added to the finish time).
- Any promotional material that YQI has asked the driver to carry to Fairbanks/Whitehorse.

In addition, eight (8) booties for each dog, either in the sled, or in use and in the sled, are required when a driver signs out of each checkpoint.

Drivers should have these items in their possession at all times. If a driver loses a required article of gear between checkpoints, he/she cannot check in at the checkpoint until he/she has acquired and replaced the lost item. In the event of accidental and unavoidable loss along the trail, the driver will be allowed to replace the missing item(s) from a public source at the next checkpoint before checking in. The driver may also obtain items from a private source with the approval of the race marshal or race judge and a time penalty of thirty (30) minutes at the last mandatory stop.

In addition to the mandatory gear listed above, items relative to the safety of the dog teams and drivers (i.e. sled brakes, mittens, etc.) may be replaced with the race marshal or race judge's approval and the thirty (30) minute time penalty assessed at the last mandatory stop.

Should any mandatory gear be missing at the finish, thirty (30) minutes per item will be added to the finish time.

A map, compass, flares, and dog blankets are recommended. Excess food or gear may be given only to residents along the trail.

3. CHECKPOINT

Check-in/sign out

Each driver must personally check in and sign out at each checkpoint before going on. The time into the checkpoint is recorded upon the team's arrival and the required gear will be checked immediately. Any driver failing to sign out, or to leave within sixty (60) minutes of signing out will be assessed a time penalty of two (2) hours at the next mandatory stop or a driver and team may return on the trail to a checkpoint to sign out without penalty. The sixty (60) minute rule may be extended with the approval of the race marshal or judge. The checkpoints will be staffed twenty-four (24) hours a day for a period of seventy-two (72) hours after the first team arrives. The checkpoint will be staffed on a limited basis after that, until all the teams have passed.

Dogs entering and leaving checkpoints

All dogs must leave checkpoints in harness and attached to the tow line. A dog may arrive at a checkpoint in the sled and leave in harness attached to the tow line.

Food and equipment

Prior to leaving the checkpoint all litter and remaining supplies must be bagged by the driver. Straw collection procedure for each checkpoint will be determined by the race marshal or race judge. After a driver leaves a checkpoint, remaining supplies may be collected by a handler with the approval of the race marshal or a race judge. Supplies remaining will become the property of YQI.

4. THIRTY-SIX (36) HOUR STOP (DAWSON CITY)

There is one mandatory thirty-six (36) hour stop at Dawson City, Yukon. Time begins when the driver checks in at Dawson City. The starting-time differential is added to the layover time here. All dogs continuing in the race must be kept in the designated holding area.

The following is allowed in Dawson City:
• Delivery of food and equipment after the start of the race.
• Assistance with feeding dogs and repairing equipment.
• Tent shelters for dogs, limited to an open ended, non-heated shelter.

The following is not allowed in Dawson City:
• Removing dogs from the holding area.
• Housing dogs in dog boxes or autos and trucks.
• Taking dogs other than those continuing in the race into the holding area.

5. MANDATORY STOPS

In addition to Dawson City, there will be a mandatory two (2) hour stop for each team at Carmacks. There will be a mandatory eight (8) hour stop at Angel Creek. During each mandatory stop, each team will be checked by a YQI veterinarian with a race official present.

6. RACE COURSE

All teams must follow the trail as marked or as instructed by the race marshal.

7. STANDARD RACE COURTESY

Standard race courtesy shall prevail. An overtaken driver and team must relinquish the trail at the request of the overtaking driver, except within one (1) mile/1.6 kilometres of the finish line in Fairbanks or Whitehorse.

8. CLEARING THE TRAIL

Drivers setting up camp must clear the trail of their dogs and gear. Build fires a safe distance off the trail.

9. LITTER

Litter of any kind may not be left along the trail or at cabins. Camps must be cleaned up before the team moves on. This is a historic trail, and its continued use for the race relies upon compliance with this policy. Failure to abide by this rule may result in disqualification, five-hundred-dollar ($500) fine and/or time penalty at the next mandatory stop.

10. ONE DRIVER PER TEAM

Only one driver is permitted per team, and that driver must complete the race with that team only.

11. TAMPERING

No driver may tamper with another driver's dogs, food or gear.

12. TEAMS TIED TOGETHER

Two or more teams may not, in any way, be tied together except to assist a driver in trouble at some immediate location. The drivers of any teams so involved must notify officials at the next checkpoint along the trail. A driver will not be penalized for helping another driver in danger for his/her life.

13. OUTSIDE ASSISTANCE

No planned help is allowed throughout the race, with the exception of Dawson City. No driver may receive outside assistance between or at checkpoints unless an emergency has been declared by the race marshal, or is subsequently so ruled. The intended spirit of this race dictates that the driver be self-sufficient and therefore able to help other drivers in case of real need. No assistance which would result in competitive advantage may be accepted or solicited.

Supplies remaining after a driver has left a checkpoint may be turned over to a handler with the approval of the race marshal or a race judge. Any items not retrieved will become the property of YQI.

14. DEMAND FOR FOOD AND SHELTER

A driver may not make demands for food or shelter along the trail or at checkpoints.

15. SLEEPING AREAS

Sleeping areas for drivers and drivers only will be designated at each checkpoint. Only these areas may be used. Hotels and lodges are not designated sleeping areas, except in Dawson City.

16. KILLING OF GAME ANIMALS

In the event that an edible game animal (moose, caribou, elk, etc.) is killed in the defence of life or property, the driver must salvage the meat for human use before proceeding along the trail. This incident must be reported at the next checkpoint. This means that a food animal must be gutted. YQI will make arrangements for further salvage. Any other animal killed in defence of life or property must be reported to a YQI race official.

17. MOTORIZED VEHICLES

In no case may a driver accept assistance from any type of motorized vehicle between checkpoints (except as allowed under Rule 30). Pacing will not be permitted.

18. CARE AND FEEDING OF DOGS

All care and feeding of dogs will be done by the drivers only, except at Dawson City. Neither force feeding nor stomach tubing is allowed. Dawson City is the only location along the trail at which the driver may be more than a few minutes away from his/her team without permission of the race marshal or a

race judge. Drivers may assist one another between checkpoints. At non-checkpoints, a driver may accept hospitality for himself or herself only. At no time during the race may a driver house dogs in heated shelters.

19. DOG MINIMUMS, MAXIMUMS AND BREEDS

Drivers must start the race with no less than eight (8) dogs and no more than fourteen (14) dogs, and must finish with no less than six (6) dogs. Dogs may not be added to a team after the start of the race. All dogs will be either on the tow line or hauled in the sled. Dogs may not be led behind the sled. An expired dog does not count as a dog for the minimum required.

Only northern dog breeds suitable for arctic travel will be permitted to enter the race. "Northern breeds" will be determined by race officials.

20. HARNESSES

The neck (and breast panel where applicable) of all harnesses must be padded.

21. MARKING/TAGGING OF DOGS

All dogs leaving the starting line will be identified by a microchip and a current-year-only YQI collar tag. Legible driver and dog names are required on each collar. Microchips are at the driver's expense.

22. SWITCHING OF DOGS

Switching of dogs between teams will not be permitted after they have officially left the start. Following the issuance of tags and acceptance of dogs for the race by race veterinarians, any exchange of dogs by the drivers must be approved by the race marshal prior to leaving the starting line.

23. TREATMENT OF DOGS

There will be no cruel or inhumane treatment of dogs. No use of whips will be allowed. The race marshal or race judges in conjunction with a race veterinarian will have absolute authority over the dog teams. Their judgement as to withdrawal of a dog or dogs from the race, or any other conditions relative to dog care on the trail, shall be final.

The health and condition of all dogs will be assessed at every checkpoint. Race veterinarians in conjunction with the race marshal or a race judge may deem it necessary to detain teams at any

Rules

checkpoint if the health and welfare of a team warrants it. No dog team will leave a checkpoint or dog drop until the dogs in that team are in condition to finish the race.

24. HAULING DOGS

A driver may not allow any dogs to be hauled by another team. A driver's dogs hauled in the sled must be hauled in a protected, humane manner.

25. DROPPED DOGS

Any injured, fatigued or sick dogs may be dropped at checkpoints or dog drops, as designated by the race marshal, without penalty. Each dropped dog must be left with food for two (2) days. Drivers are responsible for providing collars, as per Trail Procedure rule 21, and proper amounts of food for dropped dogs. A recommended amount of food is two (2) pounds/1 kilogram per day per dog. Every dropped dog must be examined by a race veterinarian.

Dogs may be dropped for emergency medical reasons between checkpoints and designated dog drops. This action must be reported to the race marshal or race judge at the next checkpoint, and the driver may be subject to an eight (8) hour penalty, regardless of the number of dogs dropped, at the next mandatory stop. The driver remains responsible for that dog and all fees incurred. The dog must be examined by a race veterinarian and accounted for within 48 hours or prior to the start of the awards banquet, whichever is sooner.

26. DRUGS

The driver must have his/her dog team free of all prohibited drugs and foreign substances from the time of the vet check until released by a race vet or race official after the team has finished the race. Dogs that are continuing in the race shall not receive any of the following:

• Any substance by injection.
• Acupuncture.
• Cold laser therapy.
• Any other treatment or therapy that, in the opinion of the head race veterinarian, is not in the best interest of a dog that is to continue on in the race.

The supervising race veterinarian must be notified of any dogs receiving allowed medication to treat an existing medical problem and a statement from the attending veterinarian describing the diagnosis and treatment must be presented with the YQI health certificate.

YQI veterinarians may randomly collect blood and/or urine samples beginning at the vet check and continuing until the finish banquet. It is the responsibility of the driver to assist the race veterinarian in the collection of the samples. The driver or the driver's handler may be present at all times during the taking and sealing of such samples. Documents evidencing the procedure shall be signed by the driver or his/her handler. No person may interfere in any way with the collection of samples or procedures conducted under this rule.

If a race veterinarian finds it necessary to treat a dog with a prohibited drug, that dog must be dropped from the race.

The following drugs will be permitted subject to the approval of the official supervising race veterinarian:

• Topical medications including DMSO.
• Wormers.
• Antibiotics (except procaine penicillin).
• Antidiarrhoeal (except those with salicylates, i.e. Pepto-Bismol).
• Ovaban and/or Cheque Drops (estrus [heat] suppressant use only).

All other drugs and foreign substances are prohibited.

The driver is required to protect and guard his/her dog team against the administration, either internally or externally, of any foreign substance. A positive test indicating the presence of a foreign substance shall give rise to a presumption that the driver has failed to meet the duties imposed upon him/her.

Fines or penalties levied for violations of this rule shall be based on the seriousness of the offence and will be assessed after completion of the race. The Rules Committee will be responsible for assessing these penalties.

The Racing Commissioner's International Uniform Classification Guidelines of Foreign Substances, dated March 9, 1992, will serve as a guideline in establishing these penalties which may be as severe as disqualification and censure from future races.

27. EXPIRED DOGS

The death of any dog may result in the disqualification of the driver, and/or prohibition from entering future races. Any dog that expires during the race for any reason must be taken to the next checkpoint or checkpoint just passed, and submitted to the race official. A necropsy will be performed on all expired dogs by a licensed veterinary pathologist or veterinarian.

28. UNMANAGEABLE TEAM

Outside assistance will be allowed only if a team is unmanageable. Whether a team is unmanageable will be ruled upon by the race marshal in each separate instance.

29. LOOSE LEADERS

There will be no loose leaders; all dogs will be in the team or on the sled. A driver must immediately make every effort to secure any dog which accidentally becomes loose.

30. LOST TEAM

A lost team will not be disqualified if the driver regains control of it, provided that the team and driver complete the entire race trail and comply with the rules including checkpoint requirements. As long as the team and driver continue on the trail when separated, the driver may remain in the race when regaining control. A driver may receive assistance from another driver in recovering his/her team A driver may receive assistance from a motorized vehicle to regain control of a lost team as long as the driver and team return to the point at which the team was lost and continue the race from that point. The incident shall be reported at the next checkpoint.

31. WITHDRAWAL FROM THE RACE

Drivers wishing to withdraw from the race may do so by filling out and signing an official withdrawal/ scratch form at a checkpoint or with a race official. Drivers are responsible for making their own arrangements for retrieving personal gear. Items remaining become the property of YQI.

32. FINISH

Subject to checking of mandatory gear, the time of a team's official finish is when the nose of the dog in lead crosses the finish line. Should any mandatory gear be missing, thirty (30) minutes per item will be added to the finish time. Dog teams must remain at the finish line or holding area until all blood and/or urine samples are collected or until the team is released by the race marshal, a race judge, or a race veterinarian.

33. STATUTORY COMPLIANCE

Any driver who violates a state, territorial, national or international law while in the race may be disqualified if convicted. Hand guns are not allowed in Canada.

34. SPORTSMANSHIP

The Code of the North dictates that all travellers be courteous, helpful, generous and honourable. Conduct yourself well enough so that the next driver will be welcomed with equal hospitality.

Rude behaviour or inappropriate actions by a driver or handler will result in a penalty.

Any competitor or athlete worthy of the name realizes that all people — officials, volunteers, media, and fans — are equal participants in this event, and that it is the driver's responsibility to define the upper limits of human performance. A true sportsman is an inspiration to all witnesses.

YUKON QUEST, ARTICLES OF INCORPORATION

The goals of the organization as stated in the Articles of Incorporation include:

• To recognize and promote the spirit that compels one to live in this Great North Land.

• To bring public attention to the historic role of the Arctic Trail in the development of the north country.

• To commemorate the international bond of "citizens of the far north," whose spirit knows no boundaries.

• To commemorate the historic dependence of man on his sled dogs for mutual survival in the Arctic environment and to perpetuate mankind's concern for his canine companion's continued health, welfare and development.

• To provide an opportunity for and encourage participation in an epic event by musher and dog without regard to the musher's sex, race, religion, national origin, age or economic standing.

Yukon Quest results by year

These are the official results for each race, including the direction in which the race was run. Times are given in days : hours : minutes.

Prize money is in U.S. dollars.

S=Scratched D=Disqualified

1984	Fairbanks to Whitehorse		
1	Sonny Lindner	12:00:05	$15,000
2	Harry Sutherland	12:04:15	$10,000
3	Bill Cotter	12:05:40	$5,000
4	Joe Runyan	12:07:51	$4,400
5	Jeff King	12:10:59	$3,300
6	Bruce Johnson	12:18:07	$2,400
7	Gerald Riley	12:21:58	$1,900
8	Jack Hayden	12:22:40	$1,500
9	Kevin Turnbough	12:23:12	$1,400
10	Pecos Humphries	13:03:07	$1,000
11	Lorrina Mitchell	13:03:08	$900
12	Senley Yuill	13:03:08	$800
13	Ron Aldrich	13:12:48	$700
14	Frank Turner	13:20:37	$600
15	Wilson Sam	13:20:38	$500
16	Mary Sheilds	14:17:19	
17	Murray Clayton	14:17:23	
18	Don Glassburn	14:23:55	
19	Nick Ericson	15:08:11	
20*	Shirley Liss		
S	Chris Whaley		
S	John Two Rivers		
S	Dave Klumb		
S	Daryle Adkins		
S	Jack Stevens		
S	Bob English		

*finished at Carmacks due to poor trail

1985	Whitehorse to Fairbanks		
1	Joe Runyan	11:11:55	$15,000
2	Rick Atkinson	11:12:15	$10,000
3	Harry Sutherland	11:13:25	$5,800
4	Jeff King	11:14:31	$4,400
5	Bill Cotter	11:15:23	$3,300
6	Dennis Kogl	12:02:31	$2,400
7	Walter Kaso	12:04:55	$1,900
8	Bruce Johnson	12:05:41	$1,500
9	Joe May	12:06:05	$1,200
10	Jack Hayden	12:06:06	$1,000
11	Jon Gleason	12:08:15	$900
12	Rick Dunlap	12:12:06	$800
13	Murray Clayton	12:15:39	$700
14	Jon Rudolph	12:16:37	$600
15	Eric Buetow	12:16:50	$500
16	Frank Turner	12:22:08	
17	Nick Ericson	12:23:07	
18	Patricia Doval	13:16:10	
19	Connie Frerichs	13:17:11	
20	Julie Collins	13:18:50	
21	Ron Rosser	14:02:00	
22	Frank Ganley	14:07:43	
23	John Mitchell	14:22:00	
24	Pete Bowers	15:02:32	
25	Jim Bennett	15:07:03	
26	Stan Bearup	15:17:59	
27	Shirley Liss	18:10:28	
28	Jim Bridges	18:14:17	
S	Richard Hayden		
S	Lena Charley		
S	Don Honea		
S	Gerald Riley		
S	Russ Ridlington		
S	Glenn Craig		

1986		Fairbanks to Whitehorse		1987		Whitehorse to Fairbanks	
1	**Bruce Johnson**	**14:09:17**	**$15,000**	1	**Bill Cotter**	**12:04:34**	**$15,000**
2	Jeff King	14:09:41	$10,000	2	David Monson	12:04:44	$10,000
3	Tim Osmar	14:10:21	$5,000	3	Jeff King	12:04:52	$5,000
4	Sonny Lindner	14:10:48	$4,400	4	Kathy Swenson	12:05:10	$4,400
5	Harry Sutherland	14:11:01	$3,300	5	Rick Atkinson	12:06:25	$3,300
6	Bill Cotter	14:11:50	$2,400	6	John Schandelmeier	12:22:16	$2,400
7	Ed Foran	14:11:52	$1,900	7	François Varigas	13:04:29	$1,900
8	John Schandelmeier	14:12:23	$1,500	8	Ed Salter	13:05:12	$1,500
9	Joe May	14:13:23	$1,200	9	Marc Boily	13:07:09	$1,200
10	Jon Rudolph	14:13:53	$1,000	10	Dean Siebold	13:08:30	$1,000
11	Mary Sheilds	14:14:59	$900	11	Ralph Tingey	13:08:37	$900
12	Bruce Lee	14:16:41	$800	12	Susan Whiton	13:16:01	$800
13	Martin Weiner	14:18:46	$700	13	Larry Johnson	13:22:48	$700
14	Tony Andreonne	14:19:57	$600	14	David Sawatzky	14:03:49	$600
15	Don Glassburn	14:20:21	$500	15	Kevin Turnbough	14:08:03	$500
16	François Varigas	14:20:21		16	Jim Wardlow	14:10:07	
17	Kathy Swenson	15:01:06		17	Karin Schmidt	14:18:18	
18	Adolphus Capot-Blanc	15:01:50		18	Connie Frerichs	15:03:57	
19	Frank Ganley	15:03:49		19	Don Donaldson	15:08:22	
20	Lena Charley	15:22:50		20	Leroy Shank	15:12:12	
21	Cor Guimond	15:23:27		21	Allen Dennis	15:15:47	
22	Bill Fliris	16:06:06		S	Rob Weathers		
23	Dean Siebold	16:06:46		S	Craig Wolter		
24	Ron Rosser	16:11:50		S	Ty Duggar		
25	Ralph Tingey	16:12:05		S	Kelly Wages		
26	Michael Schwandt	19:02:19		S	Hans Oettli		
S	Ralph Nestor			S	Larry Grout		
S	Connie Frerichs			S	Jim Reiter		
S	Frank Turner			S	Vince Stack		
S	Ed Borden			S	Lorrina Mitchell		
S	Floyd Terry			S	Pecos Humphries		
S	Rob Weathers			S	Frank Turner		
S	Arthur Church Jr.			S	Don Glassburn		
S	Bur Lydic			S	Jon Gleason		
S	Frank Robbins			D	Floyd Terry		
S	Robin Jacobsen			D	Larry Hand		
S	Jim Bridges			D	Mark Grober		
S	Dave Schmitz			D	Lolly Medley		
S	David Likins			D	Kathy Tucker		

1988   Fairbanks to Whitehorse

1	David Monson	12:05:06	$20,000
2	Gerald Riley	12:14:01	$15,000
3	Kathy Swenson	12:16:14	$10,000
4	Rick Atkinson	13:01:38	$7,000
5	Bruce Lee	13:04:22	$5,000
6	Kate Persons	13:15:02	$3,500
7	John Schandelmeier	13:15:24	$2,800
8	Dennis Kogl	13:18:53	$2,250
9	Ralph Tingey	13:21:06	$1,950
10	Jim Wardlow	13:23:13	$1,750
11	Vern Halter	14:03:28	$1,550
12	Frank Turner	14:12:15	$1,350
13	Mark Elliott	14:13:31	$1,150
14	Lorrina Mitchell	14:16:58	$950
15	Frank Ganley	14:17:09	$750
16	Mary Sheilds	14:17:15	
17	Ron Rosser	15:05:26	
18	Mark Stamm	15:05:29	
19	Ned Cathers	15:09:42	
20	Lena Charley	15:20:16	
21	Dave Dalton	15:23:01	
22	Jim Strong	16:01:50	
23	Bob Holder	16:02:12	
24	Jim Reiter	17:13:29	
25	Jeff Fisher	17:14:13	
26	Tom Randall	17:14:40	
27	James Poage	19:02:57	
28	Marc Poage	19:07:43	
29	John Ballard	20:06:26	
30	Ty Halvorson	20:09:16	
S	Jeff King		
S	Scott Poage		
S	Steve Mullen		
S	François Varigas		
S	Don Donaldson		
S	Ben LeFebvre		
S	Jim Bennett		
S	Steve Haver		
S	Adolphus Capot-Blanc		
S	Allen Dennis		
S	Dick Barnum		
S	Larry Smith		
S	Mike Kramer		
S	Bob Bright		
S	David Sawatzky		
S	Jon Gleason		
S	Clifton Cadzow		

1989   Whitehorse to Fairbanks

1	Jeff King	11:20:51	$20,000
2	Vern Halter	11:21:11	$15,000
3	Jim Wilson	11:21:56	$10,000
4	Bruce Lee	11:23:35	$7,000
5	Kate Persons	12:00:29	$5,000
6	Sonny Lindner	12:00:39	$3,500
7	François Varigas	12:02:36	$2,800
8	Linda Forsberg	13:03:06	$2,250
9	Kathy Tucker	13:03:08	$1,950
10	Frank Turner	13:04:28	$1,750
11	Charlie Boulding	13:04:52	$1,550
12	Nick Ericson	13:05:40	$1,350
13	Fred Jordan	13:06:17	$1,150
14	Harry Sutherland	13:08:21	$950
15	Ned Cathers	13:11:05	$750
16	David Sawatzky	13:11:14	
17	Larry Smith	14:01:06	
18	David Scheer	14:04:47	
19	Heath Duncan	14:06:27	
20	Bob Holder	14:08:42	
21	Ketil Reitan	14:09:52	
22	Mike Maurer	14:09:55	
23	Ralph Seekins	14:14:47	
24	Steve Barb	14:19:07	
25	John Anderson	15:03:19	
26	Dick Barnum	15:04:41	
27	Jeninne Cathers	15:13:13	
28	Scott Cameron	15:17:21	
29	Jeff Fisher	15:17:49	
30	Charles Gauthier	16:01:21	
31	Peter Butteri	16:23:34	
S	Charlotte Fitzhugh		
S	Bob Grawher		
S	Bob Bright		
S	Bob Pelling		
S	Brian MacDougall		
S	James Poage		
S	Kris Krestensen		
S	Tom Randall		
S	Marc Poage		
S	Dennis Schmidt		
S	Amy Squibb		
D	Steve Mullen		
D	Larry Johnson		
D	Gerald Riley		

1990	Fairbanks to Whitehorse			1991	Whitehorse to Fairbanks		
1	**Vern Halter**	**11:17:09**	**$20,000**	1	**Charlie Boulding**	**10:21:12**	**$25,000**
2	Jeff King	11:20:33	$15,000	2	Bruce Lee	10:21:17	$20,000
3	François Varigas	12:00:32	$10,000	3	John Schandelmeier	10:22:03	$15,000
4	Kate Persons	12:02:05	$7,000	4	David Sawatzky	11:11:37	$10,000
5	Linda Forsberg	12:11:16	$5,000	5	Linda Forsberg	11:11:40	$6,500
6	Peter Thomann	12:14:27	$3,500	6	Vern Halter	11:12:06	$4,000
7	Darwin McLeod	12:14:31	$2,800	7	David Scheer	11:15:35	$3,000
8	David Sawatzky	12:16:30	$2,250	8	Sonny Lindner	11:16:15	$2,250
9	Will Forsberg	12:18:30	$1,950	9	Jim Wilson	11:18:04	$2,100
10	Charlie Boulding	12:19:36	$1,750	10	Dave Dalton	11:21:00	$1,900
11	Ned Cathers	12:20:12	$1,550	11	Frank Turner	11:23:34	$1,700
12	John Schandelmeier	12:22:16	$1,310	12	Doug Bowers	12:00:34	$1,500
13	Larry Smith	13:03:20	$1,150	13	H. Connor Thomas	12:04:52	$1,300
14	Tim Mowry	13:10:05	$950	14	Randolph Romenesko	12:09:01	$1,100
15	Marc Poage	13:14:54	$750	15	Gene Mahler	12:14:25	$900
16	Dave Dalton	13:16:03		16	Peter Butteri	13:07:45	$850
17	William Kleedehn	13:17:16		17	Cor Guimond	13:09:45	$800
18	Jeninne Cathers	14:01:41		18	Heidi Ruh	14:13:37	$750
19	Frank Turner	14:02:04		19	Jimmy Miller	14:14:01	$700
20	Rick Wintter	15:21:52		20	Connie Frerichs	14:15:29	$650
21	Terri Frerichs	15:22:02		21	Jim Hendrick	15:05:59	
22	Paul Taylor	15:22:13		22	Tonya Schlentner	15:06:17	
23	Connie Frerichs	15:22:28		23	Beat Korner	15:06:42	
24	Bob Holder	15:22:47		S	Daniel Bourassa		
25	Jim Reiter	15:23:39		S	Jeninne Cathers		
26	Esa Ekdahl	16:11:03		S	Ned Cathers		
S	Peter Butteri			S	Jeff Currey		
S	Gary Moore			S	Will Forsberg		
S	Larry Grout			S	Roger Hocking		
S	Ron Aldrich			S	Ruedi Indermuhle		
S	Knowland Silas			S	Scott MacManus		
S	Brian Lawson			S	Marc Poage		
S	Becky Sather			S	Paul Taylor		
S	Phil Cole			S	Wayne Valcq		
S	Mark Elliott			S	François Varigas		
S	Leroy Shank						
S	Adolphus Capot-Blanc						
D	Hans Oettli						
D	Mike Maurer						

1992   Fairbanks to Whitehorse

1	John Schandelmeier	11:21:40	*$25,337
2	Sonny Lindner	11:23:10	$20,270
3	Charlie Boulding	12:01:38	$15,202
4	Linda Forsberg	12:01:45	$10,135
5	David Sawatzky	12:04:01	$6,587
6	Frank Turner	12:07:06	$4,054
7	Peter Butteri	12:14:42	$3,040
8	John Peep	13:08:30	$2,280
9	John Gourley	13:10:40	$2,128
10	Tim Mowry	13:10:59	$1,925
11	Lucy Nordlum	13:12:55	$1,722
12	Jeff Mann	13:18:35	$1,520
13	Jack Berry	14:05:40	$1,317
14	Ned Cathers	14:07:40	$1,114
15	Jeninne Cathers	14:16:34	$912
16	Jim Kublin	16:00:30	$850
17	Jeff Bouton	16:01:00	$800
18	George Cook**	16:03:19	$750
S	Dave Dalton		
S	Paul Taylor		
S	Jim Hendrick		
S	Doug Hutchinson		
S	Connie Frerichs		
S	Steven Ketzler		
S	Larry Grout		
S	Buck Williams		
S	Roger Hocking		

*   It was planned to pay prize money to 20 places, but only 18 mushers finished. The money for the remaining places was apportioned among the finishing mushers.

**   Finished south of Lake Laberge due to poor trail

1993   Whitehorse to Fairbanks

1	Charlie Boulding	10:19:09	$25,000
2	Bruce Johnson	10:22:30	$20,000
3	David Sawatzky	10:22:33	$15,000
4	Linda Forsberg	10:23:11	$10,000
5	Jay Cadzow	11:07:11	$8,000
6	Jeff Mann	11:10:23	$6,500
7	Hans Gatt	11:11:40	$5,000
8	John Peep	11:14:34	$4,000
9	Bill Chisholm	11:19:23	$3,700
10	Frank Turner	12:05:20	$3,400
11	William Kleedehn	12:05:45	$3,200
12	Tim Mowry	12:13:58	$3,000
13	John Gourley	12:14:02	$2,800
14	Ned Cathers	12:19:56	$2,600
15	Ray Brooks	12:21:50	$2,400
16	Norman Stoppenbrink Jr.	12:23:39	$2,300
17	Doug Hutchinson	13:04:00	$2,200
18	Jim Hendrick	13:05:50	$2,100
19	Ed Hopkins	13:06:33	$2,000
20	Larry Grout	13:06:34	$1,800
21	Lauralee DeLuca	13:06:52	
22	Jeninne Cathers	13:07:28	
23	Sam Nelson	13:08:39	
24	Roy Wade	14:07:30	
25	Jeff Currey	17:02:37	
S	Don Hibbs		
S	Ollen Ray Mayo		
S	Roy Monk		
S	David Scheer		
S	George Aplustill		
S	Jeff Bouton		
S	Allen Dennis		
S	Connie Frerichs		
S	Steve Mullen		
S	Peter Butteri		
S	Dave Hetman		
S	Wayne Valcq		
S	Dave Dalton		
S	Becky Sather		

1994 — Fairbanks to Whitehorse

1	Lavon Barve	10:22:44	$20,000
2	Jim Wilson	11:01:27	$16,000
3	Linda Forsberg	11:01:33	$12,000
4	John Schandelmeier	11:02:47	$8,000
5	Peter Butteri	11:03:27	$6,400
6	Kathy Swenson	11:04:46	$5,200
7	Cor Guimond	11:09:33	$4,000
8	Ed Hopkins	11:15:23	$3,200
9	Brian MacDougall	11:15:24	$2,960
10	Joe Garnie	11:19:20	$2,720
11	John Barron	11:19:21	$2,560
12	Tim Mowry	11:21:44	$2,400
13	John Peep	11:21:53	$2,240
14	Dean Siebold	11:23:19	$2,080
15	Larry Smith	12:06:07	$1,920
16	Rick Wintter	12:06:12	$1,840
17	Paddy Santucci	12:18:06	$1,760
18	Dave Dalton	12:20:50	$1,680
19	Mark May	13:03:03	$1,600
20	Gerry Kuzyk	13:03:27	$1,440
21	Suzan Amundsen	15:08:47	
22	Jim Reiter	15:18:32	
23	Barry Emmett	17:22:35	
S	Fred Jordan		
S	Dean Gulden		
S	David Sawatzky		
S	Jay Cadzow		
S	Ernest Erick		
S	Bruce Cosgrove		
S	John Langham		
S	Doug Hutchinson		
S	George Aplustill		
S	Pascal Nicoud		
S	Jim Hendrick		
S	Ned Cathers		
S	Frank Turner		
S	Lauralee DeLuca		
S	Jeff Currey		

1995 — Whitehorse to Fairbanks

1	Frank Turner	10:16:20	$15,000
2	Jim Wilson	10:17:09	$12,000
3	Jay Cadzow	10:18:39	$8,000
4	Cor Guimond	10:22:37	$4,000
5	Larry Smith	11:01:12	$3,000
6	Tim Mowry	11:15:52	$2,400
7	Bill Stewart	11:21:45	$1,900
8	Bob Holder	12:08:20	$1,500
9	Don Hibbs	12:17:31	$1,200
10	Jim Hendrick	13:01:56	$1,000
11	Mike Peep	14:10:20	
12	Ross Adam	14:11:00	
13	Dieter Zirngibl	14:20:20	
S	Henry Hahn III		
S	Paul Taylor		
S	Connie Frerichs		
S	John Peep		
S	Ned Cathers		
S	Darren Rorabough		
S	Stan Njootli		
S	Kurt Smith		
S	Suzan Amundsen		

1996 — Fairbanks to Whitehorse

1	John Schandelmeier	12:16:47	$25,000
2	Rick Mackey	12:17:45	$19,000
3	Bill Stewart	13:01:04	$14,000
4	Mark May	13:01:33	$10,000
5	Frank Turner	13:04:07	$7,000
6	Doug Harris	13:05:37	$5,000
7	Peter Butteri	13:06:37	$4,000
8	Alistair Taylor	13:09:43	$3,500
9	Paddy Santucci	13:09:54	$3,000
10	Jeninne Cathers	14:02:21	$2,500
11	Kris Swanguerin	14:10:07	$2,000
12	Dieter Zirngibl	15:02:38	$1,500
13	Suzan Amundsen	15:03:33	$1,250
14	Dave Dalton	15:07:12	$1,000
15	Alain Herscher	15:13:49	$750
16	Thomas Wiget	15:22:52	
17	Michael King	16:07:30	
18	Stan Njootli	16:21:24	
S	Dan Turner		
S	Dieter Dolif		
S	Kurt Smith		

1997   Whitehorse to Fairbanks

1	Rick Mackey	12:05:55	$30,000
2	Frank Turner	12:07:03	$24,000
3	John Schandelmeier	12:07:08	$18,000
4	Mark May	12:07:25	$12,000
5	Keizo Funatsu	12:16:12	$8,000
6	Jerry Louden	12:17:23	$6,000
7	Dave Dalton	12:23:32	$5,000
8	Ned Cathers	13:02:28	$4,200
9	Dave O'Farrell	13:12:05	$3,700
10	Tim Mowry	13:17:25	$3,300
11	Darren Rorabough	13:17:58	$2,900
12	Dave Carroll	14:01:06	$2,500
13	Jim Hendrick	14:09:02	$2,100
14	Andrew Lesh	14:15:08	$1,800
15	Ed Abrahamson	15:13:34	$1,500
16	Trevor Braun	15:13:38	
17	Ralf Zielinski	16:20:00	
D	Joni Elomaa		
D	Nicholas Vanier		
S	Jay Cadzow		
S	Peter Zimmerman		
S	Steve Mullen		
S	Ingabritt Schloven		
S	Michael King		
S	Chris Pemberton		
S	Kathy Swenson		
S	Terry Asbury		
S	Connie Frerichs		

1998*   Whitehorse to Fairbanks

- Tony Blanford
- Larry Carroll
- Ned Cathers
- Arthur Church Jr.
- Dave Dalton
- Dieter M.Dolif
- Glenn Ferris
- Connie Frerichs
- Keizo Funatsu
- Cor Guimond
- Rusty Hagan
- Doug Harris
- Jim Hendrick
- Gwen Holdman
- Michael Hyslop
- Michael King
- Keith Kirkvold
- William Kleedehn
- Bruce Lee
- Jerry Louden
- Brian MacDougall
- Brenda Mackey
- Rick Mackey

- Antonio Martinez
- Terry McMullin
- Tim Mowry
- Andre Nadeau
- John F. Nash
- Louis Nelson Sr.
- Stan Njootli
- Brian O'Donoghue
- Dave Olesen
- Walter Palkovitch
- Marc Poage
- Joe Redington Sr.
- Paddy Santucci
- John Schandelmeier
- Sebastian Schnuelle
- Kurt Smith
- Bill Steyer
- Thomas Tetz
- Dan Turner
- Frank Turner
- Amy Wright
- Aliy Zirkle

*registered as of December 1997

Note: The race begins in Whitehorse in 1998 to commemorate the gold rush centennial.

HEAD VETERINARIANS

1984	Karin Schmidt
1985	Karin Schmidt
1986	Karin Schmidt
1987	Val Stuve
1988	Del Carter
1989	Pam Gordey
1990	Pam Gordey
1991	Jeanne Olson
1992	Jeanne Olson, Rick Long
1993	Pam Gordey
1994	Clint Crusberg
1995	Wendy Royle
1996	Wendy Royle
1997	Wendy Royle, Al Hallman

RACE MARSHALS

1984	Carl Huntington
1985	Leo Oleson
1986	Leo Oleson
1987	Leo Oleson
1988	Jon Rudolph
1989	Jon Rudolph
1990	Jon Rudolph
1991	Jon Rudolph
1992	Jon Rudolph
1993	Ed Salter
1994	Ed Salter
1995	Lorrina Mitchell
1996	Dave Rich
1997	Dave Rich
1998	Dave Rich

Major Yukon Quest awards

SPORTSMANSHIP AWARD

Presented to the musher exhibiting the best in fair play along the trail. Selection made by mushers.

1984	Joe Runyan
1985	Joe May
1986	Don Glassburn
1987	Rick Atkinson
1988	Jim Wardlow
1989	Fred Jordan
1990	Adolphus Capot-Blanc
1991	not available
1992	Tim Mowry
1993	John Gourley
1994	John Barron
1995	Jay Cadzow
1996	Mark May
1997	John Schandelmeier

CHALLENGE OF THE NORTH AWARD

Presented to the musher who most exemplifies the "Spirit of the Yukon Quest." Selection made by race officials.

1984	Senley Yuill
1985	not available
1986	John Schandelmeier
1987	Susan Whiton
1988	Kate Persons
1989	not available
1990	not available
1991	not available
1992	Dave Sawatzky
1993	Jeff Mann
1994	Cor Guimond
1995	Larry Smith
1996	Doug Harris
1997	David O'Farrell

VETERINARIANS' CHOICE AWARD

Presented to the musher who demonstrates the most humane treatment and overall care for his or her dogs throughout the race. Selection made by race veterinarians. Prize is $1,000.

1984-90	not available
1991	Frank Turner
1992	Linda Forsberg
1993	Jay Cadzow
1994	John Schandelmeier
1995	Don Hibbs
1996	John Schandelmeier
1997	Ned Cathers

DAWSON AWARD

First team into Dawson City. Prize is a four-ounce poke of gold.

1984	Joe Runyan
1985	Rick Atkinson
1986	Joe May
1987	Jeff King
1988	David Monson
1989	Jeff King
1990	Vern Halter
1991	John Schandelmeier
1992	John Schandelmeier
1993	Charlie Boulding
1994	Kathy Swenson
1995	Larry Smith
1996	John Schandelmeier
1997	John Schandelmeier

Completion statistics, 1984-1997

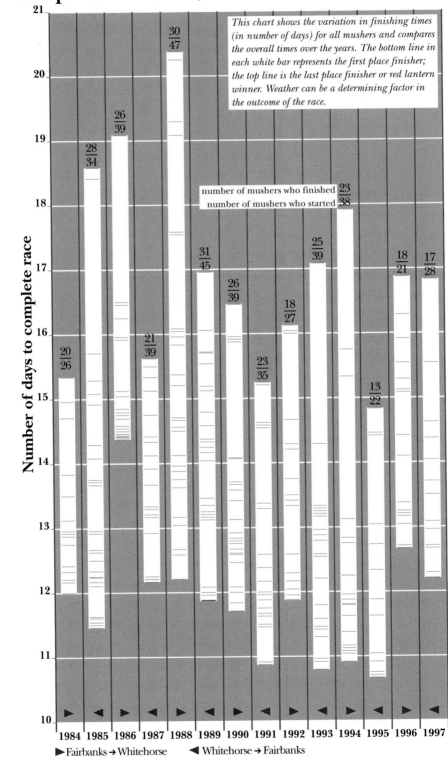

This chart shows the variation in finishing times (in number of days) for all mushers and compares the overall times over the years. The bottom line in each white bar represents the first place finisher; the top line is the last place finisher or red lantern winner. Weather can be a determining factor in the outcome of the race.

number of mushers who finished $\dfrac{23}{38}$
number of mushers who started

Number of days to complete race

1984 1985 1986 1987 1988 1989 1990 1991 1992 1993 1994 1995 1996 1997

▶ Fairbanks → Whitehorse   ◀ Whitehorse → Fairbanks

Yukon Quest musher placement, 1984-1998

	1984	1985	1986	1987	1988	1989	1990	1991	1992	1993	1994	1995	1996	1997	1998
Abrahamson, Ed (AK)														15	
Adam, Ross (AB)												12			
Adkins, Daryle (AK)	S														
Aldrich, Ron (AK)	13					S									
Amundsen, Suzan (AK)											21	S	13		
Anderson, John (AK)					25										
Andreonne, Tony (FR)			14												
Aplustill, George (AK)										S	S				
Asbury, Terry (AK)														S	
Atkinson, Rick (SCOT)		2		5	4										
Ballard, John (AK)					29										
Barb, Steve (AK)						24									
Barnum, Dick (AK)					S	26									
Barron, John (AK)											11				
Barve, Lavon (AK)											1				
Bearup, Stan (AK)		26													
Bennett, Jim (AK)		25			S										
Berry, Jack (AK)									13						
Blanford, Tony (AK)															•
Boily, Marc (AK)				9											
Borden, Ed (AK)			S												
Boulding, Charlie (AK)						11	10	1	3	1					
Bourassa, Daniel (PQ)								S							
Bouton, Jeff (AK)									17	S					
Bowers, Doug (AK)							12								
Bowers, Pete (AK)		24													
Braun, Trevor (YT)														16	
Bridges, Jim (AK)		28	S												
Bright, Bob (IL)					S	S									
Brooks, Ray (AK)											15				
Buetow, Eric (AK)		15													
Butteri, Peter (AK)						31	S	16	7	S	5		7		
Cadzow, Clifton (AK)					S										
Cadzow, Jay (AK)										5	S	3		S	
Cameron, Scott (AK)						28									
Capot-Blanc, Adolphus (BC)			18		S		S								
Carroll, Dave (AK)														12	
Carroll, Larry (AK)															•
Cathers, Jeninne (YT)						27	18	S	15	22			10		
Cathers, Ned (YT)					19	15	11	S	14	14	S	S		8	•
Charley, Lena (AK)			S	20	20										
Chisholm, Bill (AK)										9					
Church Jr., Arthur (AK)			S												•
Clayton, Murray (AK)	17	13													
Cole, Phil (AK)						S									
Collins, Julie (AK)		20													
Cook, George (NH)							18								
Cosgrove, Bruce (AK)											S				

AB	Alberta	IL	Illinois	PQ	Quebec
AK	Alaska	MINN	Minnesota	SCOT	Scotland
BC	British Columbia	MON	Montana	SW	Switzerland
FIN	Finland	NH	New Hampshire	WA	Washington
FR	France	NOR	Norway	YT	Yukon
GR	Germany	NWT	Northwest Territories		

S	Scratched
D	Disqualified
•	1998 registration (as of December 1997)

	1984	1985	1986	1987	1988	1989	1990	1991	1992	1993	1994	1995	1996	1997	1998
Cotter, Bill (AK)	3	5	6	1											
Craig, Glenn (AK)		S													
Currey, Jeff (AK)								S		25	S				
Dalton, Dave (AK)					21		16	10	S	S	18		14	7	•
DeLuca, Lauralee (AK)										21	S				
Dennis, Allen (AK)				21	S					S					
Dolif, Dieter M. (GR)													S		•
Donaldson, Don (AK)				19	S										
Doval, Patricia (AK)		18													
Duggar, Ty (AK)			S												
Duncan, Heath (AK)						19									
Dunlap, Rick (AK)		12													
Ekdahl, Esa (YT)							26								
Elliott, Mark (YT)					13		S								
Elomaa, Joni (FIN)														D	
Emmett, Barry (AK)											23				
English, Bob (YT)	S														
Erick, Ernest (AK)											S				
Ericson, Nick (AK)	19	17				12									
Ferris, Glenn (AK)															•
Fisher, Jeff (AK)					25	29									
Fitzhugh, Charlotte (AK)						S									
Fliris, Bill (AK)			22												
Foran, Ed (AK)			7												
Forsberg, Linda (AK)						8	5	5	4	4	3				
Forsberg, Will (AK)							9	S							
Frerichs, Connie (AK)		19	S	18			23	20	S	S		S		S	•
Frerichs, Terri (AK)							21								
Funatsu, Keizo (AK)														5	•
Ganley, Frank (AK)		22	19		15										
Garnie, Joe (AK)												10			
Gatt, Hans (BC)											7				
Gauthier, Charles (YT)						30									
Glassburn, Don (AK)	18		15	S											
Gleason, Jon (AK)		11		S	S										
Gourley, John (AK)											9	13			
Grawher, Bob (AK)						S									
Grober, Mark (AK)				D											
Grout, Larry (AK)				S			S		S	20					
Guimond, Cor (YT)		21						17			7	4			•
Gulden, Dean (AK)											S				
Hagan, Rusty (AK)															•
Hahn III, Henry (AK)													S		
Halter, Vern (AK)					11	2	1	6							
Halvorson, Ty (AK)					30										
Hand, Larry (AK)				D											
Harris, Doug (YT)													6		•
Haver, Steve (AK)					S										
Hayden, Jack (AK)	8	10													
Hayden, Richard (AK)		S													
Hendrick, Jim (AK)								21	S		18	S	10	13	•
Herscher, Alain (FR)													15		
Hetman, Dave (AK)										S					
	1984	1985	1986	1987	1988	1989	1990	1991	1992	1993	1994	1995	1996	1997	1988

	1984	1985	1986	1987	1988	1989	1990	1991	1992	1993	1994	1995	1996	1997	1998
Hibbs, Don (AK)										S		9			
Hocking, Roger (AK)								S	S						
Holder, Bob (AK)				23	20	24						8			
Holdman, Gwen (AK)															•
Honea, Don (AK)		S													
Hopkins, Ed (AK)										19	8				
Humphries, Pecos (AK)	10			S											
Hutchinson, Doug (AK)									S	17	S				
Hyslop, Michael (YT)															•
Indermuhle, Ruedi (SW)							S								
Jacobsen, Robin (MON)			S												
Johnson, Bruce (BC)	6	8	1							2					
Johnson, Larry (AK)				13	D										
Jordan, Fred (AK)					13						S				
Kaso, Walter (AK)		7													
Ketzler, Steven (AK)									S						
King, Jeff (AK)	5	4	2	3	S	1	2								
King, Michael (AK)													17	S	•
Kirkvold, Keith (AK)															•
Kleedehn, William (YT)							17				11				•
Klumb, Dave (AK)	S														
Kogl, Dennis (AK)			6		8										
Korner, Beat (SW)							23								
Kramer, Mike (AK)					S										
Krestensen, Kris (AK)						S									
Kublin, Jim (AK)									16						
Kuzyk, Gerry (YT)											20				
Langham, John (AK)											S				
Lawson, Brian (AK)							S								
Lee, Bruce (AK)			12		5	4		2							•
LeFebvre, Ben (BC)			S												
Lesh, Andrew (AK)														14	
Likins, David (AK)			S												
Lindner, Sonny (AK)	1		4			6		8	2						
Liss, Shirley (AK)	20	27													
Louden, Jerry (AK)														6	•
Lydic, Bur (AK)			S												
MacDougall, Brian (YT)							S				9				•
Mackey, Brenda (AK)															•
Mackey, Rick (AK)													2	1	•
MacManus, Scott (AK)							S								
Mahler, Gene (AK)							15								
Mann, Jeff (AK)									12	6					
Martinez, Antonio (NWT)															•
Maurer, Mike (AK)					22	D									
May, Joe (AK)		9	9												
May, Mark (AK)											19		4	4	
Mayo, Ollen Ray (AK)									S						
McLeod, Darwin (AK)						7									
McMullin, Terry (AK)															•
Medley, Lolly (AK)				D											
Miller, Jimmy (AK)							19								
Mitchell, John (YT)		23													
	1984	1985	1986	1987	1988	1989	1990	1991	1992	1993	1994	1995	1996	1997	1998

Statistics

	1984	1985	1986	1987	1988	1989	1990	1991	1992	1993	1994	1995	1996	1997	1998
Mitchell, Lorrina (YT)	11			S	14										
Monk, Roy (AK)									S						
Monson, David (AK)				2	1										
Moore, Gary (AK)						S									
Mowry, Tim (AK)							14		10	12	12	6		10	•
Mullen, Steve (AK)					S	D				S				S	
Nadeau, Andre (PQ)															•
Nash, John F. (AK)															•
Nelson Sr., Louis (AK)															•
Nelson, Sam (AK)									23						
Nestor, Ralph (AK)			S												
Nicoud, Pascal (FR)											S				
Njootli, Stan (YT)												S	18		•
Nordlum, Lucy (AK)								11							
O'Donoghue, Brian (AK)															•
O'Farrell, Dave (YT)														9	
Oettli, Hans (YT)				S			D								
Olesen, Dave (NWT)															•
Osmar, Tim (AK)			3												
Palkovitch, Walter (AK)															•
Peep, John (AK)									8	8	13	S			
Peep, Mike (AK)												11			
Pelling, Bob (AK)						S									
Pemberton, Chris (AK)													S		
Persons, Kate (AK)					6	5	4								
Poage, James (AK)					27	S									
Poage, Marc (AK)					28	S	15	S							•
Poage, Scott (AK)					S										
Randall, Tom (YT)					26	S									
Redington Sr., Joe (AK)															•
Reitan, Ketil (NOR)						21									
Reiter, Jim (AK)				S	24		25				22				
Ridlington, Russ (AK)		S													
Riley, Gerald (AK)	7	S			2	D									
Robbins, Frank (AK)			S												
Romenesko, Randolph (AK)								14							
Rorabough, Darren (AK)													S	11	
Rosser, Ron (AK)		21	24		17										
Rudolph, Jon (YT)		14	10												
Ruh, Heidi (SW)								18							
Runyan, Joe (AK)	4	1													
Salter, Ed (AK)				8											
Sam, Wilson (AK)	15								.						
Santucci, Paddy (AK)												17	9		•
Sather, Becky (AK)							S		S						
Sawatzky, David (AK)				14	S	16	8	4	5	3	S				
Schandelmeier, John (AK)			8	6	7		12	3	1		4		1	3	•
Scheer, David (AK)						18		7		S					
Schlentner, Tonya (AK)								22							
Schloven, Ingabritt (GR)													S		
Schmidt, Dennis (AK)						S									
Schmidt, Karin (AK)				17											
Schmitz, Dave (AK)			S												
	1984	1985	1986	1987	1988	1989	1990	1991	1992	1993	1994	1995	1996	1997	1988

	1984	1985	1986	1987	1988	1989	1990	1991	1992	1993	1994	1995	1996	1997	1998
Schnuelle, Sebastian (YT)															•
Schwandt, Michael (AK)			26												
Seekins, Ralph (AK)						23									
Shank, Leroy (AK)				20			S								
Sheilds, Mary (AK)	16		11		16										
Siebold, Dean (AK)			23	10							14				
Silas, Knowland (AK)							S								
Smith, Kurt (AK)												S	S		•
Smith, Larry (YT)					S	17	13				15	5			
Squibb, Amy (AK)						S									
Stack, Vince (AK)				S											
Stamm, Mark (WA)					18										
Stevens, Jack (AK)	S														
Stewart, Bill (YT)													7	3	
Steyer, Bill (AK)															•
Stoppenbrink Jr., Norman (AK)										16					
Strong, Jim (AK)					22										
Sutherland, Harry (AK)	2	3	5			14									
Swanguerin, Kris (AK)													11		
Swenson, Kathy (AK)			17	4	3						6			S	
Taylor, Alistair (SCOT)													8		
Taylor, Paul (AK)							22	S	S			S			
Terry, Floyd (AK)			S	D											
Tetz, Thomas (YT)															•
Thomann, Peter (SW)							6								
Thomas, H. Connor (AK)								13							
Tingey, Ralph (AK)			25	11	9										
Tucker, Kathy (AK)				D		9									
Turnbough, Kevin (MINN)	9			15											
Turner, Dan (AK)													S		•
Turner, Frank (YT)	14	16	S	S	12	10	19	11	6	10	S	1	5	2	•
Two Rivers, John (AK)	S														
Valcq, Wayne (AK)								S		S					
Vanier, Nicholas (FR)														D	
Varigas, François (YT)			16	7	S	7	3	S							
Wade, Roy (AK)										24					
Wages, Kelly (AK)				S											
Wardlow, Jim (AK)				16	10										
Weathers, Rob (AK)			S	S											
Weiner, Martin (AK)			13												
Whaley, Chris (AK)	S														
Whiton, Susan (AK)				12											
Wiget, Thomas (SW)													16		
Williams, Buck (AK)									S						
Wilson, Jim (AK)						3		9			2	2			
Wintter, Rick (AK)							20				16				
Wolter, Craig (AK)				S											
Wright, Amy (AK)															•
Yuill, Senley (YT)	12														
Zielinski, Ralf (GR)														17	
Zimmerman, Peter (YT)														S	
Zirkle, Aliy (AK)															•
Zirngibl, Dieter (GR)													13	12	
	1984	1985	1986	1987	1988	1989	1990	1991	1992	1993	1994	1995	1996	1997	1998

Index

Index

Index

About the author, John Firth

A life-long resident of the Yukon, John Firth has worked as a prospector, expeditor, journalist, public relations director and theatre manager. He is currently a financial planner. Writing is his hobby. Long distance running is his sport — he ran in the 1995 Boston Marathon. He doesn't mush dogs.

John was the only journalist to cover the inaugural Yukon Quest from start to finish. He sat on the Canadian board of directors for Yukon Quest International in 1986, 1988 and from 1991 to 1997, serving as president from 1994 to 1996. In 1997, he received the Commissioner's Award from the Yukon government for his work with the Quest.

The original printing of *Yukon Challenge* (1990) was his first book. He has also worked as editor and contributor for the original publication of Jim Robb's *The Colourful Five Per Cent Illustrated* (1984) and for the coffee table book *Fulda Yukon Quest* (1997).

About Lost Moose Publishing

Lost Moose, the Yukon Publishers, is a Whitehorse-based publisher of "books from the north, about the north." Our books are available in bookstores and gift shops, or through mail order from Lost Moose. Send for more information.

Alsek's ABC Adventure • written and illustrated by Chris Caldwell, $9.95, 1996, ISBN 1-896758-00-2

Another Lost Whole Moose Catalogue, A Yukon Way of Knowledge • by the Lost Moose Collective, $19.95, 1991, ISBN 0-9694612-0-8

Chilkoot Trail: Heritage Route to the Klondike • by David Neufeld and Frank Norris, $24.95, 1996, ISBN 0-9694612-9-1

Edge of the River, Heart of the City: A History of the Whitehorse Waterfront • by the Yukon Historical & Museums Association, $12.95, 1994, ISBN 0-9694612-2-4

Great Northern Lost Moose Catalogue • $26.95, 1997, ISBN 1-896758-02-9

Klondike Ho! • by Curtis Vos, $4.95, 1994, ISBN 0-9694612-4-0

Law of the Yukon: A Pictorial History of the Mounted Police in the Yukon • by Helene Dobrowolsky, $29.95, 1995, ISBN 0-9694612-8-3

The ORIGINAL Lost Whole Moose Catalogue: A Yukon Way of Knowledge • by the Rock and Roll Moose Meat Collective, $14.95, 1979, ISBN 0-9694612-1-6

Skookum's North: The PAWS collection • by Doug Urquhart, $14.95, 1994, ISBN 0-9694612-3-2

Whitehorse & Area Hikes & Bikes • by the Yukon Conservation Society, $18.95, 1995, ISBN 0-9694612-5-9

Wild Rivers, Wild Lands • by Ken Madsen, $29.95, 1996, ISBN 1-896758-01-0

Yukon — Colour of the Land • photography by Richard Hartmier, $29.95, 1995, ISBN 0-9694612-7-5

Lost Moose, the Yukon Publishers
58 Kluane Crescent, Whitehorse, Yukon, Canada Y1A 3G7
phone: 867-668-5076, fax: 867-668-6223
e-mail: lmoose@yknet.yk.ca
web site: http://www.yukonweb.com/business/lost_moose